HISPANIC AMERICA
AND ITS CIVILIZATIONS

Spanish Americans and Anglo-Americans

by Edmund Stephen Urbanski

Translated from the Spanish by
Frances Kellam Hendricks and Beatrice Berler

Foreword to the English Edition by Carl Benton Compton
Foreword to the Spanish Edition by Manuel M. Valle

University of Oklahoma Press : Norman

By Edmund Stephen Urbanski

Problemy szkolnictwa na Wybrzeżu (Warsaw, 1938)

Polonia, los eslavos y Europa (Mexico City, 1943)

Los eslavos ayer, hoy y mañana (Mexico City, 1944)

Historia de la literatura polaca (Mexico City, 1946)

Studies in Spanish American Literature and Civilization (Macomb, Illinois, 1964)

Angloamérica e Hispanoamérica: Análisis de dos civilizaciones (Madrid, 1965)

Hispanoamérica, sus razas y civilizaciones (New York, 1972)

Hispanic America and Its Civilizations: Spanish Americans and Anglo-Americans (Norman, 1978)

Library of Congress Cataloging in Publication Data

Urbanski, Edmund Stephen.
  Hispanic America and its civilizations.

  Translation of Hispanoamérica, sus razas y civilizaciones.
  Bibliography: p. 313
  Includes index.
  1. Latin America—Civilization. 2. Ethnology—
Latin America. 3. United States—Civilization.
4. Ethnology—United States. I. Title.
F1408.3.U6813   980   77-9116

FOREWORD TO THE ENGLISH EDITION
BY CARL BENTON COMPTON

This book deals with contemporary Spanish American society, a society made up of divergent ethnocultural groups with widely varying traits. It is a bold and clear analysis, which, though not conclusive, is based on solid anthropological and historical data and is valid for a large sector of the New World. Until now few efforts have been made at a cohesive examination of Hispanic America. Today the Spanish- and Portuguese-speaking nations of the Western Hemisphere are coming of age; hence the growing interest in their way of living, thinking, and behaving.

There are still many missing links between the nebulous prehistory and the contemporary reality of America. Americanists are attempting to reconstruct the half-legendary past through scholarly speculation aided by fragments of scientific evidence. Urbanski does not delve extensively into prehistory, though he frequently alludes to modern scholarship in the field. He also takes note of the theories of cultural transplant and diffusion to prehistoric America from other parts of the world.

Though these theories are still highly controversial, it has now been accepted by at least a slight majority of anthropologists and other students of pre-Columbian America that prehistoric contacts occurred between the peoples of the New World and those of other continents over a very long period of time. Such scholars as Gordon Eckholm, George Carter, and M. P. W. Jeffreys, as well as such authors as C. W. Ceram, Cyrus H. Gordon, and Henriette Mertz (whose contributions verge on science fiction) have attributed to chosen culture groups from the Old World, particularly from Asia, a diffusionist capacity in transplanting their cultures to America. These theorists are well known to scholars and sometimes to the general public as well, when their speculations are popularized by the communications media. The transatlantic and transpacific expeditions undertaken by

Thor Heyerdahl and others with the aim of proving the extent of ancient intercontinental communication have rekindled interest in the feasibility of such adventures in the remote past. I do not wish to deny the probability of diverse contacts among the peoples of Asia, Africa, Oceania, and America over a period of four thousand years or more. I do, however, wish to examine some aspects of such contacts in their "diffusionist" effects.

Most Americanists tend to believe that, though such contacts should have added certain culture elements to those already existing in the New World, in fact no single contact or even the sum of them had a very widespread influence. We find today persistent lifeways among the Tarahumara and Huichol Indians in northwestern Mexico that are radically different from the centuries-old agricultural customs and religious tradition of the Mayas in southern Mexico and Guatemala. We can also contrast the largely fishing and gathering economy of such groups as the Haidas, Eskimos, and Aleuts with the elaborately organized early ceremonial and governmental culture of the Andean Indians, such as the Incas and the Mohicas. Both of these civilizations contrast to the ultimate degree with the people of Tierra del Fuego, who were almost "culturally deprived" and yet kept their original customs, which were comparable to those of the Stone Age. Such wide cultural gaps hardly attest to the assimilation that could have been effected by strong culture diffusion. There were also, of course, topographic obstacles that hampered the diffusion process. By and large, therefore, we find only the most general similarities among the various pre-Columbian peoples of the Americas. Certain "extracontinental" similarities existed in only a few regions. These were manifested in the calendrical systems, the seemingly common cults of certain deities, and similarities in sculpture ornamentation, which show links between southeast Asia and Mesoamerica.

Thus, while it seems logical to accept to some degree the themes of intercontinental culture diffusion or transplant, one should not discount genuine self-development of civilizations, which follow their own course and undetermined destiny. Otherwise, diffusion would have left much stronger traces in America than those that have been discovered so far. Such intercontinental contacts were probably incidental and of short duration rather than long range and widespread. It is also possible that the "foreign" groups who brought their customs and style of life to the New World were assimilated by indigenous groups. Should they have been the original settlers, as it seems likely the Amerindians were, the breaking of ties with Asia could have led them to develop new lifeways and new cultural patterns in the adopted American soil. The change of geographic location certainly would not prevent their continued use of certain lexical expressions for plants and other elements of everyday life. The phonetic nature of those expressions is very similar to that of other geographic areas as distant as Cambodia and Polynesia. Such occurrences, of course, fortify the hypothesis of migratory movements to America from various parts of the world and, with them, the transplantation or diffusion of culture. It appears that the New World was destined to be a region of perpetual immigration.

A few sessions of the International Congress of Americanists of recent decades have been arenas of vehement scholarly controversy about the "diffusionist" versus "nativist" theories advanced about pre-Columbian America. On the one side were the advocates of intercontinental culture diffusion, mostly North American, European, and a few Latin-American anthropologists, while on the other side were the "nativists," mostly older Spanish American anthropologists and a few scholars from the United States who dogmatically defended the theory of the exclusively American origin of the pre-Columbian native civilizations. The most dramatic discussion took place during the Thirty-fifth International Congress of Americanists, which convened in Mexico in 1961. There the Austrian scholar R. Heine-Geldern in a slide lecture demonstrated similarities in ornamental design and sculpture between the products of India and Cambodia and those of Mesoamerica, particularly Mexico. He was opposed by the venerable Mexican archaeologist Alfonso Caso and his colleagues, whose uncompromising nativism has not won them much support among Latin-American scholars. No doubt this controversy will last for some time, until new anthropological evidence can substantiate the extent of the "diffusionist" foreign influence on the indigenous pre-Columbian American culture.

When Columbus discovered America at the end of the fifteenth century, some previously flourishing native civilizations were already in decay, notable exceptions being those of the Aztec and Inca empires. Many other Indian nations and tribes were subdued by the militarily superior Spaniards. The Spaniards, the Portuguese, and the English, whether as conquerors or as colonizers, superimposed their civilizations on various native Indian cultures. They were never, however, able to eliminate some native influences from the environment, or, in the territories under Spanish colonial domination, even to counter them effectively.

The European culture was a completely alien one, which had little or no relationship to the indigenous cultures of the New World. An inevitable shock took place, marking an intercultural struggle of historic dimensions. This was particularly true in what we today call Hispanic America, where Spanish culture made deep inroads and was accompanied by biological symbiosis. In contrast, cultural and social isolation was the outcome in what we now call Anglo-America.

The transplantation of these two branches of Western civilization into American soil is the subject of this book. It also describes the social and psychological conditions that accompanied the process. Above all, it stresses the molding of Spanish American character and behavior, which is reflected in the singularities of the mestizos and criollos, so distinct from those of the Amerindians and Negroes. The result is an ethnocultural drama, with all its human intricacies. An appreciation of this drama is indispensable for an understanding of contemporary Spanish American cultures.

There was extremely little literature in pre-Columbian America, though the Mayas, Olmecs, and Aztecs had effective systems of pictorial writing. The political and religious events were sometimes recorded on stone stelae, but tribal customs and legends were generally passed down orally from generation to generation. This oral tradition, although suppressed by the zealous Spaniards, was nevertheless vigorous and survived clandestinely under a thin overlay of Christianity. Fragments of the indigenous pre-Conquest tradition later infiltrated Spanish American literature in many ways. It is largely due to the efforts of anthropological investigators of the last two decades that we now have a few volumes of the oral literature of the Aztecs, Mayas, Incas, and Guaranis, translated first into Spanish and then into English and other languages. These efforts were sponsored by the Inter-American Indian Institute (Mexico), an agency of the Organization of American States.

FOREWORD TO THE SPANISH EDITION
BY MANUEL M. VALLE

Today continental and comparative approaches to Americanist studies lag far behind comparable studies of other parts of the world. In recent years archaeological, historical, and folklore investigations have expanded considerably. Ethnological, ecological, and ethnomusical studies have been less extensive, and studies of the mind and behavior of the Hispanic American have been all but nonexistent. The psychological and social area seems to be considered a mysterious labyrinth that few Americanists dare penetrate. And in truth, despite the undeniable humanist and anthropological attraction of the subject, its complexities are formidable. For that reason few books attempt to deal with the thought, motivation, and behavior of the multiethnic Hispanic society.

Broad gaps in knowledge remain, particularly in anthropological and social areas. Geographic descriptions, archaeological data, or "historic" sketches cannot fill the gaps, nor can fascinating illustrations of architectural monuments or captivating discourses on folklore that make such works resemble Baedekers for tourists. Rarely are deeper aspects of the culture penetrated. Despite the obstacles Professor Urbanski has managed to achieve a penetrating review of the Latin-American civilization, its thought, motivations, and hopes, emphasizing its enormous cultural and artistic contribution to Western civilization. He accomplishes his purpose in an objective manner, bringing to the task the devotion of a humanist who has long specialized in Latin-American studies. His work is balanced in its treatment of the diverse disciplines utilized. Above all, his presentation is notable for its clarity and comprehensibility.

In some regions of Hispanic America anthropologists and government-sponsored scholars concentrated their studies on the local indigenous groups, often with the intention of finding means to lead these groups to adopt the economic and social standards of the mestizo population. Their efforts have had varied results, one being a growing interest in the Amerindians in intellectual and artistic circles, especially in Mexico and Peru. Less thoroughly studied are other ethnic groups—mestizos, creoles, and blacks—who with the Indians make up the Hispanic American social fabric. In recent years interest has developed in *mestizaje* (the biological and cultural phenomena of racial or ethnic mixing), which now characterizes the greater part of the Latin-American population. Today we are confronted by a bewildering diversity of ethnic groups and attendant social problems.

Until now studies of these problems have been fragmented, lacking a unified, comprehensive approach to all the social strata. Professor Urbanski's book endeavors to fill this vacuum, providing a panorama of the ethnic groups that depicts their idiosyncratic contrasts and their radically divergent styles of life. It is difficult to resist his conclusion that, unlike Anglo-America, Hispanic America has no one "standardized" civilization but rather various civilizations whose "makers" are the diverse ethnic and cultural groups.

The broad Hispanic American scene is made up of multiplicity of human groups who are at times physically merged but ideologically widely separated. Americanists have paid too little attention to this phenomenon. Professor Urbanski analyzes it both psychologically and sociologically in a manner that establishes new bases for the study of Hispanic American man. The mesh of cultural multiplicity is often presented to the "outside world" in either an excessively romantic or, at the other extreme, an insufficiently dramatic manner. A more realistic view is that the Hispanic American carries within his personality many cultural "ingredients" that do not coalesce. He displays features all his own, molded by biological, historical, and geographical circumstances.

The author's methodology is the traditional European–North American approach: logical deduction supported by personal observation and experience, as well as by the work of other authorities in the field. His book is not, however, an exclusively anthropological monograph but is rather a blend of ethnology, sociology, and study of the arts—a genuinely humanistic approach to Hispanic America. Many writers and artists, rather than being presented in the conventional way, as representatives of genres, march in review as creative artists within their own ethnocultural groups and in the larger contexts of

Latin-American culture. Urbanski moves freely in the New World "cosmos" with interdisciplinary liberty, an approach that gives flexibility to his work. Frequent comparisons with Anglo-America add further dimensions.

The author inclines toward ontological revisionism, and he bases his conclusion on verifiable facts, providing them with new humanistic values. Far from being a speculative synthesis, his work is a scrupulous analysis, characterized by an independence of judgment that leads to some heterodox evaluations, as in the interpretations of interracial relations and labor problems. Without being intentionally provocative, some of his concepts will produce repercussions in the always stimulated Hispanic milieu. At the same time they can promote a favorable shift in the attitude and posture of the United States and Europe toward Hispanic America. The author's revisionism is often directed toward an examination of phenomena little known outside the Hispanic American world and sometimes not delineated even within its own.

Those who know Professor Urbanski personally or through his writings and the papers he has presented at sessions of the International Congress of Americanists have observed his persevering attachment to comparative investigation of the Hispanic and Anglo-American civilizations, as well as his absorption in study of the Amerindians. He has extended that interest to mestizos and creoles and recently also to blacks. His commitment to broaden his knowledge in these subjects has stimulated him to undertake a study of Hispanic American literature, about which he has made many contributions to the International Congress. These complementary specializations make him an unquestioned authority on complex Americanist themes free of the academic Byzantinism that still plagues some scholars. His previous works, as well as the present one, were originally written in Spanish, a feat that underscores the intellectual rapport this Polish-born citizen of the United States has with Hispanic America.

PREFACE TO THE ENGLISH EDITION

The cultural contribution of Spanish America to Western civilization
is enormous. The current of poetry known as Modernism that spread
at the end of the nineteenth century throughout the Hispanic world,
including Spain, is an expression of the Spanish American genius.
Poetry has always been a favorite vehicle of the Hispanic mind. The
rise of the essay form served as a proof of intellectual refinement.
Spanish American fiction achieved a well-deserved reputation in the
form of the realistic novel, which portrayed the natural environment,
whether of countryside, jungle, or city. The Indian and revolutionary narratives are strong statements of social protest by the
mestizo writers. The gaucho novel and theater are an original contribution of the criollos of the River Plate region, who are also
credited with originating South American drama. A noteworthy contribution is the rhythmic Afro-Hispanic poetry that flourishes in the
Caribbean area, as well as the less-well-known narrative form developed by Spanish American Negroes. In recent decades Argentinians, Chileans, Mexicans, and Uruguayans have been active in the
somewhat neglected area of Spanish American literary criticism.

The contributions listed above are prolific in literary forms and
widely disparate in ideologies. They are often characterized by un-
hampered imagination and recently by what we may call "magic
realism," elements well imbedded in the Latin spirit. All this, combined with the intensive cultivation of the fine arts, music, and
theater, is sufficient justification for the study of Hispanic American
civilization, which embraces an extensive area from the Río Grande
to Tierra del Fuego. For the inquisitive mind it is truly a cultural
epic, whose fascination cannot be diminished by behavioral and
sociopolitical disparities. Historically and emotionally the Spanish
American culture is related to Spain, but the relationship is more

complex today than it was in the past. In fact, Hispanic America has achieved its own cultural identity.

In contrast to the travelogue approach of some books, this one deals directly with Hispanic American civilization. It ties together the various ethnic groups as makers of their civilization, which is presented here from cultural, anthropological, historic, and sociological perspectives. It provides a factual background and concise analysis of the fascinating but complex melting pot that is Hispanic America, its mind, customs, motivations, and patterns of behavior. Until now these features have been overlooked or slighted, with the result that the reader is presented with a somewhat confusing and sometimes idealized picture of this important geographic area.

More than a picturesque description accompanied by geographical, archaeological, folklore, and literary information about Hispanic American countries, this book deals with the most relevant problems of their cultural experience, thoughts, lives, ambitions, successes, and disillusionments. Whenever possible, they are compared with analogous Anglo-American traits, to avoid presenting Spanish America as an isolated phenomenon. This approach was adopted following the journal *Hispania's* appeal in 1970 for a comparative approach to civilizations as being intellectually stimulating and pedagogically sounder than any other approach.

It is no easy task to characterize the civilization of America's Spanish- or Portuguese-speaking nations, with a combined population of twenty-four million people of remarkable ethnic, cultural, and social diversity. Generalizations are dangerous. No conventional approach can do justice to the human-ecological complexity of this region, often called by "outsiders" the "Land of Contrasts" and by the Latins the "Continent in Eruption." A more-or-less bucolic description would not reflect the present restlessness of the land. Reality demands a dispassionate and candid discussion of today's explosive conditions, which proceed from a rare combination of cultural anxieties, metaphysical idealogies, and racial inequities, coupled with social traditionalism, economic conservatism, and a yearning for a better future.

These issues are presented here without fear or favor, I believe, and in a balanced treatment that provides a clear and comprehensive picture of the reality of modern-day Spanish America. It is a humanistic appraisal, the "story behind the story" of the Spanish America that is close to the heart of Latin Americanists who are her devoted advocates but who also believe it their duty to tell the truth. There is no special chapter dedicated to politics in Spanish America, where politics play an important role. The few references of a political nature give the readers enough insight so that they will not confuse with democracy the dictatorship that still prevails in most of Hispanic America. Its cultural and political importance has increased tremendously in recent decades, a fact that should not be overlooked in the general panorama of the New World.

It is my intention not to simplify the complexity of the problems inherent in Spanish American civilization but rather to unfold its subtle intricacies of both spirit and behavior. Nor do I want to counter the widely accepted concept of a common sociocultural denominator that is conventionally called Spanish American civilization. I would like, however, to point out that this concept is only partly acceptable, since it is lacking in both depth and accuracy from the viewpoint of cultural and social anthropology. By definition *civilization* is in contradiction to Spanish America's rich ethnic plurality and the varied cultural and social traits displayed by her various peoples. These groups possess cultural values, mental traits, and social characteristics that they do not necessarily share with each other. That, of course, does not prevent a general linguistic and religious unity, along with *some* common characteristics, that tie all the nations of Hispanic America.

Such unity, accompanied by similar patterns of behavior, is evident in the mestizo society, the most numerous in Hispanic America. That unity does not, however, extend to other ethnic groups, especially to the Río de la Plata criollo society, whose culture is closer to Europe's than to America's and thus cannot be compared with that of other Hispanic American nations. The white, Indian, and Negro minorities cannot be identified with each other, because each group has its own style of life, very different from the others, though the groups may share the same geographic region. These circumstances seem to prove that, in terms of specific cultural traits, styles of life, and patterns of social behavior, Hispanic America has not one but many civilizations. To the rest of the world it appears as a Hispanic civilization, and sometimes also as a "branch" of the mother civilization, that of Spain. Terminology tends to obscure somewhat the distinctive sociocultural identities within this complex. I hope to clarify those identities in the pages that follow.

Many Americanists agree that its ethnocultural diversity does not lessen the spititual communion of Hispanic America. It is merely proof of Latin vivacity and intellectual keenness. Spanish American political unity is another matter, entangled as it is in quixotic regional rivalries. Not infrequently the political chaos is attributed to the legacy of bad government inherited from colonial Spain. However, almost two hundred years have elapsed since Hispanic America separation from Spain, and that argument has little validity. During that span of time Hispanic Americans have had ample opportunities to adopt forms of government that would advance their political and social aims. The military dictatorship continues to be the form that political power takes in most of Hispanic America, and the cause cannot be considered other than a form of deep-rooted ethnic atavism that turns its back on more flexible democratic ideology. Moreover, the continuing economic gaps in the various strata of the population preclude political, as well as social, cohesion.

There are some signs that contemporary Hispanic Americans are making an effort to close the gap between fantasy and reality. If they succeed, the people will change their historic destiny in the same way they succeeded in transforming their cultural and artistic life. Such a transformation may end the myth of the American utopia, bringing new spiritual and material dimensions to enrich the American "cosmos" in the challenges of the approaching twenty-first century.

Any study of Hispanic America is beset with complexities of approach and method. It is hoped that the cultural-anthropological approach taken here, similar to the one utilized in my previous book, *Studies in Spanish American Literature and Civilization*, will open new avenues for investigators.

This book is the fruit of thirty-five years of intimate association with Spanish America in long residence and regular study trips there. It is also based on extensive research carried out in Hispanic America, Spain, and the United States. It has been reinforced by comparative studies of the civilizations of both Americas, an enterprise that is of a pioneering nature. Though the thought of scholars from many American countries is unfolded in this book, the ideological formulation is mine. This approach, characterized by diversity, is aimed at mutual intellectual benefit and intercontinental understanding. The sooner we know each other, the better for all of us.

In the preparation of this book my previous interest in Slavic and Oriental civilizations was of some scholarly advantage, affording criteria for categorizing and selecting for study certain traits in Spanish American civilizations. Though as sociocultural phenomena those civilizations are presently divergent from each other, their early common Indo-Asiatic roots cannot be dismissed, nor can some behavioral attitudes that have been consciously or unconsciously retained over the centuries. While pondering the extensiveness of such an occurrence, surprisingly enough, I found characteristics shared by Occidental Slavs and Hispanic Americans: a high-pitched emotionalism, a metaphysical outlook on life, and a weak sense of what might be termed "practicality." On the other hand, a contemplative attitude, generally enigmatic behavior, a tendency toward fatalism, and passiveness in certain stages of collective distress are idiosyncrasies shared by Spanish American and Oriental cultures. I mention these traits merely to call attention to the parallelism of their existence. The present state of research in prehistoric crosscurrents, despite some noteworthy anthropological discoveries and speculations, is still in a preliminary stage. This is especially true of Hispanic America, where the physical and psychological coexistence of Amerindian, European, and African elements has been evident since the sixteenth century. To unravel these strains is to provide insight into their cultural and social significance within the framework of Americanist studies.

This book is intended for both scholarly and general readers. Because there seems to be some confusion with regard to terminology, an early chapter deals extensively with the cultural, ethnic, geographic, historic, and literary "language" of the field.

This considerably augmented edition of the original work in Spanish contains a new opening chapter on early-day European cartography of the New World, which is very revealing of the ideas the Old World had about the New. Contrary to popular belief, many other European nations shared Spain's early interest in the new lands.

I owe my gratitude to the following scholars for reading parts of my manuscript and for their valuable comments: José Juan Arrom, Yale University; Martha Adam, National University of Mexico; Richard F. Allen, University of Houston; Ithzak Bar-Lewaw, New York University; Rodolfo Cardona, University of Texas; Eugenio Chang-Rodríguez, Queens College; Angela Dellepiane, City University of New York; Lewis Hanke, University of Massachusetts; Luis Leal, University of Illinois; Ramiro Lagos, University of North Carolina; Enrique Martí, Howard University; Ángel Luis Morales, University of Puerto Rico; Martha Morelo Frosch, Ohio State University; Martin Needler, University of New Mexico; James W. Robb, George Washington University; Mario Soria, Drake University; and Wenceslaus J. Wagner, Indiana University. I am also indebted to the following distinguished Americanists for discussing with me important problems: Manuel M. Valle, of Peru; Alfredo Pareja Diezcanseco, of Ecuador; Alberto Caturelli, of Argentina; Manuel Zapata Olivella, of Colombia; and Juan Liscano, of Venezuela. Of course, I alone bear responsibility for the contents of the book.

For help in the selection of graphic material grateful appreciation is expressed to Kenneth C. Turner, Chief of the Photograph Unit, Organization of American States; Diana Muñoz, Mexican Embassy, Washington, D.C.; Natalia Macedo, Peruvian Embassy, Washington, D.C.; and Wanda M. Urbanski, whose technical advice was of great value.

I am particularly grateful to John Sarnacki for his most able assistance to me and to the publisher at the proofreading stage. His careful eye to detail was deeply reassuring and greatly appreciated.

Warsaw, Poland   EDMUND STEPHEN URBANSKI

Contents

Illustrations

Maps

HISPANIC AMERICA AND ITS CIVILIZATIONS

CHAPTER 1

THE NEW WORLD: EARLY-DAY EUROPEAN CARTOGRAPHY

Colonial notions of the New World as reflected in early cartography are strange, even baffling, to contemporary Americanists—as, indeed, were the Americas to the early explorers. Medieval cosmography was completely inadequate and was based on Ptolemaic errors—the extension of Eurasia, the invention of Terra Australis, and the geocentric system of astronomy. These concepts were adhered to for over a millennium. Then the Renaissance explorers challenged their validity in their Atlantic voyages, and Copernicus' heliocentric theory of the universe gave the death blow to the Ptolemaic theory. These events opened new ways to scientific experiments and speculations that, along with bold maritime enterprises, changed the course of world history.

The boldest event, of course, was the discovery of America by Spain in 1492. Soon, however, Spain had to compete with a more experienced Portugal, as well as with England, France, Holland, and later Scandinavia. As a result, Spanish explorations of the New World were often kept secret so that Spain would have no interference in her overseas adventures. Not surprisingly, the Portuguese behaved similarly. Nevertheless, news of important Iberian discoveries was reaching the popes, who were then the arbiters of colonial disputes. It is hard to say whether and to what degree this influenced Europeans' knowledge of American geography. But confusion there certainly was, even when printed maps began appearing. Most cartographers had no exploring experience, and many of their armchair maps were the fruits of imitation, mythology, and graphic artistry rather than geographic reality. One should keep these factors in mind while studying the early maps and charts of the New World.

Until about the middle of the sixteenth century the Mediterranean was the center of European trade with Africa and Asia. This trade greatly benefited Italy, and especially Venice, where there was a prosperous map-making business. After the discovery of America, the trade routes gradually shifted to the Atlantic seaboard, giving a tremendous economic boost not only to Spain and Portugal but also to other seafaring nations engaged in commerce with those and other countries. Cartographers followed a similar route, establishing their stronghold in the Low Countries. According to Ronald V. Tooley, early in the sixteenth century the cartographers of Belgium and Holland began to make their influence felt, and the movement began that finally wrested supremacy in map production from Italy and transferred it to Holland, where it remained for a hundred years.

From 1570 to 1670 the Low Countries produced the greatest map makers in the world.[1] Many Spanish maps, although drafted in Spain or Portugal, were published in Holland, and the Dutch and Belgian map makers issued many more of their own charts. The Seville-based Board of Trade (Casa de Contratación) not only had the monopoly of commerce with the American colonies but also was charged with supplying maps to the Spanish ships. This explains why most of the charts were drafted in Seville, although no reference was made in them to the board's patronage. Instead, they were usually dedicated to the Spanish kings as a demonstration of the makers' allegiance to the crown.

These early maps are a basic element of the Spanish exploration of the New World, for they depict the contemporary Peninsular spirit of exploration, as well as the gradually growing knowledge of the new lands. Great pride mixed with mysticism characterized those early transatlantic voyages. They reflected a kind of spiritual echo of the Spaniards' reconquest of their territories after eight centuries of Moslem occupation. This conquering spirit gave the expeditions the character of something like maritime Crusades. According to Columbus, they were destined to "bring the heathens to the Christian faith and engrandize Spain's glory and possessions in the Ocean Sea." Of course, those aims did not exclude the lust for the gold to be found in America, which became the motivating force of Spanish colonization, as it was of other European nations.

What were the reasons for the geographic misconceptions about the New World? Historians have concluded that they were due in part

[1]Ronald V. Tooley, *Maps and Map-Makers*, p. 29.

to Columbus' obstinacy, which bordered on dogmatism. Depending too much on Paolo Toscanelli's geographic calculations, which proved to be inaccurate, Columbus mistook the Western Hemisphere for the Far East. Thus, when he reached the Caribbean in 1492, he unhesitatingly decided that Cuba was a part of continental Asia. That conviction did not diminish on his subsequent voyages, even when his pilot, Juan de la Cosa, disagreed with him. Impelled by his goal of finding a shorter "northern" passage from Europe to India, he named the first discovered island San Salvador and placed it in the vicinity of the half-mythical Cipangu (Japan), which he thought was close to India.

Columbus for the same reason mistook America for India, or the Indies, and he called the indigenes Indians, a term seemingly destined to be used forever. That error, adopted by many Iberian cosmographers, persisted for a long time and was exemplified in Spanish cartographic and political terminology. Although during his third voyage Columbus sailed along the northeastern shores of South America and even sighted the Venezuelan coast in 1498, because of his "Asiatic" orientation, and because he never set foot on the mainland, he never knew that he had discovered a new continent. His error was soon rectified by explorers of the South American mainland. One of them was Amerigo Vespucci, a merchant-turned-mariner with literary inclinations. He too thought that he was somewhere in Asia, but to his Italian friends he called it the "New World." He claimed credit for its discovery, and Martin Waldseemüller, a German geographer, named that "New World" America for him. The name was soon accepted by most Europeans, though the Spaniards rejected it for a long time.

The circumstances that surrounded Columbus' New World adventures can best be explained by his almost mystical belief that divine providence had led him to discover the Indies for Spain. Similar beliefs were reflected in the early Spanish maps: many places bear the names of saints, whose images are often graphically interlaced with the contours of the newly discovered lands. Thus the first known chart of America, made by Juan de la Cosa and dated 1500, has in the background an image that looks like Saint Christopher, protector of sailors and travelers, and may also be an allusion to Christopher Columbus. This religious tone in cartography continued in the seventeenth century and into the eighteenth. An example is a symbolic map of the Hispanic world, made by Vicente Memije in 1761 and dedicated to Charles III. In it both parts of the Western Hemisphere appear united by the silhouette of a queen or Madonna from whose necklace hangs a stylized nautical compass. In one hand she holds the Spanish royal banner, and in the other a flaming sword. Her crown is symbolically placed over the Iberian Peninsula, and above her crowned head appears the image of the Holy Spirit. The cross-adorned mast of the banner cuts across the (somewhat misplaced) Line of Demarcation, which divided the American colonies between Spain and Portugal.

That important Line of Demarcation, which seldom appears on other European charts of the era, is a distinguishing feature of the early Spanish and Portuguese maps of the New World. It is an imaginary north–south line in the Atlantic, 100 leagues west of the Azores, by means of which, in 1493, Pope Alexander VI divided the American lands—those already discovered and those to be discovered—between the kingdoms of Spain and Portugal. Thus everything west of the line was to belong to the Spanish sovereigns, and everything east to the Portuguese kings. This arrangement was changed by the Spanish-Portuguese Treaty of Tordesillas in 1494. The new dividing line was then 370 leagues west of the Cape Verde Islands, with a similar territorial allocation.[2]

By the Treaty of Tordesillas, Portugal unknowingly acquired legal rights to Brazil, which, by coincidence, was discovered by the Portuguese Pedro Alvares Cabral in April, 1500, during his voyage to India. The Spanish explorer Vicente Yáñez Pinzón had arrived in Brazil a few months earlier, but no international dispute resulted. Portugal's presence in the New World was not new. In about 1495, João Fernandes, called "Labrador," explored the peninsula that was to be named for him (then called Terranova), and the Corte Real brothers explored it in 1500–1501. Portugal's earlier discovery and colonization of the Azores in the beginning of the fifteenth century had opened that country's way to America, and it tightened its bonds

---

[2]A similar Line of Demarcation was also established in the Pacific Ocean by the Treaty of Zaragoza in 1529. By the terms of that treaty the Philippine Islands became the property of Portugal, which traded them to Spain for the part of the Brazilian territory west of the Atlantic Line of Demarcation. It appears to have been a mutually beneficial arrangement.

through possession of Brazil. After that the Atlantic became the setting of accelerated Spanish and Portuguese penetration, followed soon by the French explorations and, late in the sixteenth century, those of the British.

In general, the Iberian cartographers, whose work depended on information from navigators that was not always accurately reported or understood, embellished their maps with such decorations as sea monsters, mermaids, large fish, and sailing ships (it is possible that these embellishments were added to cover up unknown details of geography). No less fascinating were the pictorial motifs, such as the four elements, American natives and animals, Indian deities, and famous discoverers, that appeared in the frontispieces of works containing such maps, or even on the maps themselves. This technique must have been very much in vogue, because it was utilized not only by the Spaniards and Portuguese but also by the Dutch, Belgian, English, French, Italian, and German cosmographers and map makers. It became a cartographic style whose exotic flavor evidently attracted European map viewers to the novelty of things American. Although inaccurate by the standards of nautical geography, the charts were often extremely impressive works of art, especially when they were executed in color.

It is not an easy task to find the early maps of the New World. They are scattered in many European and American collections. The Seventh International Conference of Cartography, held in Madrid in 1974, afforded a good opportunity to become acquainted with many of them. On that occasion an impressive exhibition, "Cartography in the Age of Explorations," was presented. It contained about 140 facsimiles of nautical maps and letters dating from the fifteenth century. They represented the work of cosmographers, navigators, and cartographers of various countries, with special attention to those of Spain.[3] One attraction of the exhibition was Ptolemy's magnificent *Cosmography*, which showed the world as it was known before the discovery of America—that is, Europe, Africa, and Asia. Another attraction was the first known chart of America (1500), by Juan

[3]Biblioteca Nacional, *Catálogo de la Exposición "Cartografía de los descubrimientos."* Other important sources are Duque de Alba, *Mapas españoles de América: Siglos XV–XVIII*; Francisco Vindel, *Mapas de América en los libros españoles: 1503–1798*; and Armando Cortesao and Avelino Teixeira da Mota, *Portugaliae Monumenta Cartographica.*

de la Cosa, which is described in detail below. Also included in this chapter are some Portuguese maps, to illustrate the uneven development of the Iberian concepts of New World geography, on which the concepts of other European nations were based. For similar reasons consideration is also given to some Dutch, English, French, German, and Italian nautical charts.

Juan de la Cosa's map, known as "Mapamundi," drafted in 1500, according to its maker, is the first known Spanish (and European) cartographic rendition of the Western Hemisphere (see Map 1). It represents a good portion of the eastern seaboard from Panama to the Amazon River region. Special attention was given to the Caribbean Sea, which was the most intensively explored region at the time. Cuba, Hispaniola, Puerto Rico, Jamaica, the Bahamas, and other Antillean islands are shown. It is interesting to note that Cuba appears as an island (not part of the mainland as Columbus had believed), which was not determined until eight years later, in 1508, when Nicolas de Ovando officially pronounced it one. To judge from these and other cartographic details, De la Cosa recorded on his map not only the first three voyages of Columbus but also those of other Spanish explorers. De la Cosa was a seasoned mariner and cosmographer. He had accompanied Columbus on his first two voyages and participated in explorations with Alonso de Ojeda and Rodrigo Bastidas. He had accumulated a wealth of geographic information that was probably superior to Columbus' and infinitely superior to that of Vespucci, who was his companion on one of Ojeda's expeditions.

Evidence that De la Cosa was aware of contemporary discoveries was his inclusion of a portion of North America explored by John Cabot in 1497, only three years before the map was drafted.[4] He described that part with its adjacent waters as "seas discovered by the English," which proves that Cabot's exploration of Nova Scotia and Labrador was not unknown to at least some Spaniards. Another curious detail on this map is that among the islands in the Atlantic, then called the Ocean Sea (Mare Oceanum), is one bearing the name Isle of Brazil. Surprisingly enough, it had previously appeared on

---

[4]Because of this detail the naval historian Samuel Eliot Morison argues that De la Cosa's chart may have been drafted later than 1500. Morison also believes that the De la Cosa who participated in Columbus' second voyage was not the same De la Cosa who had accompanied him on the first one. Samuel Eliot Morison, *The European Discovery of America: The Southern Voyages, 1492–1616*, pp. 139–40.

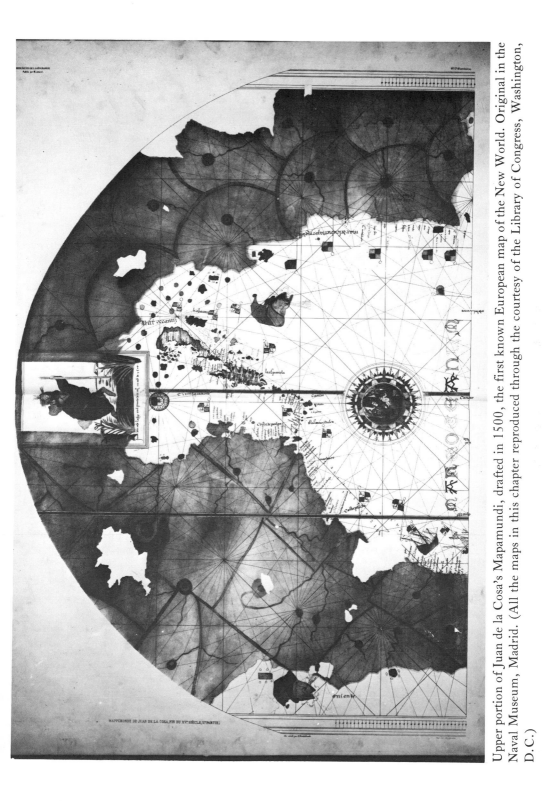

Upper portion of Juan de la Cosa's Mapamundi, drafted in 1500, the first known European map of the New World. Original in the Naval Museum, Madrid. (All the maps in this chapter reproduced through the courtesy of the Library of Congress, Washington, D.C.)

some medieval charts as one of the so-called "Fortunate Islands."
Beyond the similarity of names, however, there seems to be no
relation to Brazil itself, which was yet to be discovered and named.
The cartographer's lack of knowledge of Brazil's political identification would indicate that his map was begun before 1500 but finished
in that year in Santa María, Darién (Panama), before Pinzón and
Cabral reached the coast of Brazil.

De la Cosa's chart is crisscrossed with "mariner's rosettes," hundreds of rhumb lines running in various directions from their focal
points. They were commonly shown on nautical charts of that era,
supposedly serving as orientation guides for navigators. There are two
heavily inked parallel lines; one is marked Tropic of Capricorn, and
the other seems to suggest the Equinoctial Line. A heavy perpendicu-
lar line touches on the periphery of the New World and, like a
meridian line, separates it from other continents. De la Cosa's bold if
imperfect rendition of the Western Hemisphere is a remarkable geographic achievement, for his chart furnished previously unknown
cartographic data. It is also the first map on which America, Europe,
Africa, and a part of Asia are shown together. It is a beautiful chart,
drafted in lively colors. America is depicted in green, the color of
hope.

Chronologically close to De la Cosa's "Mapamundi" is the first
Portuguese planisphere of the New World, the "Cantino map" of
1502. Its maker is unknown, and its origin is unusual. According to
Portuguese and Italian sources, Ercole d'Este, the Duke of Ferrara,
an Italian aristocrat who was interested in cosmography and the
Portuguese explorations of America, secured the map clandestinely
through his agent, Alberto Cantino. He sent Cantino to Portugal,
where Cantino secretly commissioned a local cartographer to execute
a world map based on data that had been gathered in Lisbon. When it
was completed, in 1502, Cantino returned to Italy and delivered the
map to his master.[5]

The Cantino map depicts the eastern seaboard of the New World

---

[5]According to Cortesão, Cantino bribed an unknown Portuguese cartographer to make a chart of the
world, perhaps copied, in part at least, from the official Padrão, the standard map of the universe, on
which all the new discoveries were recorded as soon as the information reached Lisbon. Cantino paid
twelve golden ducats for the map. Armando Cortesão and Avelino Teixeira da Mota, *Portugaliae
Monumenta Cartographica*, Vol. I, p. 7.

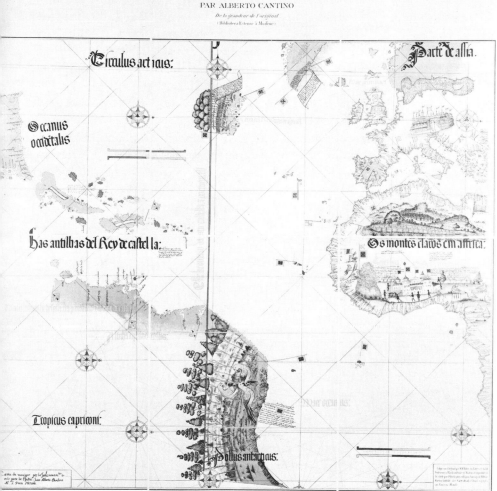

Circulus articus:

Parte de assia.

Occanus occidtalis

Has antilhas del Rey de castella:

Os montes claros em affrica:

Tropicus capricorni:

Circulus antarticus:

The first Portuguese map of the New World, drafted in 1502, known as the Cantino map. Original in the Biblioteca Estense, Modena, Italy.

differently from De la Cosa's map. South America and the Brazilian coast appear geographically isolated from the rest of the continent. This indicates an "insular orientation" that must have existed among some early cosmographers. It may have begun with Cabral's assumption, upon his landfall at Monte Pascoal on April 21, 1500, that the land he had discovered was an island situated somewhere off the coast of India. He named it Island of the True Cross (Ilha da Vera Cruz).[6] That idea was soon disproved by further explorations of the mainland by Coelho, Vas de Caminha, Vespucci, and others.

An important feature of the Cantino map is the Line of Demarcation, its first appearance in Iberian cartography. The line is evidence of a strong political awareness of the Portuguese and Spanish territorial claims in America. Not surprising, therefore, was the cartographer's omission of Cabot's discovery of North America, while recording the Portuguese explorations of Newfoundland and Greenland. Several islands discovered by the Portuguese on their way to or from Brazil and India, such as Fernão de Noronha, Ascensión, and others, were also correctly marked. On the Cantino map, however, less attention was given to depicting the Caribbean area. Although Spanish data were undoubtedly utilized, this region was presented in less detail than it was on De la Cosa's map. At the same time the Caribbean islands bear the name Antilhas (Antilles). It should be explained here that a corresponding term, Antilia, persistently appeared on medieval charts denoting faraway islands, which the cosmographers usually placed in the mid-Atlantic. According to cartographic records, the name Antilia appeared in the nautical map of 1424 attributed to the Venetian Pizigano (see Map 3) and in twenty other fifteenth-century maps. This coincidence implies a possible earlier Portuguese discovery of the Antilles.[7] The old toponymy had some followers in the sixteenth century, but most contemporary scholars consider it a part of medieval legend.

---

[6]Brazil was later named the Country of the Saint Cross and still later the Country of the Southern Cross before the name Brazil was finally settled upon.

[7]*Ilia*, the old Portuguese form of *ilha*, means "island." Thus the group known as Antilia, or Antilhas, means "In Front of the Islands" —behind which other islands or perhaps even a mainland could exist. According to Cortesão, the Portuguese had reached at least the island fringe of the New World, and possibly the mainland itself, about seventy years before Columbus hoisted the Spanish flag on Hispaniola. Cortesão based his assertion on records of Portuguese expeditions to the northern Atlantic. Armando Cortesão, *The Nautical Chart of 1424*.

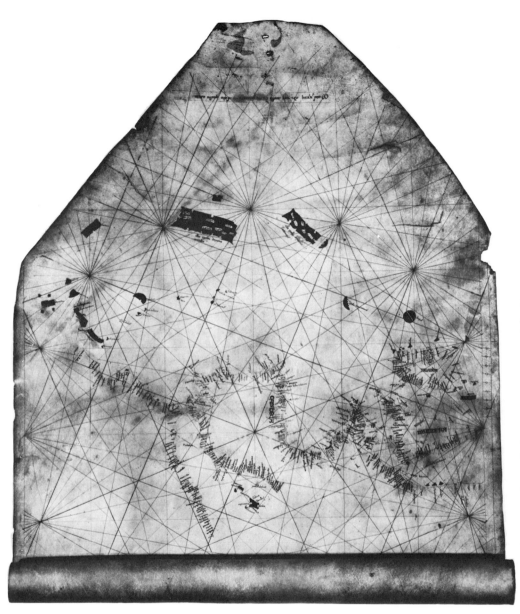

A Venetian chart of 1424, possibly attributable to Pizigano, showing the Antilles in the Atlantic.

One detail that made the Cantino map controversial was the appearance of an unnamed land mass northwest of Cuba. Contemporary geographers are still at a loss to identify it. Some believe it to be part of the Yucatán peninsula. Others believe that it represents Columbus' imagined Asian peninsula. Still others think that it is part of the Florida peninsula. Some British historians favor the last possibility, because it had been claimed that Florida had been explored by the Portuguese at an earlier, undisclosed time.[8]

The Cantino map, also beautifully colored, predominantly green and red, is profusely crisscrossed with "navigational" lines running like sea alleys in various directions, having as their centers several conveniently located rosettes. Prominent are the markings of the Arctic Circle, the Equator, and the Tropics of Capricorn and Cancer, which became the mainstays of Iberian cartography (the Antarctic Circle was added later). The Atlantic Ocean in this map is named Western Ocean (Oceanus Occidentalis), which was added to maritime terminology at the beginning of the sixteenth century.

The Cantino map, because of its pioneering character, was a noteworthy contribution to cosmography. This chart, in addition to the outlined portions of America, also depicts Europe, Africa, and Asia, the last in greater detail (especially its eastern boundaries) than in De la Cosa's "Mapamundi."

In a comparison of these first two charts of the New World, the following observations can be made. The Cantino map, conforming to contemporary Portuguese theories, especially Cabral's, depicts America as a group of islands. A similar concept persisted in Columbus' mind, though he took the insular regions to be a part of continental Asia. De la Cosa's chart, however, shows a portion of the American mainland, which the Spaniards soon afterward began exploring. It was to be some time, however, before explorers began to conceive of the New World as a continental mass. The cosmographers gave it the Latin name Mundus Novus or used Spanish or Portuguese names. Notwithstanding, the "Asiatic orientation"—misplacing America on the fringe of Asia or considering it a part of India—was still graphically evident in some Iberian nautical charts of the sixteenth and even the seventeenth centuries.

[8]W. P. Cumming, R. A. Skelton, and D. B. Quinn, *The Discovery of North America*, p. 56.

Chronologically later than the above-mentioned Iberian charts is a little-known map of America made by the Turkish admiral Piri Reis in 1513 (see Map 4). Discovered in Istanbul in 1932, it was reproduced in facsimile, in color, in 1935.[9] It is a part of a larger *mappemonde* of which only the section related to the New World has been preserved. This map, which at the time of its discovery caused an understandable sensation, depicts a good portion of the eastern seaboard of America and a few distinctive details. Contrary to the still-prevailing insular concept among explorers and cartographers, Piri Reis presented America as an unbroken continental unit. His chart comprises Central and South America, extending southward beyond the River Plate. The South American mainland, instead of declining vertically to the west-south, runs too far east-south in a circular manner.

Piri marked the Caribbean shores of the continent as Antilia, which was toponymically closer to the Portuguese than to the Spanish, but it conformed to Columbus' idea of the character of the Antilles. Central America also bears the name the Country of Antilia, and even an island off the Central American coast is called Antilia. On the margin of his map Piri stated that "the coast and island on this map are taken from Colombo's chart." It seems, however, that he leaned much more on Portuguese than on Spanish sources, because the latter never used the name but instead used West Indies. Another interesting feature of the map is the multitude of smaller and larger islands placed in what appears to be the Caribbean Sea. The tips of seven of these islands are gaily decorated with parrots, each of them with different plumage. The map makes a very pleasant aesthetic impression. On the margin of the maps are several explanatory notes systematically related to the various regions. Some are relevant; some are not.

In the category of legendary information about South America are pictures of a unicorn, an ox, and a few human "monsters" with animallike snouts. On the other hand, pictures of a jaguar,

[9]*Piri Reis Map* (Istanbul, 1935). The book contains a study of the map by Yusuf Akçura, and includes two reduced facsimile charts. Some of the explanatory notes on the margin of the original map were translated from the Ottoman Turkish into modern Turkish by Paul Wittek. The Ottoman Turkish utilized the Arabic alphabet with a mixture of Persian signs, which made deciphering the map rather difficult.

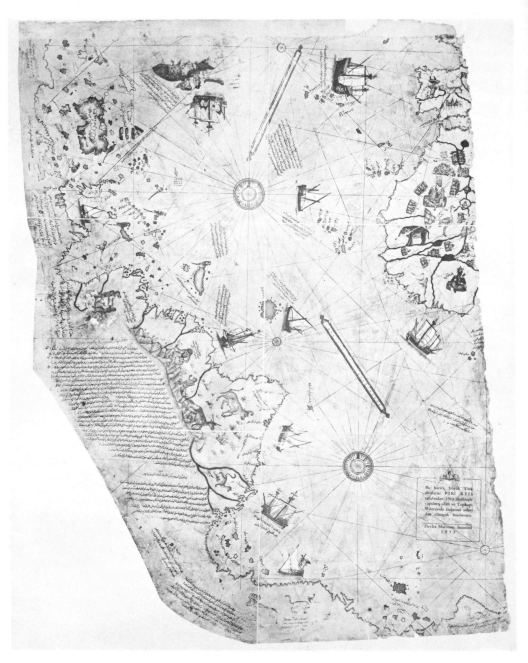

A little-known Turkish map of the eastern seaboard of America, drafted by Piri Reis in 1513, first issued in 1935 in Istanbul.

monkeys, a llama, and parrots are contributions to natural science. Also curious is a drawing, east of the Central American coast, of a big fish, on top of which two monks are building a fire, apparently thinking they are on dry land. Nearby is a vessel manned by other monks. This scene apparently refers to the medieval legend of Saint Brendan, an Irish seafaring monk who was supposed to have settled with other monks on an island named for him. Such islands always appeared on medieval maps, although their locations varied according to the map maker's whims. Antilia, Brazil, and Saint Brendan were such islands. Beautifully painted Spanish and Portuguese galleons and caravels give Piri's map a truly exploratory character.

Although Piri's eastern American coastline is not accurate, the approximate geographical distances between the New World and Europe and Africa (the western parts of which appear in his chart), is more nearly accurate than in other maps. Also fairly accurate are the positions of the Azores, Madeira, and the Canary Islands. The map is divided by a few horizontal and vertical lines. One of the latter suggests the Line of Demarcation, and in a nearby inset Piri mentions the Spanish-Portuguese territorial agreement, based on a line that he liberally placed two thousand miles west the Strait of Ceuta (Gibraltar). Piri names the New World the Western Region. He notes that "this sea [the Atlantic] is called the Western Sea, but the Frank sailors call it Sea of Spain [Mare d'España], which the Iberian navigators changed, by mutual consent, to Ocean [Oceano]." The geographic toponymy, which he borrowed from the Spaniards and Portuguese, is unrecognizable in Turkish. Except for Columbus, Piri does not mention Spanish or Portuguese explorers by name; in accordance with Moslem religious tradition he calls them "infidels."

In the variety of elements, particularly the continental concept of America, Piri Reis's map is important evidence of the cartographic development of his era. Piri had never set foot on American shores—but then neither had most Iberian cartographers.

According to Piri, his map was based on twenty charts and *map-pemondes*, four of which were Portuguese. He claimed, however, that the name Western Region was taken from Columbus' chart of 1498, because a Spanish sailor taken prisoner by the Turks in the Mediterranean in 1501 had mentioned that date (the sailor probably gave the map to Admiral Kemal Reis, Piri's uncle). The sailor said that he had participated in Columbus' three voyages to America and furnished Piri with the information reflected in his map. The question arises, however, whether Columbus prepared the chart attributed to him or whether the sailor simply mentioned Columbus' name to impress his Turkish captors, for his association with a famous explorer could improve his lot during his captivity. Another question may also be raised whether that chart could have been drafted by someone who accompanied Columbus on his trips and was more skilled in cartography. That person could have been Juan de la Cosa, of course.

Some historians attribute to Columbus considerable cartographic expertise because he and his brother Bartholomew were at one time engaged in map selling in Portugal. However, the only existing evidence of Christopher's cartographic skill is an unfinished sketch of a part of Hispaniola. Suggestions have been made about a supposed "missing chart." If it existed, was it the one obtained by Piri Reis? Or was it a chart previously made by De la Cosa? There was also a suggestion by a German orientalist that Piri's was Columbus' "forgotten chart." However, that is unlikely because Reis stated that he had utilized the material of many cosmographers, which makes his map a composite. A search of Turkish archives and museums has thus far failed to reveal the supposed map made by Columbus.[10]

According to Afet Inan, in 1528, Piri drafted a second *mappemonde*, of which only a part was preserved.[11] That map depicts the North Atlantic and the regions of North America and Central America that had been discovered in the meantime. Place names include Greenland, Labrador (as Baccalao), Terranova, Florida, Yucatán, Honduras, and the Caribbean islands. The latter are presented with greater geographic accuracy than they are in the 1513 map.

Of the Iberian maps very few of those succeeding De la Cosa's and the Cantino map have survived. Those and others undoubtedly served as the basis for the maps of other cartographers, mainly Italian and German. Most of the latter, even though displaying some imaginary

[10]Richard W. Stephenson, "The Piri Reis Chart of 1513: Its Significance and Use," *Son Cag Review* (Ankara), No. 13 (1963), pp. 22–28.

[11]Afet Inan, *Life and Works of the Turkish Admiral Piri Reis: The Oldest Map of America*, pp. 42–45.

coasts and islands, show contemporary geographic knowledge. We are less concerned here with topographic errors than with the gradual appearance of American toponymy as it was responsible for the shaping of the general concepts of the New World in Europe. This toponymy is discussed below.

In Pedro Reinel's Portuguese map of the North Atlantic (1505) the eastern coast of Newfoundland (resembling that of Cantino's map) and Greenland, appear as Lusitanian discoveries. The Portuguese fished in those Arctic waters for bacalao (codfish), for which they named Labrador the Land of Bacalao. More detailed is Pedro (or Jorge?) Reinel's map of the South Atlantic (1519). Here South America, especially Brazil, appears prominently. On the coast are shown many place names. The interior is depicted with a rich setting of flora and fauna and several busy Indians. The Atlantic is marked Oceanus. Between several horizontal parallels appear four climatic zones. They demonstrate an early interest in thermogeography.

Somewhat more detailed is another Portuguese map of 1519 (anonymous, preserved in Munich). On that map are a vertical line that seems to indicate the Line of Demarcation and a horizontal one, the Equator. A large portion of the eastern coast of North America is named Land of Bimini. The coastline extends northward, with some interruptions, to the shores of Bacalaos (Newfoundland) and "Lavrador." The Antilles are presented in some detail, as is a large portion of the Brazilian coast. An inlet corresponding to the Central American isthmus is the "Sea Seen by the Castilians," which undoubtedly refers to Balboa's discovery of the Pacific in 1513. The ownership of lands is marked by the flags of Portugal and Spain, whose impressive ships are shown crossing the ocean in various directions.

Let us now briefly examine some foreign maps of the period. The earliest known Italian printed map of the world is that of Giovanni Contarini (1506). His world is geometrically encircled by parallels, though the distance between (misplaced) eastern Asia and western Europe is closer than between America and Africa. Curiously, Newfoundland appears as belonging to Asia. The New World appears as a large, mostly unmapped land mass. On it mainly Portuguese discoveries are shown, both the northeastern and southeastern coasts, the latter identified as the Land of the Cross (Brazil). The Antilles are not far from Cipangu (Japan), which is shown at a great distance from

The 1507 Ptolemy edition of the map of the New World by Martin Waldseemüller, in which the new continent is identified for the first time as America.

Asia. Africa appears as a part of the Euro-Asiatic continent.

In the Ptolemy edition of the New World map by Martin Waldseemüller (1507) the Western Hemisphere emerges as a slim, geometrically streamlined continent (see Map 5). The northern part is joined to the southern part by an exaggeratedly long isthmus. The southern continent is identified as Terra Incognita and also as America—for the first time in cartography. The Antilles are here correctly situated east of the mainland in the Western Ocean (Oceanus Occidentalis), whereas Cipangu (Japan) is closer to America's west coast than to eastern Asia. Like Contarini's map, this one does not show many place names in North America, and the distances among the various continents are inaccurate. Even more inaccurate is the Ptolemy edition of 1508 by the Dutch cartographer Johan Ruysch (see Map 6). There South America appears as a detached land mass emerging from nowhere in the ocean, as in the Cantino map. It bears the name Land of the Holy Cross (Terra Sanctae Crucis), under which is another sign, New World (Mundus Novus), thus showing the steady extension of the latter terminology.

The so-called Olivariana map of the New World (1508–10) is controversial. In its northernmost part two islands are marked Labrador. One seems to be Greenland, and the other one is imaginary. South America is marked New World (Mundus Novus). Among the Antilles the island with the strange elephant-trunk shape is Cuba.

Less ambitious but topographically more accurate is Pietro Martyr's map of the Caribbean (1511), which includes the Antilles. Bermuda makes its first appearance in cartography in this map. Clearly marked on the Caribbean coast of South America are the Bay of Lagartos and the Gulf of Paria, as well as Margarita and Trinidad. Florida and Yucatán are also shown.

Another foreign chart of the Western Hemisphere is that of Joannes de Stobnica, included in his Polish edition of Ptolemy (1512). His general geographic outline is similar to that of Waldseemüller. The toponymy for the Caribbean and the southern part of the New World is also similar to that generally used by cartographers of the era. Stobnica, however, differs in clearly distinguishing the two oceans that encircle the New World. Nordenskiöld considers this the first complete breaking with the old theory of a single ocean surrounding Europe, Asia, and Africa.[12] That concept was soon confirmed by Balboa's discovery of the Pacific (1513).

Ruysch's early concept of the New World's territorial fragmentation was adopted by only a few cosmographers. One of them was Joahannes Schöner, a German whose globe (1515) divided the Western Hemisphere into three separate parts (see Map 7). The northern one, named Parias, is separated by a nonexistent sea passage from a large southern land mass marked America. This again is separated by another nonexistent strait from an even larger land mass in the south called Brasilie Regio, later to be known as the Antarctic. Since Schöner apparently knew about Balboa's discovery of another sea (the Pacific), he named it the Oriental Ocean (Oceanus Orientalis) as distinguished from the Occidental Ocean (Oceanus Occidentalis), as the Atlantic was then known. The Alsatian Laurent Fries's Strassburg edition of Ptolemy (1522) follows the same terminology but curiously enough bears a modified name for the sea between Asia and America—the Eastern Indian Ocean (Oceanus Orientalis Indicus). Fries depicted only a portion of the southern part of the New World, which he marked America. Among the Antilles the islands Ysabella (Cuba) and Spagnola (Hispaniola) are also shown.

The Salviati planisphere (ca. 1527) gives a more realistic presentation of the New World. This polychrome Italian map depicts, with some degree of accuracy, the entire eastern seaboard of North, Central, and South America. In addition to many place names, the entire coastline is embellished with trees. The southernmost point of South America ends, correctly, with a sea passage, separating it from another land barely outlined with a single stroke, which proves that the map's author already knew about the discovery of the Strait of Magellan in 1520. Except for the Yucatán peninsula, which appears as an island, the shape of the as-yet-unnamed Gulf of Mexico is fairly exact.

Like the Spaniards and the Portuguese, the French also early explored the New World, both north and south. For this reason new toponymy appears in the maps of the Italians Maiollo (1527) and Girolamo Verrazano (1529), both depicting the French explorations

---

[12]On Stobnica's map the surface of the earth is, for the first time, divided into two hemispheres, each of which was laid down on the projection of Ptolemy. A. E. Nordenskiöld, *Facsimile-Atlas to the Early History of Cartography*, p. 69.

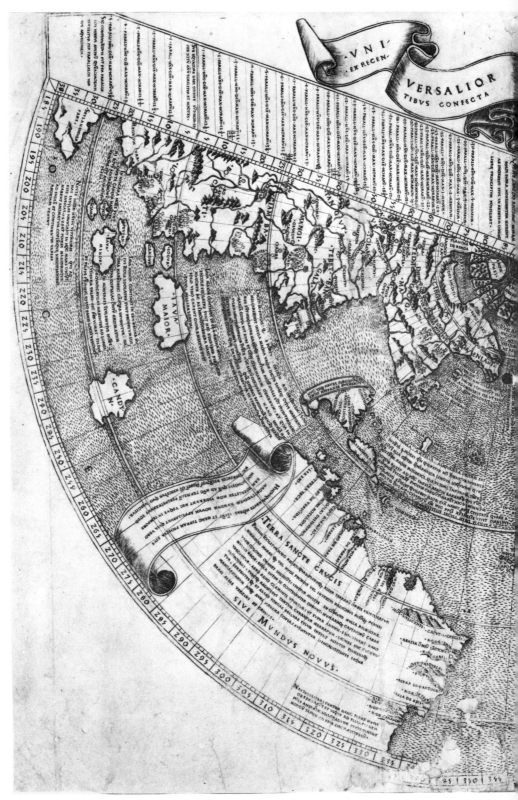

The 1508 Ptolemy edition of a map by Johan Ruysch, showing South

America as a detached land mass in the Atlantic Ocean.

Gezeichnet von K. KRETSCHMER.

Herausgegeben von der Gesellschaft für Erdkunde zu Berlin
1892.

Lith. u. Druck von GIESECKE & DEVRIENT, Leipzig u. Berlin.

Globe by Johannes Schöner, 1515, showing the New World divided into three land masses.

of North America led by the navigator Giovanni da Verrazano (see Maps 8 to 10). These maps show the coast between New England and Florida. Maiollo called the entire region Francesca and inserted the name Indian Sea (Mare Indicum) on what appears to be the Gulf of Mexico. Girolamo, the explorer's brother, named the same territory (which was to become the United States) Nova Gallia. On both Italian maps the coastline from Maine to Florida is adorned with French banners. On his map Girolamo indicated a very narrow land strip between the mainland and the Florida peninsula, which he believed separated two oceans. Except for Yucatán, which appears as an island, the shape of the unnamed Gulf of Mexico shows an astonishingly close similarity to contemporary maps. Giovanni da Verrazano, while cruising along the Atlantic coast, had spotted a beautiful, hilly, forested place, where he anchored and explored. He loved the place, which was inhabited by friendly Indians, and called it Arcadia, a name that intrigued cartographers in the mid-sixteenth century. [13]

Graphically spectacular but geographically unbalanced is the world map in Simon Grynaeus' *Orbis Novus* (Basel, 1532). Classified by Bagrow as the work of Sebastian Münster, a German, and attributed by Cumming, Skelton, and Quinn to Holbein the Younger, this map presents the Western Hemisphere in a very strange way. The geographic outline is similar to Waldseemüller's, after whom the author named the southern part of the continent America, but he also added Terra Nova and Prisilia (Brazil). Surprisingly, the continent's northern part bears the name Terra de Cuba. Another novelty is that the Central American isthmus shows an unnamed sea passage, where the Panama Canal was built almost four centuries later. North of the Antilles is an island named Terra Corterealis after Schöner and others. It suggests a greatly reduced Greenland. New names also appear for the Atlantic, whose northern part is called the Great Ocean (Oceanus Magnus) and whose southern part is labeled the Southern Ocean (Oceanus Meridionalis). These seas are conspicuously infested with large sea monsters, and the map's oval border is adorned with cannibals, animals, and hunters. Münster's map "Novae Insulae"

[13]This mysterious Arcadia has been identified by Morison as Kitty Hawk, North Carolina. Samuel Eliot Morison, *The European Discovery of America: The Northern Voyages, A.D. 500–1600*, p. 195.

An Italian chart drafted by Vesconte de Maiollo in 1527, showing the
French explorations of North America led by Giovanni da Verrazano.

A manuscript map of North America and the Gulf of Mexico, showing the French explorations led by Giovanni da Verrazano between 1524 and 1529. The map was drafted by his brother, Girolamo da Verrazano, in 1529 and corrected in 1540. Original in the Borgia Museum, Rome.

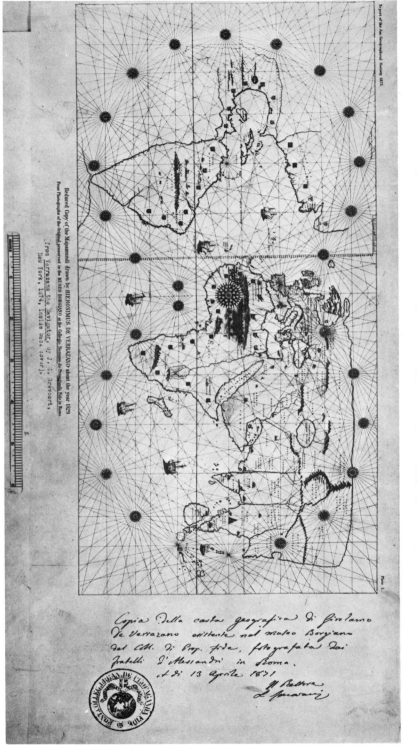

Reduced Copy of the Mappamundi drawn by HIERONIMUS DE VERRAZANO about the year 1529
From Photographs of the original, preserved in the MUSEO BORGIANO at the Collegio Romano de Propaganda Fide in Rome.

[From Verrazano the Navigator, by J. C. Brevoort's,
New York, 1874, inside back cover.]

Plate I.

Copia Della carta geografica di Girolamo
de Verrazano esistente nel Museo Borgiano
del Coll. di Prop. fide, fotografata dai
fratelli d'Alessandri in Roma.
A dì 13 Aprile 1871
Il Rettore
L. Spazzani

World map of 1529 by Girolamo Verrazano, showing the results of the
French explorations of North America led by his brother, Giovanni.

(Basel, 1540) displays a considerable growth in his knowledge of America (see Map 11).

Incomparably superior to Münster's chart and not far removed in time is the world map of the Italian Battista Agnese (1536). Its main features are the more realistically drafted east and west coasts of South America. Agnese marks the circumnavigation of the world by Magellan and Elcano (1519–22) with a continuous line and shows, south of the Strait of Magellan, a land mass that suggests Tierra del Fuego. The northeastern seaboard of North America is also shown. The outline of the Gulf of Mexico leaves much to be desired, but Florida's shape is correct. Another continuous line marks the Spanish trade route from Seville to Panama and across the isthmus to Peru. I saw another of Agnese's maps without the contours of the western South American coast, except for its northern portion.[14] Here, however, the place names on the mainland are Peru Provintia, Mundus Novus, and Brasil, which prove that Agnese knew about Francisco Pizarro's conquest of the Inca empire (1531–35). In a later map of South America, probably drafted in the second part of the sixteenth century, both western coasts are depicted, and Pizarro's route of conquest is presented with many geographic details. Also, the identification of Río de la Plata proves that he knew of the explorations of Juan Díaz de Solís and Sebastian Cabot of the Río de la Plata region.

In the era of exploration Spain and Portugal had the so-called Padrón or Padrão, the standard map of the world on which each geographic discovery was recorded under state supervision. It is doubtful that all these data were available to most cartographers, because on their maps one sometimes finds grossly inaccurate details. Among the earliest charts closely related to America is the world map of Juan Vespucci (Seville, 1526), Amerigo's nephew. Its distinguishing feature is the continental unity of the New World, which goes beyond Waldseemüller's rather simple concept of the shape and territorial distribution of America. Vespucci's South America, in spite of many uncertainties, emerges better shaped topographically. Both coasts are also better delineated, though large

---

[14]This map of America, Africa, and Europe is in the possession of the Hispanic Society of America. Identified as an early-sixteenth-century work of Agnese, it is included in Edward L. Stevenson, *Portolan Charts: Their Origin and Characteristics*.

A German world map from Sebastian Münster's

VNIVERSALIS

Aquilo

Latitudo Septene.

Oceanus Hyperboreus

Cæcia

INDIA Superior

Cathay regio

Temiscitan

ASIA MAIOR

Cat

INDIA

Collicut

OCEANVS
Orientalis

Zi
pāgri

Subsolanus

Ta
pro
ba
na

Gilolo

Porne

Iaua

Madigascar

Aequinoctialis Circulus

Tropicus Capricornu

| 100 | 110 | 120 | 130 | 140 | 150 | 160 | 170 | 180 | 190 | 200 | 210 | 220 | 230 | 240 | 250 | 260 |

Zanzibar

Insulæ Grifonū

Calensuan

Mare pacificum

Vulturni
Eurus

Latitudo merid.

Eurodus ster

1540 edition of Ptolemy's *Geographia*.

portions are unnamed. The eastern coast of North America is too eastward-bent.

A northern island marked Tierra de los Bacalaos suggests Newfoundland. The Mexican Gulf and mainland are depicted somewhat more accurately, proof that Vespucci knew about Cortes' conquest of Montezuma's empire (1519–21) from official sources. A large mountain range is shown along the still-unexplored Pacific coast of South America. The Strait of Magellan divides the mainland from the still-unnamed Tierra del Fuego. Central America has an unusual shape, but the Caribbean is fairly well depicted. The Pacific is called Mare del Sul (Southern Sea), and the Atlantic, Mare Oceanum. A Spanish coat of arms placed over the newly established Viceroyalty of New Spain, as Mexico was known during the colonial period, reflects the political character of this map (now in the possession of the Hispanic Society of America.)

Chronologically closest to Vespucci's is a world map by a Portugese, Diego Ribeiro (Seville, 1527). It outlines the entire eastern seaboard of the New World, whose southern part bears the name El Brasil. A more descriptive polychrome edition of the map, dated 1529, identifies its author as a cosmographer to King Charles V of Spain (see Map 12). The map's most conspicious feature is the detailed presentation of the eastern coast of America from Greenland to the Strait of Magellan. Many place names are included, such as Labrador, Cortereal, Estévan Gómez, Garay, Cortés, and Solís. Among regional place names Guatimala, Castilla del Oro, Peru, Brasil, and Tierra de Patagones appear, as does the Río de la Plata. Ribeiro (who signed this map Diego Ribero) utilized the information available in the Seville-based Padrón, which he himself helped develop. Characteristically, on the western seaboard of South America only the Peruvian coast is outlined, which proves that Vespucci had more data at his disposal than did Ribeiro. The latter, however, utilized more names. Thus the Pacific is identified as Mar del Sur, the North Atlantic as Oceanus Occidentalis, the South Atlantic as Mare Ethiopicum, and the waters south of South Africa as Oceanus Meridionalis. The names Arctic and Antarctic also appear on this ungraded but unique chart. Ribeiro's ornate map is cartographically very impressive. In addition to geographic data, it gives navigational information.

A Spanish chart of the New World, drafted in Seville in 1529 by Diego Ribeiro, Portuguese cosmographer to Emperor Charles V. Original in the Vatican Library.

California's discoverer was the conqueror of Mexico, Hernando Cortés, who sighted it in 1535. At his order it had been explored by Domingo Castillo, who thought it to be a part of Quivira[15] and so denoted it on the first map of California (1541). Another navigator, Francisco de Ulloa, while reconnoitering California's coast in 1539, named it Tierra de Santa Cruz (Land of the Holy Cross). Ulloa called the present Gulf of California Mar Bermejo (Vermilion Sea) for the reddish water discharged from the Colorado River. A more systematic exploration of the coast was undertaken at the order of Viceroy Mendoza by Juan Rodrigues Cabrillo (1542–43), who gathered much information on the future Golden State. It is curious to note that Lower California was mistakenly depicted as an island as late as the eighteenth century.

Maps related to other discoveries in the New World are contained in *Islario,* by Alonso de Santa Cruz (1541). One map depicts Estévan Gómez' exploration of New England from Cape Cod to Desert Island (1525) in search of the "northern passage to Cathay." Gomez also entered the Penobscot River (labeled in Portuguese Rio dos Yslas). Another map illustrates Sebastian Cabot's expedition to the Río de la Plata (1526–40), in which Santa Cruz participated as cartographer. This particular chart contains inaccuracies similar to those of Cabot's world map (1544). Especially informative is Santa Cruz's coastal map of northern California.

Pedro de Medina's nautical chart of the New World in his *Arte de Navegar* (Valladolid, 1545) shows only the east coast of North America, from Labrador to Florida, and the Viceroyalty of New Spain. The isthmus bridges North America and South America, of which only the meridional part is shown. It is marked Peru, with Ciudad de los Reyes (Lima) and Cuzco as its cities, proving the existence of the Viceroyalty of Peru. The northeastern region of the southern continent is named Tierra de Canibales (Land of Cannibals), and Amazonas (Amazon River) is shown flowing in a serpentine course. Clearly marked are the Mar del Sur (Pacific) and the Demarcation and Equinoctial lines. Medina's other map, "Mundo Nuevo," in-

---

[15]The legendary region Quivira, sometimes identified as the Land of the Seven Cities of Cíbola, is known from Coronado's expedition. It supposedly embraced a large territory between Texas and the Pacific. José Pichardo, "La Quivira (1768)," in *One Hundred and Six Manuscripts, Autographs, Maps and Printed Books* (Washington, D.C., 1929), p. 75.

cluded in his *Grandezas de España* (Seville, 1549), shows South America in its entirety. As on Medina's earlier map, Peru is the only country named on the southern continent. There are also place names for the Río de la Plata and the Estrecho de Magallanes. The latter separates the mainland from Tierra del Fuego, which is named Tierra Incognita on Medina's other map. Both South American coasts are delineated here.

The world map of the Catalonian Joan Martines, known as "Typus Orbis" (1587), is graded and shows more detail about America than the earlier Iberian maps (see Map 13). Here both seacoasts of the New World are fully depicted. The northern continent (not shown), identified as America, is exaggerated in size as compared with the southern continent. The continent's toponymy is more abundant than in other charts.

The Caribbean region and the Central American isthmus are presented as on other charts. The northern coast of South America is called Caribana, a name derived from the Carib Indians, who lived in the region. Among other place names Tisnada, Charcas, Picora, Patagonum, and Chica appear. Under the name Brasil is the date 1504, which proves that Martines knew of the exploration there by the Frenchman Palmier de Gonneville. The Amazon is called Paguana and also Orellana River, for Francisco de Orellana, who explored it. Peru's location is more nearly accurate than in other contemporary maps. The estuary of the Río de la Plata and the Paraná River are shown. The names Chile and Quito also enter cartography here. The Strait of Magellan divides the mainland from a southern land mass above the Antarctic Circle that is named Tierra del Fuego. Its extension northwest is Terra Incognita. Some names seem to indicate that the author was acquainted with the South American explorations of Pizarro, Cabeza de Vaca, Pedro de Mendoza, and Fernández Ladrillero. Altogether it is an impressive map. Martines' earlier chart, drafted in Messina in 1562, is toponymically less detailed, but the geographic configuration of South America is more exact than in his 1587 map. Not surprisingly, Martines' many topographic and toponymic features appeared later on other charts, especially in Langeren's "South America" (1595).

Graphically spectacular and toponymically rich is the Spanish map of America by Diego Gutiérrez, issued in Antwerp in 1562 (see Map

The South America portion of "Typus Orbis," from an

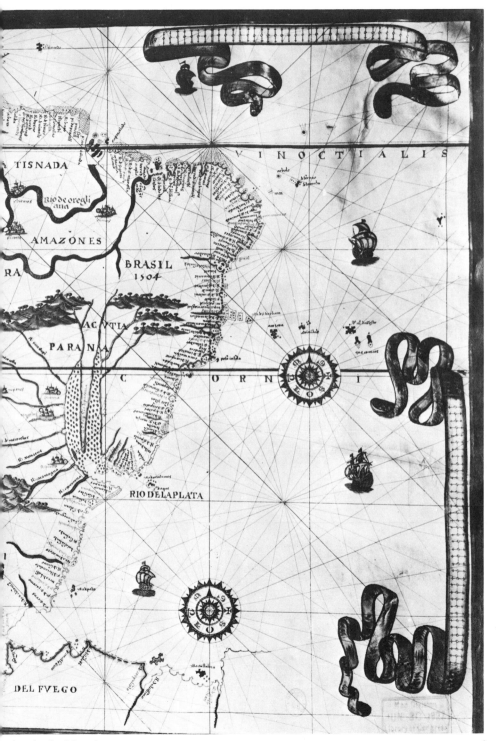

atlas drafted by the Catalonian Joan Martines in 1587.

Spanish map of the New World by Diego Gutiérrez (Antwerp, 1562).

14). South America looks almost like an upside-down Christmas tree, a cartographic peculiarity of many sixteenth-century charts. As a royal cosmographer, he introduced many new place names available in the Padrón and eliminated some imaginary old ones. In naming bodies of water, he retained Oceanus Occidentalis and Mar del Sur. He named the southern Pacific, Mare Magellanicum; the northern Atlantic, Oceanus Septentrionalis; and the southern Atlantic, Oceanus Australis. Apparently impressed by Francisco Orellana's exploration of the Amazon (1541–42), he depicted that mighty river in the characteristic snakelike course.

Gutiérrez' North America embraces only the eastern shore. Looking north to south, one finds a misplaced Gronlandia (Greenland), Picnemay (the Pygmies?), Labrador, Bacalaos, the mysterious Norimberga (known as Norumbega from Verrazano, 1529), and Nueva Galicia (central Mexico), the region of the Chichimeca Indians. Nueva España (Mexico) is placed in Central America along with Guatemala and Nicaragua. In South America, Nova Andalusia (Venezuela) makes its first appearance in cartography. The name Gigantum Regio for Patagonia relates to the popular myth about the gigantic size of the Patagonian Indians. To Tierra del Fuego the author gave the name Tierra Magellanica and presented it as a continental land mass. The best-depicted area is the Caribbean. The seas are filled with Spanish and Portuguese ships, sea monsters, and mythological figures.

Among the Portuguese maps of America related to that period are those of Lopo and Diogo Homem and of Vas Dourado. Lopo Homem's world map (1554) depicts eastern North America from approximately the southern trip of Greenland to Florida. Running uninterruptedly through the Central American isthmus, it delineates both coasts of South America. Only the southernmost part is missing (the Portuguese had not yet explored it), but the nearby area is identified as the Magellan Sea. The northern continent bears the name Fourth Part of the World (Quarta pars Mundi), and the southern one is named New World (Mundus Novus). The St. Lawrence River and the Bay of Fundy, as well as New England, are outlined, proving that Lopo knew of Jacques Cartier's discoveries (1534–42). He undoubtedly also utilized reliable Spanish sources, for Peru is properly marked.[16] The meridional part of South America is named Silver Land (Terra Argentea), which obviously refers to the future Argentina. Among new names the Antillean Sea (Mare Antiliarum), the Brazilian Sea (Mare Brasilis), and the Great Southern Sea (Mare Magnum Meridionale) appear on the Atlantic waters. The Peruvian Sea (Mare de Peru) and the Magellan Sea (Mare Inventum per Magalhães) are shown in the Pacific. Another characteristic of this chart is the markings for three climatic zones, important guides for navigators.

The map of North America and the Antilles by Diogo Homem (1558) is ornate and elaborate and has many place names. The Caribbean area is more detailed than it is in Lopo's chart, but the Florida peninsula is too broad. New England, the Bay of Fundy, the St. Lawrence waterway, with its inland islands, and the Paramantium Sea are cartographically attractive. Diogo considered Newfoundland an agricultural land. The Portuguese terminology utilized in this chart seems to confirm the map maker's acquaintance with João Alvares Fagundes' previous explorations of the New England and Canadian coastlands. Among new names Diogo introduced the Sea of Terranova (Mare Terre Noue) for Newfoundland coastal waters and Paramantium Sea for the inland water system east of the St. Lawrence. Surprisingly, he used the old name Spanish Sea (Mare Hispaniae) for the Atlantic waters touching the western coast of the Iberian Peninsula.

Also more detailed than Lopo Homem's chart is Fernão Vaz Dourado's map of the New World (1568). It depicts both coasts of South America. Graphically appealing but topographically less exact is the section depicting Patagonia and Tierra del Fuego. The archipelago is presented with some detail, but the water distribution in the Strait of Magellan is inaccurate. To judge from the toponymy, the map maker was acquainted with Cabeza de Vaca's southern exploits (1540–43) and with Sebastian Cabot's map of 1544, in which that region also shows some imperfections. Pictures of Indians with bows and arrows and the local flora and fauna somewhat compensate for these shortcomings.

[16]The name Peru appears on Iberian and other maps in a variety of spellings, such as Piru, Pyru, and Perus.

Of historical and toponymic note is the French world map by Pierre Desceliers (1546), especially the North America section. It presents the east coast from Labrador to the Gulf of Mexico, with a good portion of the adjoining inland area. It gives prominence to New England, Nova Scotia, the St. Lawrence Bay, and Newfoundland. Among new place names appear the legendary kingdom of Sagney (with a king seated on a throne), Ochelaga (the name given to the St. Lawrence River), La Terre du Laboureur (Labrador), and, several times repeated, Canada (an Iroquois-Huron word meaning "settlement"). This usage demonstrates that the map maker was acquainted with Cartier's three explorations of that area. It is the first known appearance on a map of the name Canada.

Other names introduced by Desceliers are Mer d'Espaigne (Spanish Sea) and Mer de France (French Sea), denoting certain parts of the Atlantic, which is named La Mer Occeane (the Ocean Sea). In Desceliers's planisphere (1550) the land on both sides of La Rivierede Ochelaga is marked Canada three times (see Map 15). In the region between Ochelaga and Sagne is a fort, and below it is a Frenchman who is speaking to some pygmies. At a distance are some Indians hunting large birds. Though the coastlines and rivers are not well defined, this disadvantage is outweighed by the rich French and Indian terminology. This terminology, soon appeared on other maps (including French ones, of course) with some modifications. Thus Nicolas Vallard's chart (1547) denotes the St. Lawrence River in Portuguese fashion as Rio do Canada. He also depicts a multitude of French settlers in the background, possibly an allusion to the opening of Robersval's fur trade in the region in 1542. Several European maps showed an increased interest in Canada after that.

An anonymous Portuguese map (ca. 1555), which presents the eastern coast from Labrador to the Strait of Magellan, adapts Vallard's French terminology for the St. Lawrence Bay region.[17] In the Belgian Jean Bellère's world map (Antwerp, 1554), which appeared in López de Gómara's *Historia de México*, the Canadian toponymy is based on Estévan Gómez' and Fagundes' explorations, rather than on Cartier's. Bellère's map is important, however, because the shape of

---

[17]This manuscript map, titled "Tierra de Lavrador," has been reproduced in Derek Howse and Michael Sanderson, *The Sea Chart*, pp. 35–36.

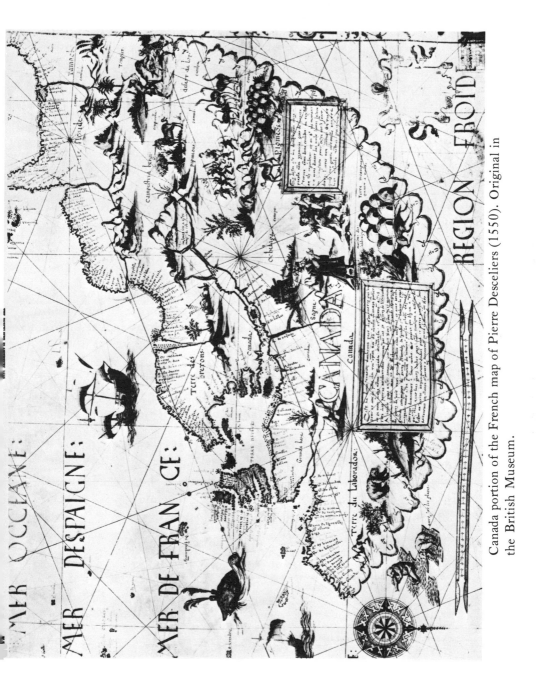

Canada portion of the French map of Pierre Desceliers (1550). Original in the British Museum.

South America is fairly well delineated, and the nomenclature on both coasts is applied correctly. Florida appears both as a peninsula and as a territory, and Hispania Nova (Mexico) is correctly located. Owing to the map makers' interest in orography, the Rocky Mountains and the Andes, though unnamed, are conspicuous. There are some errors: the Amazon flows from the south rather than from the west, and Mexico, Brazil, Peru, Chile, and Andalucía Nova (Venezuela) appear as separate territories.

Other non-Iberian maps that deal with the New World—and possibly molded the Old World's concepts about it—are the charts of the Italians Sebastian Cabot, Gastaldi, and Zaltieri, as well as those of Mercator, Ortelius, and Langaren, of the Low Countries.

Sebastian Cabot's world map (1544) depicts the New World along the eastern coast from Newfoundland to the Strait of Magellan and the western coast from California southward (see Map 16). In the northern portion of eastern North America, Cabot's terminology bears a close resemblance to the maps of Diego Ribeiro (1529) and Nicolas Desliens (1541), as well as to their topographic outlines.[18] New Spain, the Caribbean, and other American regions are presented with conventional details based on the Padrón, which were accessible to Cabot as the Spanish *piloto mayor*—the nautical supervisor of "ships going to the Indies." The territory north of Nueva España (New Spain) is marked Terra Incognita. The outline of the northern part of South America is somewhat too narrow, and some details of Patagonia, which Cabot explored (1526–39), are missing. This chart furnishes a lot of useful toponymic information. It is, however, controversial, for in his description Cabot boastfully attributed the discovery of North America jointly to himself and to his father, John, whom he had accompanied in 1497 as a boy. John Cabot did not leave any records or maps from his American exploration for England, and there are some contradictions in Sebastian's story.[19] The date

[18]This is the opinion of Morison, who compared Cabot's map with those of Ribeiro and Desliens. Morrison, *The European Discovery of America*, pp. 197–98. Cabot's explorations and map were earlier discussed by Henry Harrisse, in *Jean et Sebastien Cabot* (1882); by G. P. Winship, in *Cabot Bibliography* (1900); and by other historians.

[19]The only mention of John Cabot's exploration of North America in 1497 is found in Juan de la Cosa's "Mapamundi" of 1500. Nobody knows, however, how and from whom De la Cosa obtained this information or whether the English flags on his map were later added by someone else. Such later "corrections" were not unusual.

of the map is also in dispute. It was apparently changed from 1493 to 1497. This too casts doubt on Cabot's authorship of the map.

The *mappemonde* of Giaccomo Gastaldi (Venice, 1560) presents North America still united to Asia, a concept that had already been rectified by cosmographers of lesser fame (see Map 17). By his intercontinental "blending process," the misplaced Colorado River also flows in Asia. The mythical lands of Topira and Seven Cities are recorded, as well as areas that were already known, such as Labrador, Canada, Nova Ispania, and Florida. It is evident that Gastaldi used widely varying sources for North America, while frequently misplacing the toponymy of South America. The shape of the latter is similar to the inverted Christmas tree outline of other cartographers.

Gerhard Mercator, breaking with the Ptolemaic tradition, introduced in his maps the increased cylindrical projection, by means of which the parallels and meridians cross each other at right angles. This technique is displayed in his world map (Duisberg, 1569), which outlines the New World with fixed borderlines on both coasts. In utilizing this new approach, Mercator could not avoid topographic distortion, and his North America, even though fairly accurate, appears disproportionately large. Mercator's toponymy is rich and based on data of Spanish, Portuguese, and French explorations, which give his map credibility. The name S. Laurentii for the Bay of St. Lawrence appears for the first time, and the Appalachian Mountains appear southwest of Canada, titled Apalchen as on other maps. An inset inscription near Guanahani (San Salvador) explains that Columbus discovered the New Indies—that is, America—in 1492, which nullifies Vespucci's claim to the discovery.

Another important feature is Gerhard's inset picture of the Arctic region with the North Pole at its center. This concept was followed with more details in Rumold Mercator's world map (1587). The map, while very similar to Gerhard's map, contains new place names (see Map 18). Thus the northern continent is called America or New India (America sive India Nova), the southern portion of the Mar del Sur is named Mar Pacifico, and a huge continent is shown southeast of Tierra del Fuego with the name Terra Australia, a name also used by other cartographers. This map is impressive. Mercator's new cylindrical projection was followed by Ortelius, Delisle, and others,

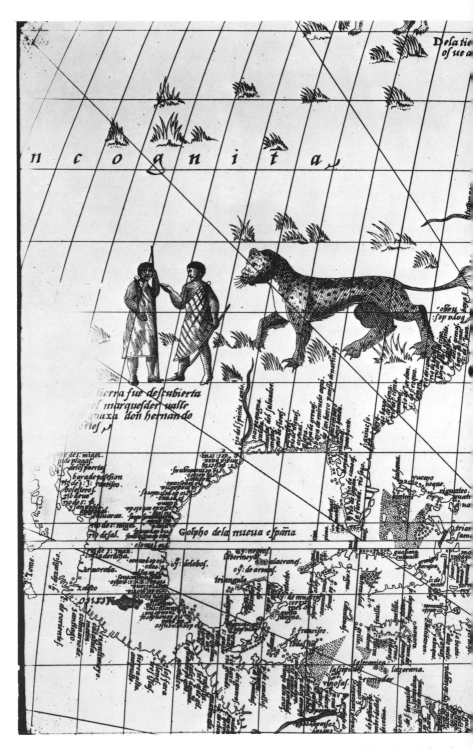

n c o g n i t a

Dela tie
of sue a

sierra fue defcubierta
el marquefdel ualle
quaxa don hernando
ortes

Golpho dela nueua efpaña

Spanish map of North America and the Antilles by Sebastian

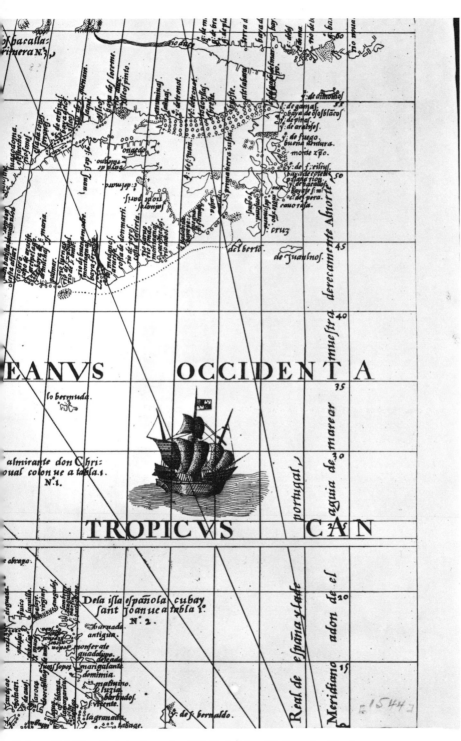

Cabot (1544). Original at the Bibliothèque Nationale, Paris.

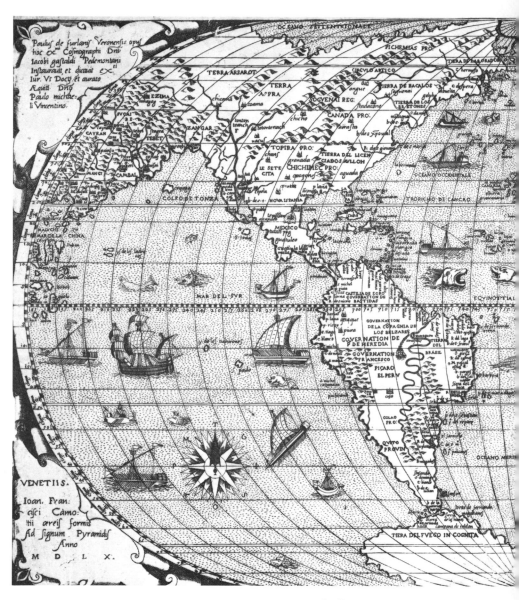

Italian world map by Giacomo

Gastaldi (Venice, 1560).

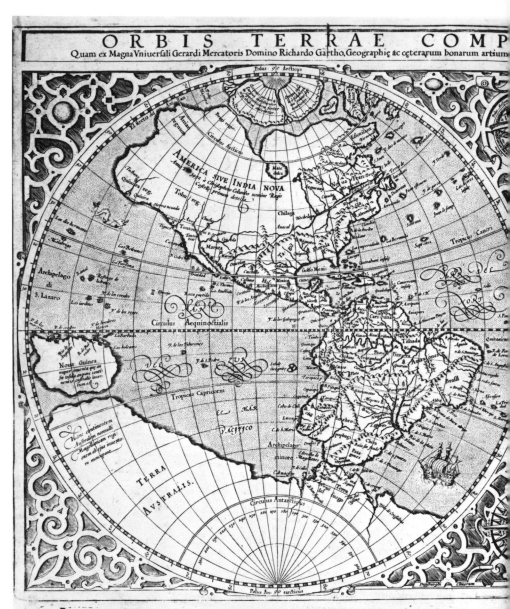

ORBIS TERRAE COMP

Quam ex Magna Vniuersali Gerardi Mercatoris Domino Richardo Gartho, Geographiæ ac cęterarum bonarum artium

DE MVNDI CREATIONE ac constitutione breuis instructio.

Studiosus Geographiæ ante omnia considerat mundi creationem, hoc modo. Deus constituto puncto, quod nunc mundi centrum est, pro sede et quiete gѕauium, massam liquidam informem creans, quã chaos uocant, illi eam imiecʼt, excitauitóʒ, uehementi spiritu eam agitauit, agitando crassior ѕ grauiora ѕʒ discreuit, quæ centro se ad æquilibrium applicantia, terram ac mare in unã corpus figuræ sphæricæ dederunt, cuius centrũ punctus ille qui sedes est grauium existit, supra hoc corpus ut leuiora et nobiliora quæ ѕ; ita superiorem locum obtinuerunt, lucidæ, materiam globoѕ paulatim collectã, lunam, solem, stellas ѕʒ reddidit, quæ ratione primi mobilis, supremi inquam cæli super polis æqui- noctialis siue mundi ab ortu in occasum rapiuntur, noctem diem ѕʒ diuidentes, at super alij̄s polis, eclypticæ uidelicet, proprio motu ab occasu in ortum, aliæ citius, aliæ tardius circumuoluuntur. Vt autem terra habitationi animalium accommoda fieret, spiritus ille quo placuit Deo undas in altum attollens, alibi montes & altiorem terræ æ ream con- gessit & solidauit, albi ѕʒ cauit uras & sinus effecit, in quos fluxilis aquæ descenderet, & quo in æquilibrio penderet tota machineѕ nostræ continentis quæ Asiam, Africam et Europam comprehendit alteram quam Americã siue no- uam Indiam uocant ex opposite obiecit, & quia hæ duæ continentes pro maxima parte supra æquinoctialem uersus polũ arcticum sunt sitæ, ideo his sub polo antarctico tertiam continentem opposuit, maribus undiѕʒ inter se commu- nicantibus, ut tota terra & mariѕʒ, machina undiѕʒ, æquilibrie esset & consisteret, omneiѕʒ, partes ex quauis regione adnusѕʒ ables redderentur. Hæc obiter ex Patri mei in suam Cosmographiam lucubrationibus annotare uolui, ut naturali orbis speculatione imbueretur Lector, & ad altiora etiam conditi mysteria aditum nanciscatur.

huius em sphærici corporis conuexam superficiem contemplaturus Geographiæ studiosus, astru illud subli- illorum situ uarsa ipsi accidentia contingere obseruet, quæ ratione circulorum, quibus astrorum motus, dis- tempora deti minantur, illi oburniunt. Sunt autē circuli ad Geographiam cognitu necessary, Aequinoctie ѕ Parallelei siue æqui distantes, & Meridiani. Porro quia hi circuli in plano non rodem modo quo in sphæra possunt, quod sphæræ superficies in planum seruata eade partium ad inuicem habitudine depingi nequeat, ѕʒ nos tamē compledende sphæræ rationem secutos esse, quã Gemma Frisius in suo planissphærio adinuenit, quæ longe optima est. Et si enim gradus à centro uersus circumferentiam crescant, utin gradibus æquinoctia- tamen latitudinis longitudinisѕʒ, gradus in eadem à centro distantia eandem ad inuicem proportionem seruê in sphæra, et quadranguli inter duos proximos parallelos duos ѕʒ, meridianos rectangulam figuram habent modum in sphæra, ita ut regiones undiquaѕʒ, omnes natiuam figurã obtinent sine omni tortuosa distractio- cente tamen uersus exteriora magnitudine, propter graduum latitudinis latitudinis ѕʒ, incrementum, atⁱ quo etiam fit ut paralleli, qui in sphæra æquatori sunt æquidistantes, hic circularei apperent, ѕ ѕ æquator- linea, permedium hemisphæri j̄ media inter utrumѕʒ, polum distantia ductã, quæ diuiditur in 180. gradus æquiⁱ diui tantum æquinoctialis in uno circulo, dimidium alterum in altero continetur, quia dimidium totius sphᶜ perficiei tantum in uno circulo comprehendi potest, nequaquã tota, ita uno circulo totam ueteribus cognitã tinentem comprehendimus, nimirum Europam, Asiam & Africam, Nouum autem orbem siue Indiam non circulo, Continentem interim australi in utrumѕʒ, circulum incidens. Dicitur autem æquinoctialis circulus ѕ noctia, quod solem tum peruenies efficit quod bis in anno contingit, quã 11. diem Martij & 14. Septem.

Flemish world map from Rumold Mercator's

Atlas Sidi Cosmographica (Duisburg, 1587).

Abraham Ortelius' *mappemonde* showing the New World (Antwerp, 1570).

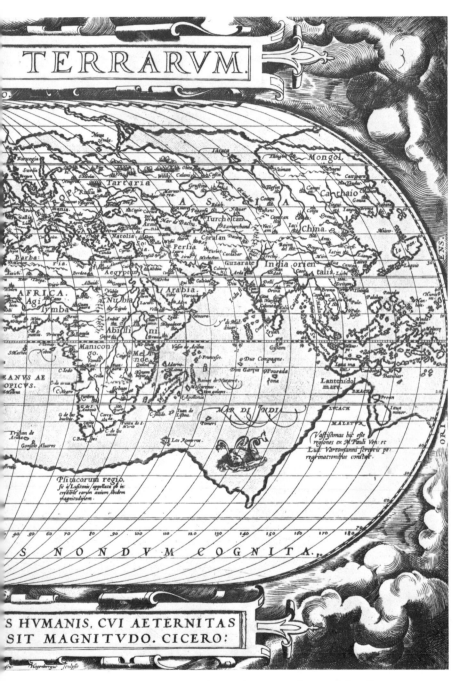

Original in the National Maritime Museum, Greenwich, Conn.

Dutch map of South America by Arnold F. Van Langeren
Voyages into the East and West Indies (London, 1598).

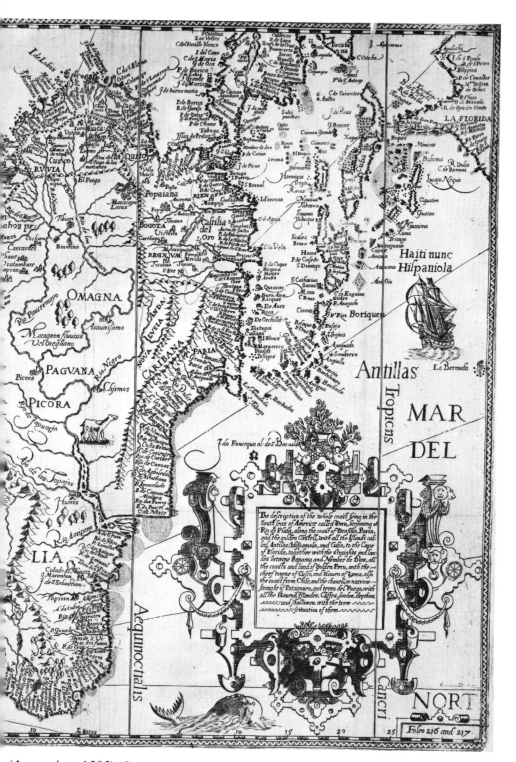

(Amsterdam, 1595). It appeared in Jan H. van Linschoten's famous

and greatly influenced the cartography of his time.

Topographically similar to Gerhard's chart is Abraham Ortelius' world map known as "Typus Orbis Terrarum," issued in Antwerp in 1570 (see Map 19). Its prominent feature is an extensive glacial continent girding the world on the southern perimeter. Called Terra Australis, it ranges from the Tropic of Capricorn to the South Pole. Two northern tips of this land mass are marked Tierra del Fuego and Plitacorum. Another, unnamed, glacial continent makes its appearance in the Arctic, separated from America, Europe, and Asia by sizable sea passages. In Ortelius' 1579 edition of the same map, the two main parts of the New World seem, for the first time, to be distinguished as North and South America, which was a notable contribution to geography. In addition to Mare Pacificum, the name Mare Atlanticum also makes its appearance in modern cartography. Ortelius also made maps of various Spanish colonies in America. Among them a chart of Peru (1574) depicts its river and mountain systems, with Lake Titicaca appearing prominently. Ortelius' maps denote the various climatic zones. A very prolific cartographer, Ortelius issued his map in many Dutch, Italian, Latin, French, German, and Spanish editions. According to experts, his atlas, *Theatrum Orbis Terrarum*, of which "Typus Orbis" formed a part, was the single greatest step in the evolution of a standard geography.

Arnold Van Langeren's map of South America (Amsterdam, 1595) presents a kind of toponymic variation (see Map 20). Among major regions identified by him are Castilla del Oro, Paraná, Brasilia, Chilem and Peruvia. The fabulous wealth of the latter must have impressed the author greatly, because he placed the name Peruviana in the center of South America. The Caribbean islands are called Antillas in the Portuguese-French fashion; one of them has two names, Haiti and Hispaniola.

Another chart of that period is George Best's "Map of the World," issued in London in 1578 (see Map 21). On it two glacial continents, one in the north and another in the south, are marked Terra Septentrionalis and Terra Australis. Best sketched a passage between the Arctic and the northern shores of North America and named it Frobisher's Straites, relating it to Martin Frobisher's three voyages to the Arctic (1576–78). His map includes only five regional place names in the entire New World. Its topographic configuration is

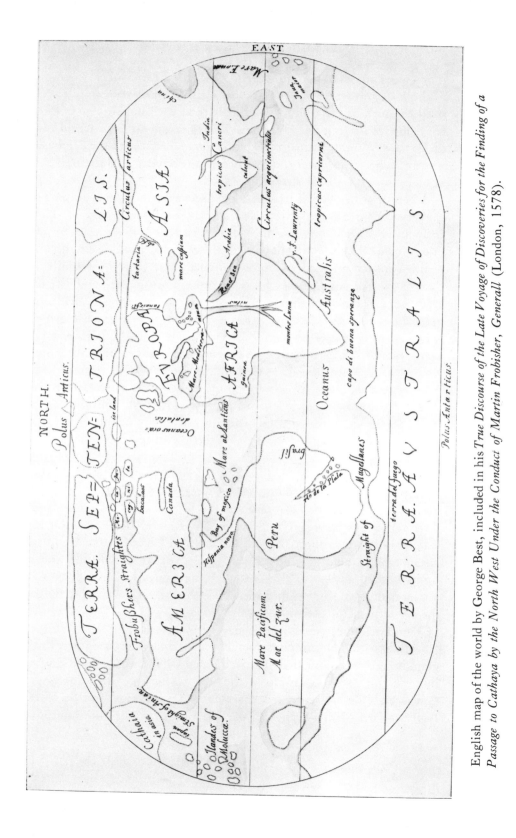

English map of the world by George Best, included in his *True Discourse of the Late Voyage of Discoveries for the Finding of a Passage to Cathaya by the North West Under the Conduct of Martin Frobisher, Generall* (London, 1578).

inexact and attests to the rather primitive state of English cartography of the time, despite a few remarkable British maritime exploits. Not until the turn of the century would there be an English chart of any consequence dealing with the New World. Such was the world map of Edward Wright, issued in London in 1600 (see Map 22). Based mostly on Spanish sources, it conformed to conventional cartographic knowledge with all its virtues and flaws.

A century after the official date of discovery, European notions of the New World were still based mostly on Iberian maps. They influenced other charts and the general concepts of America in the Old World. The colonization of the Americas throughout the sixteenth century resulted in more knowledge of them, especially of the coastal regions, where the Spaniards, Portuguese, and French established their strongholds. Exploration of the interior had also begun, but communications with the colonies were restricted, which explains the disparity in names and locations. On the whole, however, the Iberian cartography of the seventeenth century was somewhat better oriented. South America, instead of being presented as an inverted Christmas tree, slowly emerged in more or less its actual shape. In the maps made during the early English colonization of North America, disparities in geography were abundant.

Let us now examine some seventeeth-century cartographic developments. The map of South America included in Antonio de Herrera's *Descripción de las Indias Occidentales* (Madrid, 1601) outlines the southern continent fairly well—better than it does the northern one. Surprisingly, among the territorial place names only three territories are marked: New Spain, Brazil, and Peru, the last extending through most of South America. Chile is also recorded, but not prominently. The map is graded only for latitude and is limited in names, but on the west coast the Andes are located, though not named. Two lines of demarcation—the eastern in the Pacific and the western in the Atlantic—are prominent.

The Portuguese manuscript navigational chart of the Western Hemisphere by Dominguos Sanches (Lisbon, 1618) shows topographic configurations that approach geographic reality, though some imperfections are noticeable in the northeastern coastline of South America. This partly graded chart depicts a good portion of North America, with Nova França (Canada), Virginia, and Florida prominently outlined. Central America is accurately presented, as is the Caribbean region. The northern part of South America bears the conventional name Tierra Firme. The locations of Brazil and Peru are correct; the other territories are identified mainly by urban place names. The hydrographic outline of the interior of South America is fairly accurate, except for the inclusion of a large nonexistent lake in northern Brazil, which also haunted other cosmographers. Tierra del Fuego is shown with a degree of accuracy. The distances between America, Africa, and Europe are fairly realistic. This map is adorned with Portuguese and Spanish coats of arms placed over the various regions. There are also a few silhouettes of saints.

Other Portuguese maps relating to America are those of Teixeira and Peres, each of which has distinctive features. In the colored manuscript atlas of João Teixeira (Lisbon [?], 1630) the contours of the New World are far from exact, but it has an unusual abundance of names (see Map 23). Like Sanches' map, Teixeira's depicts New England and Virginia, and in the Arctic region Grunlanda (Greenland), Islanda (Iceland), and Frislanda make their appearance. The map follows Desceliers's terminology, naming the St. Lawrence River the Rio de Canada. Among new place names are Acapulco in Mexico. Charcas, Mendoza, and Paraguay appear as territorial units. Another novelty in this map, besides the inclusion of the Strait of Magellan, is the Strait of Le Maire, which proves that Teixeira knew about the circumnavigation by Schouten and Le Maire (1615–16), during which this new southern sea passage was discovered. Besides some mythical place names, many more real ones are shown, demonstrating that the cartographer utilized new geographic data. Indication of the climatic zones shows the Portuguese preoccupation with climatology.[20]

Curiously, Indians also made maps before and immediately after the Conquest. Those charts, included in some Aztec codices, depicted mostly the interior of Mexico, with Lake Texcoco and its island, on which the ancient Tenochtitlán was located. While those codices are anonymous, there is in existence a signed native Peruvian map of the

[20]Teixeira's manuscript atlas, bound later, has lettering on the spine indicating that it belonged to the collection of secret maps of America in Portuguese archives. To judge from a Castilian preface written in 1692, it then fell into Spanish hands and lay forgotten for several centuries. It was purchased by the United States Library of Congress in 1921.

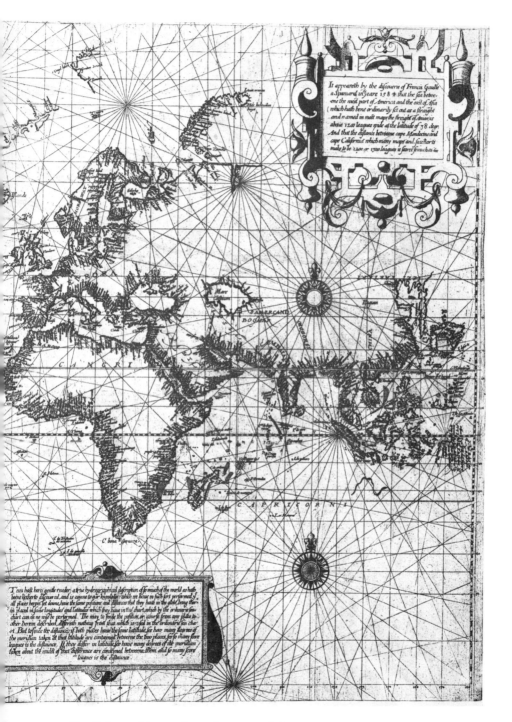

It appeareth by the discouerie of Francis Gaulle a Spaniard in y.e yeare 1584 that the sea betwe-ene the west part of America and the east of Asia (which hath bene ordinarily set out as a straight and n amed in most maps the streight of Anian) is about 1200 leagues wide at the latitude of 38 deg: And that the distance betweene cape Mendocino and cape California which many maps and sea char ts make to be 1500 or 1700 leagues is scarce so much as 100

Tou hast here gentle reader, a true hydrographicall description of so much of the world as hath bene hetherto discouered, and is comen to our knowledge: which we haue to such art performed, of all places beyond the lande, haue the same positions and distances that they haue in the globe, how there in placed is their longitude and latitude which they haue in this chart which by the ordinary sea chart can in no wise be performed. The way to finde the position, or course from any place to other herein described, differeth nothing from that which is vsed in the ordinarie sea char ct. But to finde the distance; if both places haue the same latitude, see how many degrees of the meridian taken at that latitude are contayned betweene the two places, so so many score leagues is the distance. If they differ in latitude see how many degrees of the meridian taken about the midst of that difference are contayned betweene them, and so many score leagues is the distance.

English world map by Edward Wright (London, 1600).

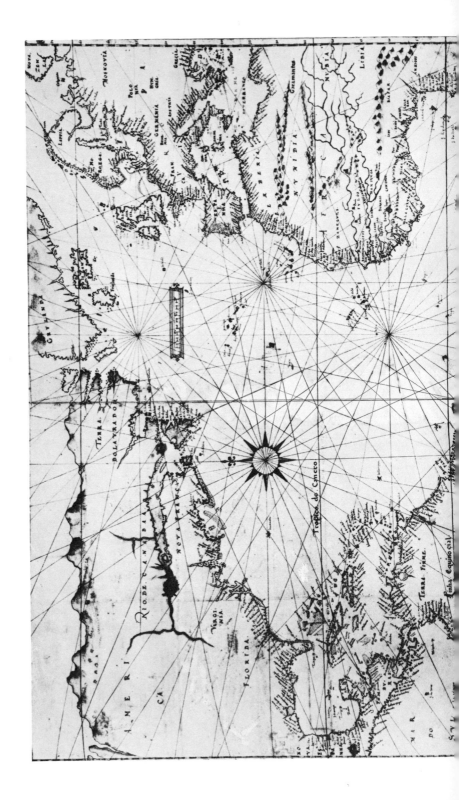

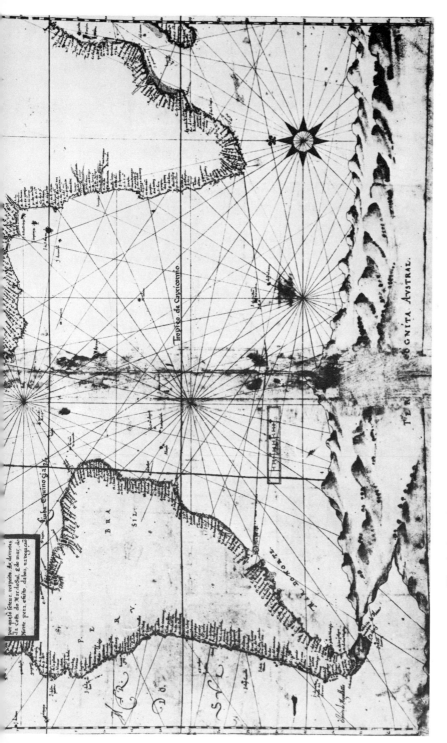

North America and the Caribbean, by João Teixeira, of Portugal (1630).

Inca empire, drafted at the beginning of the seventeenth century (see Map 24).[21] Its maker outlined the western coast of South America from Guayaquil to Santiago de Chile. Special attention was paid to Peruvian cities and rivers, and a few drawings of prominent Inca monarchs are shown. The tropical jungle is filled with wild animals and Indians, and the sea with whales, mermaids, and Spanish galleons. The unnamed Andes are presented as very high mountains, for which the map maker deserves credit—though not for locating them on the Atlantic coast.

Another map of South America was issued in Peru by Lucas de Quirós (Lima, 1618). The general shape of the southern continent is somewhat more accurate than it is in most contemporary European charts, except for the curve on the central part of the Brazilian coast. It shows South America from Panama to Tierra del Fuego. The unnamed Andes extend along the west coast, but the other mountain ranges are shown too geometrically. Río de la Plata, Orinoco, and Paraná are shown; the Amazon appears with the name Río Orellana. A nonexistent lake with twelve islands is shown in northern Brazil. The Line of Demarcation is also shown. Among the many place names are those on the west coast, which correspond to the present-day Ecuador, Peru (here named Piru), and Chile. This ungraded manuscript map is in color, with a predominance of yellows, blues, and browns. Toponymically and topographically De Quirós' work compares favorably with contemporary Spanish charts.

According to José Aguilar, De Quirós had a map-making shop in Lima, one of the first in colonial South America and perhaps in the Western Hemisphere.[22] De Quirós, who also made a color navigational chart of Callao, was the son of a Portuguese captain in the service of Spain, Pedro Fernandes de Quirós. The latter and Váez de Torres, sponsored by the Count of Monterrey, the viceroy of Peru, sailed from Callao and discovered Australia in 1605. De Quirós' family settled in Lima.

In his two sea charts of New England and the St. Lawrence region

---

[21]The map appears in Felipe Guamán Poma de Ayala, *Nueva crónica y buen gobierno* (Paris, 1936). Utilizing a framelike descriptive technique, the map maker indicated all four parts of the Inca empire: Chinchasuyo, Kollasuyo, Cuontinsuyo, and Antisuyo, calling them native kingdoms.

[22]José Aguilar, *Historia de la Cartografía*, pp. 177–80. De Quirós' map is in the Library of the Royal Palace, Madrid.

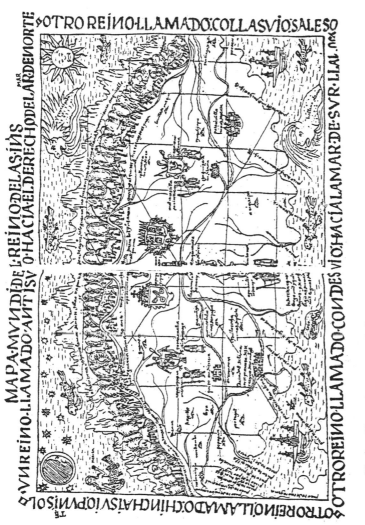

Native Peruvian map of the Inca empire drafted at the beginning of the seventeenth century. It appeared in the manuscript of Felipe Guamán Poma de Ayala, published as *Nueva Crónica y buen gobierno* (Paris, 1936). Reproduction furnished by Manuel M. Valle, Lima.

(Paris, 1612, 1632) Samuel de Champlain delineated the coast between Labrador and Vineyard Sound. The Great Lakes region west of Lake Ontario has many new place names and is accurately presented for the first time. It was Champlain who permanently established the name St. Lawrence for the river and bay.

Continuing Champlain's pioneering work was another Frenchman, Nicolas Sanson d'Abbeville, author of the map "Amerique Septentrionale," issued in Paris in 1650 (see Map 25). This map shows new details of the Atlantic seaboard from the Arctic to Florida, including eastern Canada, Mexico, Florida, the Caribbean, and Lower California, which is shown as an island. D'Abbeville's later maps of Canada were even more detailed.

While most sixteenth-century maps were executed in black and white, polychrome charts became more frequent in the seventeenth century. In addition to the Italian and Portuguese color maps, which were noted for their attractiveness, many Dutch, French, and English color maps appeared. The new pictorial elements broke the monotony and possibly diverted attention from the continuing uncertainties about geography. The endless imitation by map makers of each other contributed little to the development of knowledge.

The earliest known English polychrome venture was in the first English atlas (London, 1627), which was prepared by John Speed. It contains his map of the New World, drafted in 1626 and reissued in 1651 (see Map 26). Like the conventional topographic outlines, Speed's continents stretch too far northward. The novelty of his map is that one continent bears the name North America or Mexicana, the other, South America or Peruana. The new English northern discoveries, such as the Hudson Bay and Hudson Strait (1610), as well as Button Bay and the Queen Elizabeth Foreland, are named. California appears, again as an island. The vaguely contoured Antarctic region, named Magellanica, and the Southerne Unknowne Land are references to Magellan and Plitacorum.[23] The Atlanticke Ocean is marked so only in the vicinity of Europe; west of the Azores the name is changed to Mar del Nort, while west of Africa it is called

---

[23] Speed's inset inscription reads: "Plitacorum regio is the Country of Parrots soo Called of by Portugals from the extraordinary and almost incredible bignes of those birds there." The allusion is undoubtedly to the flightless penguins, inhabitants of the Antarctic, about which Speed, as a tailor-turned-cartographer had only a nebulous idea.

Westerne Ocean. Likewise, the Pacificke Sea bears two additional names, Mar del Zur and Ocean of Peru. Following other cosmographers, Speed marked three climatic zones around the circular frame of his map. His chart is embellished with allegorical color presentations of the four elements, the heavens with a coastline, and the medallion busts of four discoverers: Drake, Magellan, Van der Noort, and Cavenish (sic). The earth and the water are symbolized by two naked women. All of this decoration compensated somewhat for the map's topographic deficiencies.

With the passing of time and the growing exploratory experience, geography was also slowly but steadily advancing. The older maps were now challenged by a public seeking more details, as well as by painstaking cosmographers. This transitional period was marked by the appearance of some informative charts, which brought the image of America into better geographic focus. Thus Guillaume Delisle map "L'Amérique Septentrionale" (Paris, 1700) presents North America in a realistic way. It delineates with a high degree of exactness, the eastern and middle western territories of today's Canada and the United States, as well as Mexico, Central America, and the Carribean.

Among the Spanish maps of the New World from the beginning of the eighteenth century are one by Sebastián Fernández de Medrano and another by Juan de Torquemada. Both are black-and-white, graded charts. Fernández de Medrano was a Spanish general on active duty in Flanders, where cosmography was highly developed. His world map is included in his *Geografía o Moderna Descripción del Mundo* (Antwerp, 1709). It appears to have been modeled after some Flemish maps, because it displays similar topographic features in both hemispheres. It depicts the New World with some degree of clarity. The western seaboard of North America is only partly delineated. Lower California appears as an island, a detail soon to be corrected by Juan de Torquemada, a monk who lived in Mexico.

Torquemada's map "Las Yndias Ocidentales" appeared in his work *Monarquía Indiana* (Madrid, 1723). The outline of South America is fairly realistic and resembles that of Herrera. This map, however, has more place names, such as Terranova, Sierra Nevada, Mississippi, Lucayas, Martinique, Juan Fernández Islands, and Chiloé Islands. The northern delineation of North America extends to approximately 60° latitude, which indicates the map maker's exclusive

French map of North America by Nicolas

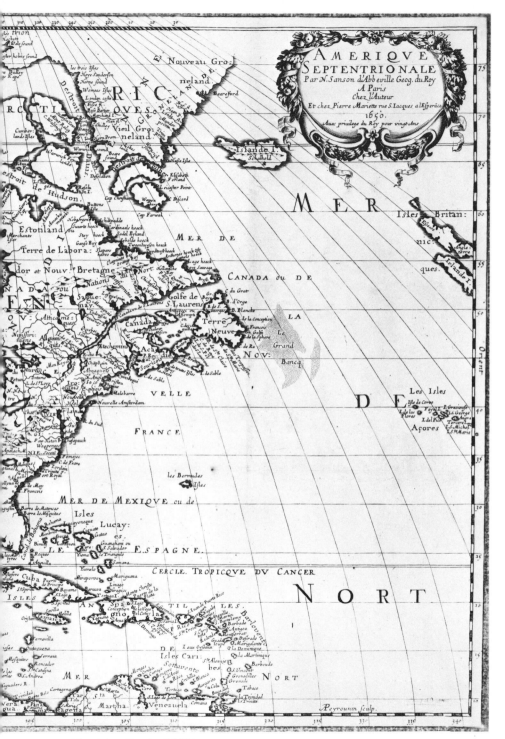

Sanson d'Abbeville (Paris, 1650).

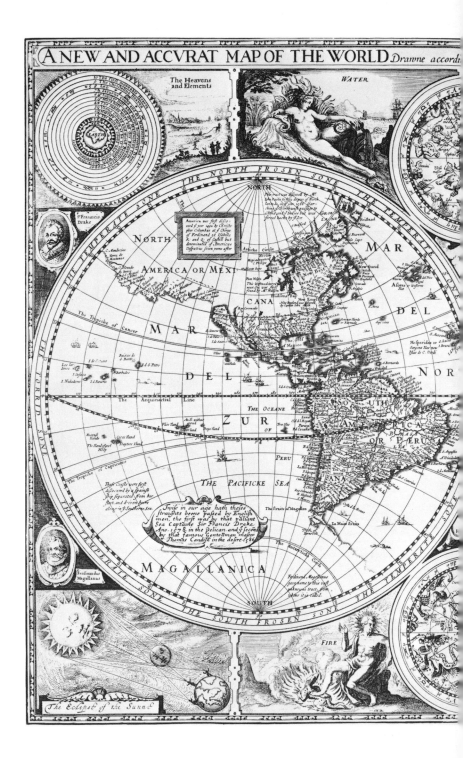

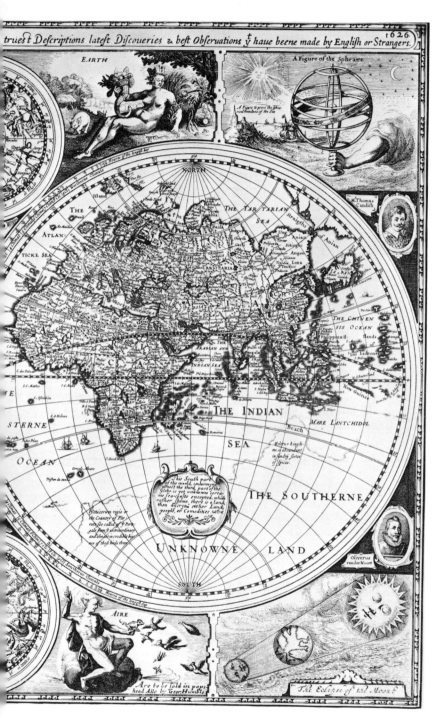

English map of the world by John Speed (1626).

interest in the Spanish possessions of the New World. The map also indicates climatic zones.

More detailed maps of America began appearing early in the second half of the eighteenth century. Examples are José A. de Villaseñor y Sánchez' "America Septentrional" (Rome, 1754), the world map in M. Pluche's *Espectáculos de la Naturaleza* (Madrid, 1757), and Tomás López' *mapamundi* in his *Atlas elemental* (Madrid, 1792), which delineates the New World in an approximately accurate shape. Tomás López included an abundance of names, most of them correctly placed. Canada, the thirteen states of the new United States, and New Spain are correctly located, as are the South American and Caribbean colonies of Spain, Portugal, England, France, Holland, and Denmark. The geographic mythology has almost disappeared. The scales of distances, presented in Spanish, English, and French nautical miles, demonstrate that López was a professional geographer. He brought Spanish cartography to a competitive level.

In summary, many explorers, including Columbus and Cabral, upon arriving at the shores of the New World, thought it to be India, Cathay (China), or the land of the Great Khan, known vaguely from the thirteenth-century description of Marco Polo. Cabot, while searching for a northern sea passage to the Spice Islands, assumed that the land he found on his way was somewhere on the outskirts of China or Japan. These explorers' assumptions invariably related to Asia, known from Ptolemy's medieval *Cosmography*. The Iberian explorers considered the newly discovered lands to be insular or peninsular parts of the Asiatic continent. This orientation persisted for some time. Thus one can understand why Columbus named the lands he discovered the Indies, a term adapted by many as the West Indies. In 1507, Waldseemüller introduced the name America, a misnomer since Columbus discovered the new continent, not Amerigo Vespucci. Vespucci visited the New World several years later, in 1499, accompanying the Spanish explorer Alonso de Ojeda. Both geographic names, the Indies and America, have been used in cartography since then. Columbus' American exploration was properly recorded, and thus he became the "official" discoverer. But history also mentions other little-documented pre-Columbian voyages. Two of them are discussed later.

Was the New World a burdensome reality or an earthly paradise? Some explorers seemed to believe the latter, finding the American flora and fauna luxuriant and the precious metals abundant. Also, the many Indians seemed rather docile and innocent, which prompted Chateaubriand to evoke the romantic image of *le bon sauvage*— though in truth some native tribes proved to be rather fierce. Viewing the toponymy on the early American maps, one notices references to paradise, as well as the names of mythical kingdoms and biblical names. This indicates that some discoverers were imbued with mythology and religious tradition, which they transplanted through names to the newly discovered lands.

The Iberians, ignoring the Amerindian languages and cultures, which they considered pagan, gave many cities and rivers Peninsular names. Some of the names were changed a few times, with resulting confusion. Examples are Santo Domingo and Haiti for Hispaniola, Spagniola, or Española; Juana and Isabela for Cuba; and Lucayas for the Bahamas. Some native Indian names were retained—Cuba, Cuzco, Haiti, Guayana, Jamaica, and Texcoco—though they were sometimes Hispanized or mutilated orthographically. Adherence to Indian toponymy started only after the missionaries learned the native languages. Several legendary kingdoms or regions, such as Anian, Quivira, and Norumbega, survived well beyond the seventeenth century. The geographic reality of America, both toponymically and topographically, emerged in European maps a century later.

Comparing the Iberian maps of America of the sixteenth and seventeenth centuries with the Italian, Dutch, and French ones of the same period, one notices that, with very few exceptions, the latter were more informative. Why was it that the nations that were not involved in the American exploration adventures (with the exception of France) were able to produce more nearly exact maps than Portugal and Spain? How did they obtain their data, and why were they so eager to know about Iberian activities in the Americas? Historians of cartography rarely touch upon this question. One should understand that during the era of explorations maps were important sources of information and were of commercial and political value. The precious metals and the colonial products sold by Spain and Portugal on European markets produced envy and rivalry among the buying nations. Those nations wanted to enrich themselves also by purchasing such goods directly from the American colonies or establishing their own trading posts there. Spain and Portugal knew about those foreign intentions and, to protect their interests, established tightly organized trade monopolies. Logically, therefore, they would not release informative maps of their colonies.

The competing nations then began sending their own expeditions to the New World to establish footholds there. Since most of those expeditions proved costly or unsuccessful, they resorted to piracy. That practice brought fantastic revenues in confiscated cargo and even ships. History records the English pirates as among the fiercest. Their looting of Spanish ships contributed considerably to the wealth of the emerging British Empire. Germán Arciniegas said that most of the gold and silver extracted from "America's womb" thus found its way to the banks of London, Amsterdam, and Venice. That, of course, seriously undercut the legend of the fabulous wealth of colonial Spain. Sometimes the pirates established themselves in less-inhabited or less-guarded territories, especially on strategically located islands, from which they could easily intercept Iberian ships. Some of those colonies, of course, were also established for economic purposes. That explains the appearance of English, French, Dutch, and Danish colonies in the Caribbean and on the South American mainland (called the Spanish Main).

Spain and Portugal scrupulously recorded their overseas discoveries on well-guarded royal maps (in Spanish, the Padrón; in Portuguese, the Padrão). The death penalty was imposed for disclosing such state secrets. As a precaution, there existed very few detailed manuscript maps designed for royal use. One of them was João Teixeira's manuscript atlas of 1630. It belonged to the secret collection of American maps at the Portuguese court—until it inexplicably appeared in Spain in 1690. Another such map was the Cantino map of 1502. No doubt there was an organized foreign intelligence service in Madrid and Lisbon whose purpose was to secure valuable cartographic information about the Iberian explorations of the New World. This information ultimately found its way to many non-Iberian cartographers.

Another possible source of data was the navigators themselves. Quite a few foreign sea captains were in the service of Spain, and we know that not a few of them also sailed under other flags. Nor should we discount the Vatican. At that time the popes played a unique political as well as religious role as arbiters in colonial disputes. Thus they were receiving information about various discoveries, sometimes accompanied by maps, which also showed the location of missionaries. The Vatican Library still holds many such "first" maps, while others were drafted by Italian cartographers on commission. It would be interesting to know from whom they secured their data.

In view of all these circumstances it is not surprising that some "foreign" cartographers had more exact data at their disposal than did those who were allowed to use official Iberian maps. But even in the official maps one perceives some differences between the more informative Portuguese and the less informative Spanish maps. Seemingly, the quality depended on the degree of liberty of map makers during the seventeenth century among the Portuguese, whose American colonies were somewhat less exposed to foreign rapacity than the Spanish ones. An interesting feature of many Portuguese maps is the delineation of the various climatic zones, which was soon copied by Spanish, Dutch, English, French, and other map makers. While Iberian cartography was deeply involved in legal aspects of American colonization, the other European maps were mostly concerned with political and administrative aspects.

Another reason for the relative "backwardness" of Iberian cartography was the strain the colonization of the New World placed on the Iberian nations, especially upon Spain. In the time between the discovery of America in 1492 and of Australia in 1605 much of Spain's human and financial resources was exhausted. Concentrating mainly in America, Spain was not able to pursue colonization of the world's sixth continent, which was more systematically explored by Holland and later by England, which finally took it over. Spain's round-the-world maritime activities ceased in the second part of the seventeenth century. Its exploratory zeal diminished almost in direct proportion to the increasing Dutch, British, and French maritime operations.

In one way or another this was reflected in the decay of Spanish cartography. The opposite may be said of Holland, which in the sixteenth and seventeenth centuries achieved its cartographic "golden age," supported by flourishing foreign trade and colonial enterprises.

Colonization also became a major interest of the British, who gradually gained in knowledge of geography and map making. French cosmography was also beginning to develop. Except for its colony Brazil, Portugal spread mostly to distant colonial outposts in Africa, Asia, and Oceania. Owing to the close ties with them, Portugal produced a voluminous cartography that never stopped developing, even if it was not always accessible to the outside world.

Cartography profited considerably as its practicioners moved from one country to another, implanting their ideas and techniques or following the patterns of the adopted country. Thus the Genoese Nicolay de Canerio's early map of America (ca. 1502), which bears a certain resemblance to the Cantino map (1502), seems to indicate that both map makers utilized the same Portuguese sources and that Canerio had spent many years in Portugal. Baptista Boazio's drafting, in London, of the map of Sir Francis Drake's pirate voyage to the West Indies (1588) indicates that at least some Italian map makers were active in England. Indeed, they introduced the art of cartography to the English. Leo Bagrow says, in his *History of Cartography*, that Spain and France attracted Portuguese pilots and chart makers into their service during the sixteenth century. These men assuredly brought Portuguese charts with them, and those charts undoubtedly served as models for Spanish and French maps, as shown by the use of Portuguese terminology. Likewise, during the sixteenth century, owing to religious conflicts and political discontent in the Low Countries, which were still under Spanish rule, some Flemish cosmographers and map makers migrated to England, Germany, and Switzerland, where they continued their activities and shared their knowledge. In addition, the Flemish masters of map making engraved or edited many sixteenth- and seventeenth-century foreign-drafted charts in Holland and Belgium, although many were also appearing in Italy and other countries.

Cartography is a mirror of geographic discoveries, but not all of those discoveries are recorded. Those forgotten, but perhaps no less important, explorations of America are obscure because they involved navigators who failed to return or because the countries who sponsored them that did not attach enough importance to them. Such an instance was reported by L. A. Vigneras, a French historian, in 1956. It concerned a pre-Columbian voyage to America by men of

Bristol, England. He found, in the Spanish archives in Simancas, a letter from one John Day, an English merchant residing in Seville, to Columbus, written in 1497. While giving Columbus an account of John Cabot's successful voyage, Day wrote: "It is considered certain that the cape of the said land [found by Cabot] was found and discovered in *other times* by the men of Bristol who found 'Brasil,' as your Lordship knows. It was called the Ysle of Brasil and it is assumed and believed to be the mainland."[24] British historians J. A. Williamson and D. B. Quinn, after scrutinizing the royal exploration grants awarded to British merchants, speculate that such an expedition could have taken place before 1480 or between 1481 and 1494. This assumption was to a certain degree supported by a letter from the Spanish ambassador in London, Pedro de Ayala, to Ferdinand and Isabella in 1498. While reporting to them on Cabot's expedition, he said, "For the last seven years the people of Bristol have equipped two, three, or four caravels to go in search of the island of Brazil and the Seven Cities, according to the fancy of this Genoese [Cabot]." These places were still considered to exist well after the discovery of the New World. Vigneras' discovery of Day's letter to the Great Admiral spurred historical interest but disturbed some of Columbus' staunch partisans, especially Morison, who had already denied the validity of some recorded pre-Columbian Portuguese explorations.

Another unrecorded pre-Columbian Spanish voyage to America was said to have been undertaken by Alonso Sánchez de Huelva, called the "Unknown Pilot" by some historians. An account of that expedition appeared in *Colón no descubrió América*, by Manual López Flores (Madrid, 1964). It is based mostly on stories persistently repeated in Andalusia and backed by references of Spanish and Portuguese historians. According to the author, Sánchez, who was engaged in trade shipping between Spain and the Azores, made the western trip in 1481. He reached Quisqueye (Hispaniola) and reconnoitered other islands, Siboneys (Cuba) and Tureyqueri (Santa María de Guadalupe). At the latter he lost his ship and was compelled to build another one, which delayed his return to Spain.

On Sánchez' homeward voyage, according to Flores, a storm

---

[24]Louis André Vigneras, "New Light on the 1497 Cabot Voyage to America," *Hispanic-American Historical Review*, Vol. XXXVI (1956), pp. 506–509.

wrecked his new vessel in the waters near the island of Madeira. Sick and battered, Sánchez and four sailors reached the island, where Columbus was staying. Columbus took him to his home. There, on his deathbed, Sánchez gave an account of the islands to Columbus, who immediately left Madeira for Spain. There he offered to the crown his plan for discovery of the Indies. If the story is true, it would explain Columbus' certainty about the location of the distant lands. One might even raise the question whether that was not the beginning of Columbus' insular concept of America. The chronicler-missionary Las Casas, who shortly after went to live on Hispaniola, stated that he heard from the natives about the previous presence of white men on the island. Was not the wreck of Sánchez' ship, said to have been found by Columbus on the coast of Guadalupe, of the same construction as his own caravel? We can only regret that Sánchez left no map.

CHAPTER 2

AMERICANIST TERMINOLOGY AND RELATED CONCERNS

From the time of its "official" discovery, America—the New World countries. Surprisingly enough, Ibero-Americans themselves, have included geographical as well as cultural and political terminology. As discussed in Chapter 1, because Columbus believed that he had reached the Asiatic archipelago of India when he landed on San Salvador, Spaniards adopted *Indias* (*Indies*) as the name for America and called the natives *indios* (*Indians*). Spaniards who lived in the Indies a long time came to be known as *indianos*. Those names appeared in colonial documents and also in the first chronicles and histories. The legislation compiled in *Derecho Indiano* and *Leyes de Indias* also used the names. The voluminous official documents concerning the Spanish colonies in America are preserved in Seville in what is still called the Archivo de Indias.

By rights the new continent that Columbus had discovered should have been named for him. Instead, as we have seen, a later navigator, Amerigo Vespucci, was given that honor. Though *America* gradually became the popular name in many European nations, Spain continued for a long time to use the name *Indias*. The English adopted *America* without reservation, and so did the Anglo-Americans. The Anglo-Americans continue to use the name for their country, as well as the official name, the *United States of America*. Their appropriation of *America* is sometimes resented by their fellow North Americans, the Canadians and the Mexicans, but customs are sometimes stronger than geographical facts.

Americanists—students of New World matters—generally agree that United States citizens do not have exclusive rights to the name *American*. It belongs by fact and by right to the citizens of all New World countries. Surprisingly enough, Ibero-Americans themselves, as well as Europeans, call the people of the United States *North Americans*, which seems more appropriate. It would be preferable to substitute "United Statians" (*estadounidenses*) for North Americans, but that solution presents lexicographical and grammatical obstacles. The word *estadounidense* is used in Spanish as an adjective, not as a noun, so that its use is largely descriptive, as in such expressions as *costumbres estadounidenses*.

In geographical terms the New World is relatively clearly defined. *America* includes *North America*, *Central America*, *South America*, and the *American Antilles*. Within those divisions are clearly defined geographical regions. For example, *Mesoamerica* includes part of southern Mexico and most of Central America. *Amazonian America*, or *Amazonia*, takes in the basin of the Amazon River and its tributaries, which extend into various tropical countries of South America, and includes parts of Brazil and the forested areas of Venezuela, Colombia, Ecuador, Peru, Bolivia, and Paraguay. *Tropical America*, or *Equatorial America*, incorporates principally the tropical regions within the Amazon basin, as well as the Guianas and the islands of the Caribbean. There are, however, tropical zones in other countries with varied climates, such as Mexico and Central America and some South American coastal zones on both oceans.

Andean America, predominantly mountainous in character, takes in countries dominated by the Andes: Colombia, Venezuela, Ecuador, Bolivia, Peru, and Chile. *River Plate America* is composed of Argentina and Uruguay, countries of the Río de la Plata. Because the Paraná River, a tributary of the Río de la Plata, also crosses Paraguay, that country is sometimes included within the designation. *Antillean America* includes both the Greater and the Lesser Antilles, in the Caribbean Sea. The British named some of these islands the *West Indies*. In this they imitated the Spaniards. After the Conquest of Mexico, Indians continued to inhabit the islands for a time. Among them were the Caribs, from whom the geographic zone took its name. It is somewhat ironic that, when the English became involved in the area, practicing piracy and establishing their insular colonies, there were almost no Indians left. Like the Spaniards, the English settled their Caribbean islands with African slaves. They in turn were followed by immigrants from India and China, who also became important settlers of Guiana.

The English rulers' terminology for the Caribbean seems to have only one explanation: they wanted to distinguish the Caribbean

Archipelago—that is, the *West Indies*—from the Malayan-Indian Archipelago—in the *East Indies*. For that purpose they set up trading companies bearing the respective names. In that instance commercial considerations outweighed geographic and ethnocultural ones. Frequently the name *Caribbean America* is applied to the Caribbean or Antillean islands and those adjacent to them and sometimes, in acknowledgment of their sphere of influence in custom and culture, the coastlines of Colombia and Venezuela. During the era of the pirates the Caribbean region was called the *Spanish Main*, a name still used by some English historians.

The remaining geographic regions of the New World are *Arctic America* and *Antarctic America*. They are the American segment of the north and south polar circles.

If the terminology of Latin American geography is varied, even more so is that of Latin American anthropology, in its ethnic, cultural, linguistic, and historical perspectives. With respect to these elements, there are many Americas. What we are accustomed to call *Latin America* is made up of the southernmost part of North America, Mexico, and Central America and all of South America. Linguistically it is divided into two parts: *Spanish-speaking America* and *Portuguese-speaking America*. Some scholars believe that the term Latin America has linguistic justification since Spanish and Portuguese belong to the Romanic linguistic family, which is based on Latin. The colonists were carriers of a culture whose Latin roots filtered through America, and it is logical that they and their civilization should be called Latin. Other Americanists, however, think that the name is inappropriate and is even confusing, since many millions of American Indians—Amerindians—live in the same region. Many of them speak their ancestral languages, which have no relationship to the cultural "Latinity" of the Spaniards and Portuguese. Indians speak Peninsular languages but continue to follow their indigenous customs and beliefs, which cannot be considered Latin. Of course, most of the aboriginal peoples are affected one way or another by Spanish influences.

Still other Americanists conclude that, since the colonizers came from the Iberian Peninsula (and are thus often called *peninsulares*), the territory they settled would more accurately be called *Ibero-America*. The term incorporates the New World and is not limited to the Latin of the Old. It does not, however, incorporate the Indians of the region, many of whom sometimes live physically and culturally apart. Some of the *indigenists* —experts in the various fields of indigenous affairs—still prefer to call this ethnically mixed region *Indo-Ibero-America*. Another term, *Indigenous America*, or *Indian America*, extends geographical boundaries to include Indians in Anglo-America.

Some Americanists divide Latin America into population segments. *Mestizo America* is the term they apply to the *mestizo* (Spanish-Indian) population, which makes up 70 to 80 percent of the total American population. *Creole America* denotes the population of pure Spanish descent. The regions of the River Plate, Chile, and Costa Rica are inhabited almost entirely by creoles, but their ethnocultural enclaves are found throughout Hispanic America. Creoles living in Mestizo America make up a minority about equal to the numbers of Indians residing there. *Negro America* includes the regions of the New World peopled by blacks and influenced in varying degrees by their civilization. In addition to the heavy concentration of blacks in the Caribbean region and in the Guianas, there are also Negro groups in Central America, South America, and the United States. In those areas they live as minorities in blocs or in racially and ethnically mixed areas. Depending on the cross-cultural influences in a given geographic area, it is possible to speak of *Hispanic Negro America*, *Saxon Negro America*, *Portuguese Negro America*, and even *French Negro America*, since in some Caribbean islands and in French Guiana the French language is dominant.

Still another means of defining the areas of Hispanic America is linguistically. The term *Hispanic America* itself is largely used in reference to the people and affairs of the regions where Spanish is spoken, regardless of the racial or ethnic population. That term, in fairly widespread use among Hispanic American intellectuals, is better accepted than *Spanish America*, the term generally used by Spaniards. Hispanic Americans who wish to divest themselves of the vestiges of their former colonial dependence on Spain avoid the term. Those who prefer it are mostly historians of the colonial epoch and *Hispanophiles*—advocates of everything Spanish. Less controversial is the term *Spanish-speaking America*, currently used by linguists and literary historians on both sides of the Atlantic. It is current among

Hispanists, that is, experts in the affairs of the Hispanic world (which includes all the countries where Spanish is spoken). Hispanic Americans, depending on their emotional response and nationalist aspirations, favor *Hispanic America*, *Latin America*, or *Ibero-America*. Usage also varies with educational level. The term *Hispanic Americanists* (or sometimes *Latin Americanists*), denoting scholars in Hispanic American affairs, is derived from this term.

The adjective *Hispanic* is derived from *Hispania* (España), a name given to the Iberian Peninsula in ancient times, when it was a part of the Roman Empire. Thus both *Hispanic* and *Iberian* refer to the traditions, culture, and customs of the people of the entire peninsula. When the Spaniards and Portuguese colonized the New World, all they took with them came to be synonymous with their enterprise. Hispanic elements were merged with indigenous, resulting in an ethnic and cultural symbiosis of two distinct races, each with its own idiosyncrasies.

Logically *Hispanic American* as an ethnic term becomes a subtle designation for natives of the New World who biologically mixed with the Spaniards and who adopted many of the Hispanic ways of living. Similarly, as the colonists arrived from Portugal (called Lusitania in ancient times), the Brazilians' civilization came to be termed *Luso-Brazilian*, to indicate the mixed European and American origin. Brazilians speak Portuguese (though some of their customs differ from those of the *peninsulares*) and are not pleased to be called a "Hispanic people." They do not object to the term *Ibero-American*.

The convenience of the word *Hispanic* is obvious, since it does not separate Hispanic America from Spain, the "mother country" to some Hispanic Americans. The term *Hispanidad*, as used to denote, among other things, a political bond between Spain and Hispanic America, is more controversial. In the judgment of some contemporary Spanish ideologists, Spain is the "great arena" for Hispanic America, and Madrid the metropolis of the Hispanic world, a point of view that annoys many Hispanic Americans. Even those who recognize the Peninsular contribution to Hispanic American culture consider the idea of a return of their countries to Spanish influence, especially in politics, utterly unacceptable. Not all attitudes have been so dogmatic. The position taken by the Spaniard Ramiro de Maeztu on Hispanidad was balanced, egalitarian, and pro–Hispanic American. It contrasted with the concept formulated in Spain during World War II, which aroused Hispanic Americans' suspicion and wounded their national pride.

Spaniards, apparently realizing the unsavory implication that *Hispanidad* could have for Spanish American nations, have recently changed the name of *Instituto de Cultura Hispánica* in Madrid to *Centro Iberoamericano de Cooperación*. It is the consequence of a visit King Juan Carlos paid to six Spanish American nations in 1977, showing thus a spirit of reconciliation and friendly cooperation between Spain and Spanish America. Since then, October 12, which previously has been known as Day of the Race or Day of the Americas, has become known, symbolically, as Day of Hispanidad, to which no one has any objection. In the United States this date is, of course, known as Columbus Day.

Anthropological terminology, as it is applied to ongoing biological and cultural mixtures, will be defined in the chapters dealing with the various ethnocultural groups. These groups generally are examples of *acculturation*—the transfer of cultural and spiritual values of an individual or social group to another individual or social group of a different ethnic origin. It is appropriate to note here the three-way Hispanic, Negro, and indigenous acculturation—that is, the fusion of Hispanic peoples with black and indigenous peoples. That extraordinary tricontinental phenomenon is one of the manifestations of the Hispanic American racial melting pot.

Over the years scholars have introduced a body of ethnic terms into studies of the New World. Such terms have, of course, geographical, cultural, and historical implications. *Indo-America* encompasses the indigenous society of the New World. *Euro-America* signifies everything related to the transplantation of European culture to the New World, as well as to the European-American mixture in Hispanic America, which is different from that in Anglo-America. *Afro-America* refers to the peoples of African origin or descent and to Negro American affairs in their continental context.

The terms *Anglo-Saxon World* and *Latin World* are frequently used to distinguish between the two great ethnocultural groups of America. The *Anglo-Saxon World* is made up of the United States of America and Canada, in which Anglo-Saxon civilization emanating from Great Britain predominates. The typical personification of that world is naturally the United States. Ibero-Americans sometimes call it the "Colossus of the North" because of its economic power and international political influence. The *Latin World* takes in all the nations in which Spanish or Portuguese is the predominant language. Sometimes included is the large French-speaking minority in Canada, which, feeling no affinity for the "Saxons," claims a connection with the other "Latin" nations. With a few exceptions the cultural classifications of the ethnic groups are based chiefly on language. Thus the Anglo-Saxon world includes the former British possessions in the Caribbean, which are today small, independent republics having their own cultural identity.

Anglo-America and *Anglo-Saxon America*, which are other terms for *Anglo-Saxon World*, identify the English cultural roots, which have been reinforced by those of other northern European countries. Linguistically the terms are valid, especially for the United States, where the linguistic base dominates the ethnic base. Like Ibero-America, the United States rightly calls itself a melting pot. The racial mixture in Ibero-America developed "freely," while that of the United States has evolved principally among similar "white" ethnic groups. Owing to its absorption of immigrants of many blood lines, the United States is gradually losing its Anglo-Saxon ethnicity, but not its cultural heritage. Nor is Canada's ethnic structure based on a single strain; one-fourth of the population is of French descent and has a traditional French culture. This Canadian bi-ethnicity brought about bilingualism, with both English and French as official languages. Paraguay is another bilingual country; there both Spanish and Guarani, the language of the indigenous people adopted by the mestizo society, are spoken.[1]

From time to time new terms appear in Hispanic American studies. An example is *Eurindia*, which is applied to the racial mixture that began with the arrival of Europeans in the Indies. The term was introduced by Ricardo Rojas as a parallel to *Eurasia*, alluding to the ethnic convergence of Europe and Asia through very early intercontinental migrations. Rojas saw in Eurindia a similar "ethnogenic

[1]Another linguistic curiosity is Papiamento, a Lingua franca of some Dutch-owned islands of the Caribbean. It is a mixture of Spanish, Portuguese, Dutch, English, Carib, and African languages. It shows a tendency toward the linguistic "Hispanization" of those who speak it.

mystery" and called Argentina "the most fecund agent of that ethnic creation." Yet the systematic annihilation of the Indians in Argentina eliminated racial mixture there and consequently prevented the creation of an American civilization with an indigenous base. (The same fate overtook the Indians of Anglo-America, though many more aborigines have survived there than in the River Plate country.)

Some European Americanists use terms that have anthropological and geographic connotations but sometimes carry overtones of ethnic bias. Examples are *Asiatic America*, *African America*, and *European America*. They are correct when used to refer to particular Asiatic or European elements in the prehistoric or historic formation of the New World civilizations. But to use those restrictive terms is to risk disregarding other elements in the evolving American civilizations. The multiethnic New World requires equal attention to all its racial, cultural, and social components. Otherwise it is not possible to form a clear picture of what America was and is.

In New World studies we find terms denoting the national tendencies of various countries and serving to identify their cultural or political aspirations. Examples are *mexicanidad*, *argentinidad*, *bolivianidad*, and so on. Some highly expressive terms and expressions come from the popular language of the country. These regionalisms, called, depending on their country of origin, *mexicanismos*, *argentinismos*, *bolivianismos*, and so on, are highly significant, belonging to the people's way of expressing themselves and therefore revealing their attitude of mind and spirit. The *mexicanista*, *argentinista*, or *bolivianista* is a specialist in the affairs of the given country. The term *Americanist (americanista)* signifies the expert in American affairs in the intercontinental sense.

As with other aspects of Hispanic American culture, language and vocabulary—the subtleties of meaning and connotation—are of great complexity. Literary English of the United States bears a close relationship to the English of England, although each preserves its own distinct lexicon. The most obvious differences between United States English and British English are principally in pronunciation. By and large, however, the Anglo-Americans and the English readily understand each other. Within the United States there are differences in pronunciation from region to region. The speech of the populous Middle West is considered the standard speech and is perhaps the most widespread. Consequently, it is the usual pronunciation of trained actors, speakers, and broadcasters. The speech of New Yorkers is the most diversified, owing to the cosmopolitan nature of the city.

United States English, in common with languages of other countries, has many idioms and regional expressions. Yet, in spite of the immense territorial expanse of the country, such expressions are usually understood by people of widely separated regions. That, in addition to the basic lexical unity, affirms the linguistic conformity of the United States. Slang, the popular jargon, is widely used in daily speech and journalistic writing. United States English, almost totally lacking in indigenous influences, except for isolated words and phrases, exercised little significant influence on Indian languages. It is, however, rich in words and expressions from its multiethnic population. Nevertheless, the process of Anglo-Americanization, to which successive waves of immigrants submitted voluntarily, is stronger than their linguistic impact on the language of their adopted country.

Their contribution to the vocabulary of United States English was described by H. L. Menken in his discussion of the lexical pluralism of the language in *The American Language* (1919). He set forth the concept of an "American language," but that is not a linguistically exact term. The key to the continuous development of United States English is the constant progress of technology and modern science, which assures the language much lexical flexibility. A similar evolutionary process, though in varied forms, has been experienced by other languages. Such inevitable linguistic metamorphosis is evidence of the vitality of a nation.

The Spanish language of Hispanic America has more complexities than the English of Anglo-America. Of course, Hispanic men of letters and intellectuals use literary Spanish, which differs little from that used by their counterparts in Spain.

Reading a work written in this cultivated language, whether by Spaniard, Mexican, Argentinian, Colombian, or Peruvian, offers no difficulties. A strange notion still exists that two languages are spoken in the Hispanic world, Castilian and Spanish. The truth is, they are the same, and the terms may be used interchangeably. Although in the Iberian Peninsula the term *Castilian* is preferred, in

Hispanic America one hears it less often than *Spanish*. When the Spaniards brought the language to America, it had already been linguistically refined. In the fifteenth century the kingdom of Castile reunified Spain, which had been divided by the Arab occupation. The Spanish language of the Castilians consequently gained prestige. Antonia de Nebrija defined the rules and uses of that tongue in his *Gramática castellana* (1492), the first grammar of a vernacular tongue. The language penetrated the American colonies. Among the colonists were not only Castilians but also Andalusians, Estremadurans, and Galicians, whose pronunciations differed from Castilian. For a long time dialectic traces comparable to those in Spain remained in America. Some still persist today, as does usage of many words that are archaic in Spain. Pronunciation does not cause as many problems in Hispanic American Spanish as do the influences of indigenous languages, which were varied and inevitable. Many indigenous words infiltrated Peninsular Spanish, which had no terms for many New World plants, fruits, animals, and so on, not found in Spain. Spaniards adopted the names used in the native languages, such as Nahuatl, Quechua, Taino, Maya, and others.

Some indigenous words were promptly accepted and used throughout the colonies and even in Spain. Examples are, from Taino: *canoa* ("canoe"), *maní* ("peanut"), *cacique* ("chief"), *hamaca* ("hammock"), *maíz* ("corn"); from Nahuatl: *aguacate* ("avocado"), *cacahuate* ("peanut"), *chocolate* ("chocolate"), *petate* ("sleeping mat"), *tomate* ("tomato"); from Maya: *huracán* ("hurricane"), *henequén* ("henequen"); from Quechua: *alpaca* ("alpaca"), *chacra* ("small piece of land"), *llama* ("llama"), *pampa* ("pampa"), *palta* ("alligator pear"), *papa* ("potato"), *puna* ("tableland"), and *curaca* ("chief"). Taino, Nahuatl, and Quechua were the principal sources of *Americanisms*—indigenous American words—perhaps it would be more appropriate to call them *indigenisms*. These terms, added to other local expressions, give color to regional narratives, but extensive use of regional vocabulary often requires a glossary to ensure understanding. Such lexical variety appears in novels dealing with indigenous themes, such as those about the gauchos or the jungle peoples. In the Río de la Plata region early-day creoles of the pampas utilized gaucho jargon, while today the poor of Buenos Aires continue to speak *lunfardo*, the port city argot, which was especially influenced by Italian.

Vulgarisms were commonly adapted from the speech of later immigrants. According to the celebrated linguist Tomás Navarro Tomás, in South America vulgarisms were used even by cultivated people, except those of Colombia, Mexico, Costa Rica, and the cities of Lima and La Paz, where the educated groups spoke Spanish most properly. To the indigenous influences were added the "foreign" influences, French and English. Hispanic America, after achieving independence from Spain, adopted France as its cultural Mecca. Gallicisms were fashionable during most of the nineteenth century, especially those relating to cuisine, women's fashions, and perfumery. At the turn of the century the influence of the English language increased, principally in the terminology of sports, mechanics, and the sciences. Adoption of these Anglicisms or Americanisms was a consequence particularly of the rapid technological and scientific development of the Anglo-Saxon world, whose products and terminology spread through modern Hispanic America, as well as other countries of the world. (All the expressions borrowed from foreign languages were considered barbarisms by linguists.)

Navarro Tomás believes that, while Hispanic American Spanish is much more uniform than that of Spain in the pronunciation of consonants and in the classification of words, the Spanish spoken by the masses in Hispanic America is "inferior" to that spoken by the masses in Spain, who preserve their lexical cohesion. While it would be an exaggeration to say that no cohesion exists in Hispanic America, the lexical uniformity is being progressively weakened owing to variations in vocabulary from country to country and sometimes from region to region. These modern-day regionalisms abound, as illustrated by the wide variety of words for birds, fruits, plants, and food dishes. The Honduran Hispanist Rafael H. Valle once commented that the fowl known as *pavo* ("turkey") has at least a dozen different names in the American countries where Spanish is spoken. Such ingenuity has caused many confusions. If the trend toward regionalism continues, Hispanic American Spanish as we now know it may disintegrate, to be supplanted by new tongues in the various Hispanic nations. That would endanger Hispanic American unity. The possibility inspired fear in the linguistic "purist" Andrés Bello a hundred years ago and disturbed linguist Pedro Henríquez Ureña some decades later. It is doubtful that the Royal Spanish

Academy and the corresponding academies in Hispanic America have sufficient influence to stay the trend. Indeed, the Hispanic American academies began to display their independence from the Royal Academy on linguistic matters as soon as they became national institutions.

In concluding these reflections on New World linguistic matters, I wish to stress the international importance of their languages as compared with that of European languages. Today English is spoken by more than 220 million Anglo-Americans and by more than 300 million people on other continents. Spanish is spoken by more than 250 million Hispanic Americans and by more than 30 million Spaniards. The two languages are among the five official languages of the United Nations and the four official languages of the Organization of American States. Portuguese, another important language and one of the official tongues of the OAS, is spoken by more than 100 million Brazilians and 9 million Portuguese.

Some New World concerns are a source of pride; others arouse disquiet. One of the former is the chronology of the founding of educational and cultural institutions in each of the Americas. In that chronology Hispanic America has played an impressive role, as indicated by the dates of the establishment of institutions of higher learning: the University of Saint Thomas Aquinas, in Santo Domingo, 1538; the Royal and Pontifical University of Mexico, in Mexico City, 1551; the University of San Marcos, in Lima, 1551; the University of Saint Ignatius, in Córdoba, 1613; and the University of San Carlos, in Guatemala, 1676. Corresponding dates in Anglo-America are: Harvard University, 1636; the College of William and Mary, 1693; Yale University, 1701; the University of Pennsylvania, 1740; and Princeton University, 1746. The first presses were established in Mexico City in 1535; in Lima, in 1583; and in Cambridge, Massachusetts, in 1639. The first book published in Spanish America was *Breve y más compendiosa Doctrina Christiana en lengua mexicana y castellana*, which appeared in Mexico in 1539. The *Bay Psalm Book*, published in Cambridge, Massachusetts, in 1640, was the first book published in English America. In comparing these dates in the colonial calendar it should be recalled, of course, that Spanish colonization of America began in the sixteenth century, while English colonization did not begin until the seventeenth.

The cultural rivalry existing within the Hispanic world gives cause for some concern. As mentor of colonial America, Spain molded its literary and artistic life for more than three centuries. Accustomed to that dominant role, Spain has found it difficult to recognize the cultural achievements of Hispanic America during the century and a half of independence. For a long time outstanding achievements were considered an extension of Spanish culture, as when prominent Hispanic authors were numbered in the body of Peninsular writers. On the whole, however, Hispanic American literature did not enjoy much prestige in Spain. That attitude has changed in recent times as Spanish publishers have begun publishing Hispanic American works, and literary critics have assumed a more benevolent and even respectful attitude toward them. Spanish universities, however, have paid little if any attention to Hispanic American letters, though the literature of Spain continues to be taught in American universities.[2] One gains the impression that Spain has no interest in Hispanic American culture. It is tempting to accuse the Spaniards of lack of universalism or exaggerated national pride.

That separatism appears even stranger when one observes Madrid's unilateral efforts to improve its relations with Hispanic America. Such separatism has been reflected also in the attitude of Hispanists in Europe and Anglo-America whose interests center on Spanish Peninsular culture and who lack understanding of Hispanic American cultural achievements. They are noted for their professional "sectarianism." After World War II, North American scholars began specializing in Hispanic America, and native Hispanic American specialists began occupying chairs in universities in the United States. Spanish culture has always been of academic interest in the United States. A similar interest is developing in Hispanic American artistic and intellectual accomplishments. There is now promise of a better balance in cultural studies of the Hispanic world.

[2]A chair in Spanish American literature was established at the University of Madrid in 1967; only in 1974 was such a chair established at the University of Seville. On Spain's present interest in Hispanic American culture see Edmund Stephen Urbanski, "A Cultural Report from Spain," *Vida Hispánica: Journal of the Association of Teachers of Spanish and Portuguese in Great Britain*, Vol. XXII, No. 1 (1975).

CHAPTER 3

THE NEW WORLD AND ITS EUROPEAN SETTLERS

The discovery of the New World by Columbus in 1492, North America by John Cabot in 1497, and Brazil by Pedro Cabral in 1500 opened the door to colonial expansion by Spaniards, English, and Portuguese. After them came the French, the Dutch, and the Scandinavians, but on a smaller scale. Contemporary chroniclers termed the lands "virgin" because they were little cultivated—at least by European measures. The Indians inhabiting the regions seemed less "civilized" than the European colonists, who, ignorant of the achievements of the aboriginal civilizations, consequently called them "savages." It was also supposed that the population density was less than that of Europe. It is estimated that the indigenous population of the Americas in the era of discovery was between thirteen and sixty million. The mean of their estimated numbers does not appear to be much lower than that of Europeans at the end of the fifteenth century and the beginning of the sixteenth. The notion of the virginity of the New World was, therefore, somewhat inaccurate.

The European colonists closed the indigenous epoch and initiated the era of European domination. African Negroes soon appeared as well. Thus the American continents became the scene of a historic encounter and the linking of three races: white, Indian, and black, who have since continued to fertilize the New World. It is a sort of ethnic triangle, with America, Europe, and Africa forming the bases.

The colonization of America was an important event of the Renaissance. That movement, which initiated modern culture and made way for the new scientific and geographic discoveries stimulated by their interaction, also promoted the development of the humanities in the countries engaged in New World enterprise. The current of the Renaissance in Roman Catholic Spain, however, was soon transformed into a trend toward religious orthodoxy, which inspired the *peninsulares* with an evangelizing spirit in the newly discovered lands. Religious orthodoxy combined with national vigor produced the magnificent cultural and political achievements of the Golden Age and facilitated the rise of the Baroque. Yet Spanish conservatism snuffed out the development of a more brilliant and universal culture. Renaissance humanism in Protestant England, however, survived and progressed. Its strongest expressions were manifested in speculative philosophy rather than in purely aesthetic literary production. Instead of seeking intellectual glory, English liberalism fortified the consciousness of destiny achieved through duty fulfilled. It opened new avenues to human knowledge and practical inventions. All these mental and spiritual motivations were transplanted from the Old World to the New on the caravels that brought the Spanish and English colonists.

Thus America gained two new civilizations, one with an Iberian character, the other Anglo-Saxon. In occupying New World territories, the Iberians early assumed the character and role of conquerors, while the Anglo-Saxons chose the role of colonizers. These roles determined the course of New World history, which would reflect the motivations and aspirations of each group. Each was determined on conserving its language, religious beliefs, customs, social attitudes, and political institutions, all of which molded the colonial mind. For obvious reasons the pre-Columbian heritage is not included here. The indigenous civilizations almost disappeared with the Conquest, though certain linguistic influences and customs remain among groups with considerable Indian blood.

The history of colonial America indicates the various elements that determined its structure. Each ethnic group, whatever the "European" labels, exhibited distinct human, psychological, and social characteristics. The vital sources of Hispanic American civilization came from the union of Spanish blood with Indian and the Indians' acceptance of the language and religion of the conquerors. To the north the situation was entirely different. The rejection of English feudalism—that is, its hierarchic system, not its juridical and moral one—together with the growing consciousness of the common destiny of the colonists, laid the groundwork for a vigorous

Principal Pre-Columbian indigenous civilizations

Spanish colonies and their administrative divisions, sixteenth to eighteenth centuries

Hispanic America and Anglo-America today

Anglo-American civilization. It did not face linguistic obstacles because almost all the settlers spoke the same language and lived apart from their Indian neighbors.

The carriers of each civilization exhibited many distinctive characteristics. Some drew them together, and some divided them. The one common American characteristic was the Christian religion, observed in various forms from the time of the discovery of the New World. They also shared a commitment to the ideals of liberty and independence, which, suppressed during the colonial epoch, burst forth when they threw off the yoke of English and Spanish domination and became independent nations. They shared a strong sense of individualism, jealously guarded, capriciously and obstinately cultivated by Hispanic Americans and intuitively and rationally exhibited by Anglo-Americans.

New World individualism is manifested in rhetorical "I-ism," in supreme confidence in one's own power, or in a posture of indisputable knowledge. Yet, despite its egocentrism, that individualism, joined with intellectual curiosity, has promoted many innovations in the service of humanity. Given the relative youthfulness of the New World peoples, this combination of individualism and curiosity may be considered a part of the "American intelligence." It cannot be claimed that there is any sense of hemispheric unity, although there is plenty of evidence of intercontinental solidarity, especially when the security of all the peoples of the New World is endangered.

It is the divergent features of the two predominant influences on New World civilization that claim our attention here. The settlers from England and the northern European countries on the one hand and those from the Iberian Peninsula on the other were utterly unlike in their colonial "behavior," largely because of differences in occupation. The Spaniards were principally soldiers, adventurers, government functionaries, ecclesiastics, and, in fewer numbers, farmers and peasants. The settlers from England and northern Europe were predominantly farmers, artisans, and merchants. They had economic vigor and a sense of relative independence, whereas the Spaniards entered the New World dependent upon the Old, supported by government positions, land privileges, or religious orders. Representatives of the king, soldiers, and missionaries were sent to conquer lands and indigenous peoples in the name of Spain and of Christ, while the Anglo-Saxon settlers came of their own will and with the aim of cultivating the land, establishing new homes, and enjoying religious freedom.

There were few intellectuals in either group. Adventurers predominated, which explains the turbulent character of the early colonial period in America. The Spaniards conquered territory militarily and then colonized it, while the English, who did not have to wage wars of conquest, were for the most part peaceable colonizers. Spanish soldiers of fortune and some noblemen, adventurous and ambitious for power, reduced the Indians to slaves so that they could live as masters, directing the exploitation of the mineral and agricultural riches. English colonists, mostly of humble origin, worked the land for themselves and utilized the available resources skillfully and independently, without any need or desire to enslave the natives. These divergent attitudes toward work were to have an important influence on the social behavior of Hispanic America and Anglo-America.

Spanish missionaries, the "spiritual conquerors," converted the Indians to Christianity through remarkable evangelizing and educational efforts. In this connection the names Toribio de Benavente, Bernardino de Sahagún, Bartolomé de las Casas, and Vasco de Quiroga come to mind. The men of war also considered their mission a "crusade," one that reminded them of the reconquest of Spain from the Moors and that should, therefore, be carried to a conclusion by the sword, the harquebus, and the Gospel. Many Spaniards arrived in the New World intending to enrich themselves and then return to Spain (those who did so became known in Europe as *indianos*).

Emigrants who left England because of religious and economic oppression came to the New World intending to forget the past and make their economic future secure and to establish permanent homes in the new land. They came not in search of treasure but with a robust will to work that enabled them to forge a strong, independent character. Since the English did not wish to return to their native country, their colonizing efforts involved long-range planning that was lacking in Spanish colonization, at least at the beginning of the American adventure.

The Spanish conquerors and colonists left their women in Spain.

They lived with indigenous women, and *mestizaje*—extensive racial mixing—was the inevitable consequence. The English colonists brought their wives and families with them, and there was little racial mixing. A homogeneous society was soon established in the English colonies, which developed a uniform social standard and economic stability. In contrast, the heterogeneity in the Spanish colonies produced social strata so widely separated that it was impossible to achieve socioeconomic integration. It did result, however, in the formation of a new and vigorous mestizo society, which today constitutes the ethnic trunk of the Hispanic American people.

Spaniards came as propagators of a Hispanic–Roman Catholic culture that had been modeled on conservative and combative traditions dating from the medieval struggles against Muslim power. Their Roman Catholicism had strengthened and renewed in the fervent Counter Reformation spirit of the Council of Trent. It was distinguished by a deep-rooted religious dogmatism and idealism that bordered on absolutism and was therefore spiritually adjusted to politicotheological authoritarianism. A preoccupation with metaphysics and aesthetic sensibility gave impetus to the plastic arts, to music, and to architecture. The body of colonial literature, though modeled on the Spanish, included ambitious works of poetry, prose, and drama, some of which equaled their Peninsular models in quality.

The English brought to the New England colonies the Anglo-Protestantism born of the Reformation, with its affirmation of liberty of conscience and social and economic liberalism combined with that Puritan restraint, a rigid moral and religious system. It synthesized a rigorous theological and legal system based on Calvinism, whose doctrines demanded a repression of earthly pleasures. The colonists substituted hard work, whose ultimate goal was the establishment of a "spiritual commonwealth." Within those restrictions men were free to carry out those duties that combined the useful with the rational. Modest in character, the Anglo-American colonial literature consisted of almanacs and books of Psalms, some works on history and exploration, and a very little poetry. The hardships of colonial life were obstacles in the way of cultural development, at least in the northernmost colonies. Yet the Anglo-Americans achieved a fair degree of spiritual unity and altruism.[1]

The collective psychology of a people evolves from its customs, lifeways, and political convictions. Thus the Anglo-American settlers were strongly community-oriented, supporting laws that strengthened the community, disregarding or violating laws they believed unjust, and affirming social equality both in fact and by right. They were determined to manage their own political destinies and did so by means of elected town governments.

From the beginning social and economic inequality prevailed in colonial Spain, expressed in the landlords' abuse of the Indians, blacks, and mestizos. It is worth noting that those groups without privileges, who constituted the majority of the colonial population, did little to try to better their fate. There was a sensibility for the arts and for literature among the educated few. Personalism—exaltation of the values of an individual regardless of the legal and social rights of the masses—predominated. The deterministic principles of religious life that permeated colonial society were accepted without challenge. Moreover, political regionalism, characterized by unquestioning obedience to the rulers, was cultivated—and is followed to this day. Yet that superficially disciplined society had a potential for rebellion, as time would show.

Hispanic American pride and Anglo-American dignity were other distinctive New World characteristics. Hispanic American pride, stemming from Spanish pride of birth and race, was diffused throughout Hispanic America. Anglo-American dignity originated in the satisfaction produced by individual and collective achievements, not usually from lineage or past history.

The New World civilizations were nourished by the legacies from the Old. The Spaniards brought a store of knowledge of architecture and the arts that enormously enriched Hispanic colonial culture. Colonists from England and other Anglo-Saxon countries lacked a deep traditional culture, and they did not bring friars and learned men of the sort from whose spiritual work the Spanish colonies benefited. But they came with a fixed attachment to the common law and moral

---

[1]These comments do not invariably apply to the colonies lying south of New England. There Church of England colonists were in the majority, and their religious strictures were much less stern, as were their codes of conduct and their lifeways.

austerity and with a capacity for work and social organization. They knew how to utilize those endowments in accommodating themselves to new conditions of life.

The evolution of Hispanic American civilization is viewed in radically different ways by Anglo-Americans and Hispanic Americans. To Anglo-Americans colonial Hispanic American culture evolved from a movement inspired by the wealthy from which the masses did not benefit. Owing to the subjugation practiced by the ruling class, the indigenous peoples, as well as the mestizos and even many creoles, lacked any concept of equal rights. Their social and economic emancipation was delayed, leaving them at a marked political disadvantage and in an almost chaotic situation after political separation from Spain. The effects were apparent for a long time after independence, during a time when Anglo-Americans were establishing the principles of equality of human rights that were to appear in their democratic system.

Hispanic Americans perceive the evolution of their culture quite differently. They acknowledge that the masses did not know how to read poetry, history, or philosophy. But they did have a folk culture, including music and theater. Thus they did participate in the arts, if indirectly. The cultivated minority left the masses illiterate but fostered in them an aesthetic sensibility and an almost mystical admiration for arts and letters. The colonial artists and writers played their part in laying a foundation for the rich popular art of later centuries. It was different in the social sphere. Though Hispanic America achieved political emancipation, it is still endeavoring to achieve true social and intellectual emancipation.

The radically different cultural developments of the American colonists stemmed from the cultural climates in the centers of trade and learning in their homeland. Those centers were in the midst of the Renaissance, the transcendental cultural movement that produced not only a return to cultivation of the classic humanities but also transformation of civilization in all its human aspects. The budding civilizations of the New World were rooted in the fundamentals of Occidental civilization upon which the Renaissance had been superimposed. How the Renaissance affected the cultural and social life of Spain and England explains how it influenced their respective colonies. A brief examination of the development of the Renaissance in those countries is necessary in order to understand what was transplanted to America.

A literary Renaissance could not fully develop in Spain because nationalistic attitudes were in conflict with Italian currents and because conservation of Spanish epic, cosmological, and theological values was of overriding concern. Those concerns were a Peninsular individualism that reached new heights with the conquest of America. The conservation of those values during the Golden Age contributed great brilliance to cultural Spain and imperial splendor to its stature in the international political arena. However, the religious orthodoxy that tied those achievements together did not allow the colonies full exposure to Renaissance ideology, and they were prevented from discarding the spiritual conservatism of the mother country. It was feared that the "paganism" of the Greco-Roman culture, which nourished the Renaissance, would weaken the Catholic faith. Nevertheless, the short Renaissance period produced excellent literary and artistic works, especially in Mexico, Peru, and the viceroyalty of New Granada (now Colombia, Panama, Venezuela, and Ecuador), which were surpassed only by the more ostentatious monuments of the Baroque Era. Universities and schools established in the colonies soon became centers of cultural and artistic life, providing inspiration for creole and mestizo artists. All of this gave rise to a colonial Humanism that was watched over by the ecclesiastical censors, with the result that topics of a speculative nature were rarely discussed. Too, within the atmosphere of cultural exclusivity, the education of the masses was neglected.

The intellectual flexibility and inquiring nature of the English allowed the Renaissance to flourish in England. The Renaissance spirit was manifested in a variety of literary works that raised philosophical, moral, theological, and scientific questions and offered speculative answers. Yet the Renaissance did not bear fruit in the New England colonies. There it was stunted by the theological stance of the Puritans. English colonial architecture in New England, which exhibits utility but little artistic beauty, is evidence of the overriding Puritan influence. Nor was humanistic literature well received; the Calvinists and Lutherans, who were influential in colonial education, opposed it. Except for a few writers, a few well-designed buildings, and a limited number of schools and theological colleges that later became universities, colonial culture in America was rather simple. It did, however, express moral and social values that emanated from the Renaissance. The colonists left those values to succeeding generations. Everyone participated actively through work and education. In contrast to the Hispanic American exclusivity and predominance of the few, Anglo-American civilization became a movement of the majority. To oversimplify, if religion and art molded the Hispanic America, work and the school produced Anglo-American civilization.

America was colonized during the ideological and religious struggle on the Continent between Catholic dogmatism and Protestant rationalism. The result was a fundamental divergence in spiritual attitudes in the New World. Spanish conservatism was the outcome of constant preoccupation with purity of the faith, which in colonial times was identified with good citizenship. Equally important were the egocentrism of the privileged class and the mysticism of many learned men, to which must be added a certain individualism among the people. These elements determined the activities of a large segment of the Spanish population. Other ingredients were a preoccupation with aesthetics, a tendency toward contemplation, and ever-present emotionalism. Of course, not all these features were of equal influence in the Hispanic American nature. Most of the people, confronted with the reality of the daily routine, did not think of reducing it to aesthetic terms. Consequently, to speak of the "spirituality" of those simple people seems somewhat exaggerated, or at least resolutely optimistic.

English ideology incorporated aspects of both Puritanism and rationalism. The rationalist philosophy has often provided the English with more material success than intellectual glory, which, in fairness, the Anglo-Saxons did not seek. Rationalism has frequently been the inspiration for British colonization, as well as for all sorts of speculative ventures, social theories, and, of course, mechanical inventions. The Anglo-American spiritual and philosophical outlook thus produced a union of what was real and what was attainable by the most readily available and least esoteric means. In short, the Anglo-Saxon attitude was less doctrinaire and more pragmatic. It should also be remembered that colonial Hispanic Americans, particularly those of the privileged classes, because of their fidelity to the crown, remained very closely tied to Spain. The Anglo-American colonials, whose ties to England were more commercial than emotional, gradually grew independent of the mother country.

While it is possible to speak of colonial Hispanic America as a political unit, in social and economic structure there were actually two Hispanic Americas: the wealthy landowning urban society and, at the other end of the economic scale, the large rural indigenous and mestizo society. The first was the Hispanic America of the powerful leisure-class minority, whose refined tastes and sophisticated airs were visible to the outside world. The second was the Hispanic America of the poor, who were hidden in the interior and therefore invisible. Colonial Anglo-America, with its insignificant percentage of aristocrats and with a rural and urban population of settlers with similar ethnic origins, cultural backgrounds, and social ideologies, had a more or less uniform structure. Its utilitarianism, proceeding from the English civil and moral heritage, took root in the Anglo-Saxon colonies and produced the image of a people alert and united in purpose.

CHAPTER 4

COLONIZATION: ITS HUMAN AND ECOLOGICAL
ASPECTS

Colonization of the New World, which the Spanish undertook extensively in the sixteenth century and the English in the seventeenth,
was a rich experience in human history. Colonists from each country
brought their own cultural traits and customs, which were altered and
supplemented as required by life in the New World. Examination of
group behavior provides insight into the similarities in the colonial
experience. Violence was attendant upon both Spanish and English
colonization. The Spaniards succeeded through force of arms. The
terror they inspired with weapons and behavior effectively subjugated
the indigenous peoples. English colonization, begun peacefully and
largely without force, almost from the beginning prompted violence
by the Indians.

The violence took various forms. In Hispanic America it was
manifested in the arrogance of the masters toward the Indians, who
were seldom rebellious. In Anglo-America the English colonists,
peaceable at first, began responding to the continued harassment by
the Indians with determined defense and later offensive action.
Harsh treatment was meted out by both sides. The English colonists
consequently faced a more dangerous situation than did the
Spaniards, whose policies toward the Indians, mestizos, and Negroes
gave them complete domination.

In addition to territorial conquest, Spanish colonization had a
missionary aim. One of its goals was converting the natives to Christianity, which meant propagating the Castilian language and con-
structing thousands of churchs, convents, and palaces. Many of those
works, principally in Baroque style, are gems of colonial architecture, built by the indigenous peoples under the direction of the
peninsulares. The Indians who erected these monuments were the
victims of economic and social slavery, in unhappy contrast to their
ancestors, whose magnificent pyramids and other great pre-

Columbian monuments were products of their own art and culture. The Spanish missionaries were very effective among the Indians and the Negroes. One recalls among the missionaries Bartolomé de las Casas, missionary to the Indians, and Peter Claver, "Apostle to the Africans."

Anglo-Saxons, in contrast, paid little attention to the Indians, beyond defending themselves against sporadic attacks. Lacking missionary zeal, they had no interest in drawing the natives into Western civilization. They concentrated their efforts almost exclusively on cultivating the land or working as artisans. Spiritual aspirations were manifested in religious teachings and in the construction of simple churches like those still standing in the states of the eastern seaboard.

To their credit the Spanish masters acknowledged that Indians were human beings, even though they constantly abused them and valued them only as a labor force. In this connection it is necessary to weigh against maltreatment by the soldiers and *encomenderos* the Christian charity of the missionaries. They defended the Indians and supported laws designed to protect their rights. The good intentions of the *Derecho Indiano* were generally observed, however. On some royal *cédulas* ("orders") that came to the colonies, functionaries wrote the ominous words, "I obey but do not execute." Such disobedience of imperial law, far from the seat of government, did not encourage respect for regulations dealing with other colonial matters.

The English did not voluntarily mix with the Indians, though it was impossible to avoid some contact with them. Most confrontations were violent. The Indians attacked and burned white communities and terrorized the colonists with their atrocities. The result was mutual animosity and almost total separation of the two peoples. Those attitudes were often reflected in Sunday sermons, as when a New England minister thundered, "The Puritans hope to find the Pequot Indians in heaven, but they wish to keep apart from them in this world; it is better to exterminate them on earth!" Such attitudes made it certain that there would be little missionary work among the Indians. Moreover, in Puritan New England religion was considered a private matter and a message revealed only to the chosen, not to be imposed on the uninformed. The Puritans did not, however, neglect their own spiritual life. Their religious activities and passion for schools were sources of inspiration and unity in the struggle against the wilderness. Unlike the Spaniards they did not try to conquer or subjugate the Indians. They had no aversion to hard work and were determined to win the land and cultivate it.

Free of problems of social and economic integration of heterogeneous groups, the English colonists were able to achieve an equitable participation in local affairs. They held elections for town councils and played active parts in government through their representatives. The municipal bodies that made New England famous were evidence of local autonomy that the distant seat of government had to accept. They early formulated principles of free expression and equal rights that were later the basis of the democratic form of government of the United States.

In the Spanish colonies, where the crown sold public offices, including municipal offices, at auction, the citizens played a very limited role in their town governments and therefore had little political influence at the local level. Political, administrative, and judicial power was almost exclusively in the hands of Peninsular functionaries. Toward the end of the colonial era, however, the urban dwellers were given an opportunity to exercise their rights in *cabildos abiertos*, open meetings of municipal bodies. Those meetings were later used to further the cause of independence.

Political and social conditions in the cities were less favorable in the Spanish colonies than in the English colonies. The rigid, almost medieval concepts that the *peninsulares* imposed on colonial society made possible the suppression of the Indian and the exclusion of the mestizo and, for a long time, the creole from ruling posts in government, church, and commerce. The result was constant discontent. In the English colonies, in contrast, the rise of the middle class and the liberal cast of the institutions encouraged social and political progress. When independence came, the people were economically and politically ready for self-government.

The rise of cities in the two Americas also took different directions. While the benefits of urban civilization were extended gradually throughout the English colonies, in the Spanish colonies the rural interior remained on the margin of civilization. The Portuguese colonists, descendants of a nation of navigators, sought likely coastal areas in which to found their port cities. The vast interior of Brazil remained relatively sparsely populated. Spaniards went from the islands of the Caribbean to the Atlantic Coast and then plunged into the interior, exploring and conquering extensive territories. They erected new cities on the ruins of the centers of indigenous civilizations (Mexico City, Cuzco, Cholula) and founded settlements in mining regions (Guanajuato, Potosí, Taxco). They also appeared on the Pacific coast, establishing settlements from Chile and Peru to California. The latter cities, however, rarely became economic centers because the Board of Trade of Seville, which controlled Spain's external commerce, designated only certain American ports—Veracruz, Porto Bello, Cartagena—for that purpose. (The Board of Trade, established in 1503 and originally called the House of Trade, Casa de Contratación, was in effect a Spanish commercial monopoly.)

On the other hand, Anglo-American cities were founded both on the coast and in the interior and grew with the needs of the population. They evolved through their own vitality as centers of work, commerce, and civilization, growing constantly in numbers, and served as indispensable ties between agriculture and trade carried on by private English companies. Prosperity grew, especially in Boston, Philadelphia, and New York, port cities that became important centers of commercial exchange with Europe. Along with other North American cities they also became known as industrial, cultural, and political centers. Although, according to the 1790 census, 90 percent of the United States population was rural, the emerging urban concentration contributed to the developing Anglo-American civilization, though remaining dependent upon the necessities produced in the interior. As a consequence of urban development a middle class developed early and was consolidated as a bourgeoisie, which conserved its wealth and interests without excluding the masses. The middle class, whose activities were based on free competition, created a society based on commerce, with a genius for mechanical inventions that advanced production and trade.

The opposite occurred in Hispanic America, where priority was given to the establishment of sumptuous capitals for the viceroyalties, with palaces, churches, and universities. The potential for commerce and crafts, from which a large middle class could have risen, was neglected. The rich agricultural areas were only partly utilized, and rural communities remained apart from the cultural life of the cities.

The great landholders, preferring to live comfortably in the cities, left the business of their estates to managers, who in turn became the *caciques* ("political bosses") of their regions. Except for a few bourgeois groups, most of the people lived a rural or infraurban life, and the principal centers were the great haciendas. This was the result of the failure of colonial Spain to achieve socioeconomic integration, a situation that was not remedied during the era of independence, and even today conditions typical of a frontier civilization prevail. The socially conservative elements often oppose modernization, which delays the transition from a rural civilization to an urban one.

The contrasts of urban and rural civilizations are better understood when we become acquainted with the natural bases of sociocultural development. Those factors—above all, the interrelations among climate, physical setting, and human conduct—have been studied by a number of Americanists. Their conclusions shed much light on the interdependence of man and nature. Perhaps we owe the most suggestive presentation of that interdependence to Peruvian ethnologist Manuel M. Valle. In his *Dualismo Racial* he offered two scientific concepts: *morphorace* and *thermorace*.[1]

Morphorace is concerned with the study of ethnic groups according to traditional racial typology and characteristics of skin color in relation to their conventional geographic distribution. That concept is, Valle believes, somewhat superficial in that it does not take into account the evolutionary ethnic factor and implies a division of the human community that is excessively schematic and therefore arbitrary. Thermorace deals with ethnic groups that are not only marked by similar physiological features but also linked by biological and ecological adaptation. This harmonious relationship of the natural order, including the climatic adaptability of plants and animals, Valle considers the transcendent phenomenon of human groups within a climate zone.

Basing his study on the latter concepts, Valle reconstructed the bioterminology of Tahuantinsuyo (the "Four Quarters of the Inca Empire"). The Incas' biothermic adaptability was the key to their outstanding administration of what was the largest and best-organized

---

[1]Other words by Valle dealing with the ecological-ethnic theme are *Yunga, Quechua y Kolla* (1956), *Biological Bases of Race, Culture and History* (1964), *Two Concepts of Race* (1964), and *Method to Formulate an Integrated Science of Man* (1968).

state of pre-Columbian America. The Spaniards, lacking such knowledge, used the European compass to divide the conquered Inca empire into four administrative parts. They did not correspond to the biothermic divisions and were therefore ineffective. Such interpretations as Valle's, equally applicable to other geographic areas, permit new ways of viewing the uneven rates of development of New World civilizations.

Similar research also helps us understand the conditions surrounding man's transplantation from Europe to America. It shows, for example, how most of the immigrants of Anglo-America, living in climatic and geographic zones similar to those of Europe, were assured of not only ready adaptation but also high productive potential. But the same people, despite their exceptional energy, could adjust in only a limited degree to unaccustomed climatic conditions. That is illustrated in the "tropicalization" of some Europeans and Anglo-Americans who, after living in Central or South America for some time, gradually acquire traits typical of the natives and lose much of their "temperate-zone energy." Thus the fact of "belonging" to a specific zone is, in principle, a matter of considerable importance.

Spanish civilization of the New World resulted in part from the movement that prompted men, impelled by the human migratory instinct, to leave the Iberian Peninsula to settle in similar climatic zones in America. Neither the glacial cold of the extreme south nor the inhospitable heat of the tropical forests was attractive to the Iberian people. They concentrated principally along the coasts of South America, leaving the interior only partly occupied. The extensive areas of Amazonia and the high regions of the Andes remained almost uninhabited. Iberian settlers invariably put down their roots where conditions were favorable and avoided or withdrew from less suitable regions.

The geography of the New World and the natural riches of its lands are rightly accorded their importance in the colonial era in the Americas. Hispanic America encompasses a broad range of geographic features and varied climates, from cold to temperate to tropical. Most of the densely populated areas are in the plateaus and highlands, where the climate is cool or temperate. But many people also live on the plains, in the valleys, and along the coastal strips

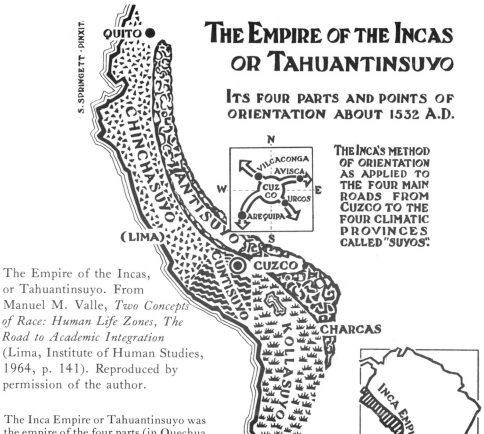

THE EMPIRE OF THE INCAS OR TAHUANTINSUYO

ITS FOUR PARTS AND POINTS OF ORIENTATION ABOUT 1532 A.D.

THE INCA'S METHOD OF ORIENTATION AS APPLIED TO THE FOUR MAIN ROADS FROM CUZCO TO THE FOUR CLIMATIC PROVINCES CALLED "SUYOS".

S. SPRINGETT · PINXIT.

© M.M. VALLE. 1962
APARTADO 1255 LIMA

The Empire of the Incas, or Tahuantinsuyo. From Manuel M. Valle, *Two Concepts of Race: Human Life Zones, The Road to Academic Integration* (Lima, Institute of Human Studies, 1964, p. 141). Reproduced by permission of the author.

The Inca Empire or Tahuantinsuyo was the empire of the four parts (in Quechua *tahua* four + *suyu* part). It was not divided according to four points of the compass as mistakenly thought, since the compass familiar in Europe was unknown to the Incas. They had their own notion of the world and of its different parts. The misconception, however, has lasted four hundred years; let us see now the new perspective. They divided empirically the land, plants, animals, and even human types and cultural styles into three kinds: *yunga* of hot climate, *quechua* of temperate climate, and *kolla* of cold climate. The *yunga* portion was split in twain by the Andes, on the one side the rainy Amazonian jungle, on the other the sandy deserts of the Pacific coast. From Cuzco, the capital, four roads lead to each of the four climatic provinces. And four well-known places, near Cuzco, served in each road as points of orientation: Vilcaconga, Avisca, Arequipa and Urcos. Quito and Charcas were great and famous enough to be used as the distant points of reference, indicating as far away as the empire had stretched in the popular thought. Of course, the divisions of the Tahuantinsuyo were neither exact nor perfect, as they could not possibly have been in the world's most abrupt and changing territory. Still, considering the empire's cultural level, the solution was adequate, effective, even brilliant. Four zones or *suyus* were obtained, tied up to the climate, flora and fauna, in consequence, somewhat homogeneous and stable. This was the magic scheme permitting the efficient administration of such vast an empire. In fact the Inca's classification of temperature-adapted human types and the resulting political divisions, formed the most important contribution of the Americas to world civilization. (From Manuel M. Valle, *Two Concepts of Race*, p. 142).

where it is very hot. For the most part the climate of the two Americas is comparable. It is inaccurate to describe Hispanic America as "tropical." Although three-fourths of South America and a large part of Mesoamerica are included in the Tropic Zone, because of the elevation those regions do not experience the unrelieved tropical conditions of the Caribbean islands, the Guianas, and the Amazon Valley.

The natural riches of Hispanic America were, of course, the key to its colonization. Gold and silver attracted the Spanish conquerors and provided the impetus for settlement. Precious metals were intensively mined and lodes exhausted long before the end of the colonial era. Those riches created the myth of the fabulous wealth of Hispanic America. Mineral resources are still present, of course, in petroleum, copper, platinum, and iron that are yet to be exploited on a large scale. Gold and silver are still extracted in limited quantities. Over all, however, Hispanic America cannot be said to possess great riches. Abundant resources, yes, when agriculture is taken into account. But to overstate its natural resources out of national pride is to run the risk of viewing Hispanic America too optimistically and thereby failing to perceive economic reality.

Some Americanists discuss the ecological thesis from the aspect of the interdependence of man and the natural setting. However convincing this approach may be, it does not explain the psychology of human conduct as regards attitudes toward effort and collective work. Some Slavic and Oriental colonists in South America, though coming from radically different climatic zones, were able to transform tropical regions into productive agricultural ones (for example, Paraná and Santa Catarina, in Brazil, and Misiones, in Argentina). Hispanic American and Asiatic immigrants in Canada and the United States adapted themselves to temperate or cold climates and worked as productively as other ethnic groups. Such examples demonstrate the overriding importance of initiative and the will to work, whatever the climatic conditions. The ecological factor, though important, is not invariably the determining one.

It remains necessary to explain the varying creative potentials of Anglo-Americans and Hispanic Americans in the colonial era. After the discovery of the New World—a genuine Iberian epic—the

Spanish and the English colonists took different directions in the colonizing process. They were equals in audacity and initiative but, as noted earlier, differed markedly in their attitudes toward work. The English for the most part performed their own labors, while the Spaniards directed the labors of others. Such attitudes could not be without influence on the creative capacity of the two peoples.

In Anglo-America arduous work and the struggles with nature and the Indians produced an independent character and initiative in settlers of both sexes. Unlike the Spaniards, they did not put the Indians in bondage. Later, of course, many landholders in the South owned African slaves. Given the territorial extent of the English colonies, however, Negroes did not equal in number or proportion the indigenous multitudes subjected to servile conditions in the Spanish colonies. Anglo-Saxon pioneers soon established a frontier civilization marked by determination, force, and aggressive expansionism. Later immigrants adopted similar attitudes and behavior. Thus evolved the frontier epic begun by the peaceful Pilgrim Fathers with their unquenchable vitality and energy. From these traits developed a citizen conscious not only of his duties and destiny but also of his prerogatives, which he jealously guarded. He took pride in his ability to confront any sort of obstacle and to rely on his own efforts and those of his community. There was little time or opportunity for "cultural refinement."

In colonial Hispanic America the Indians worked for the Spanish and creole masters in slavery-like servitude. Dispossessed of their lands, they lost much of their vitality and energy, and perhaps also their spiritual vigor, a loss to be reflected later in mestizo attitudes. The mixing of Spaniards and Indians gave vigorous support to the colonial ethnic structure but did not solve the problem of lack of creative potential and of social and economic integration. The mestizo inherited features of both peoples that resulted in a psychological dualism. In the mestizo the slowness and lack of ambition of the submissive indigene was in conflict with the racial pride and imaginative sensitivity of the Spaniard. The conflict often resulted in indecisiveness and slowness of action. The semifeudal practices in land tenancy stupefied the Indians, who could not conceive of individual land ownership. The mestizo was artistically and culturally productive, but economically much less so. Hispanic Americans, more attuned to the spiritual than to the practical, moved but slowly from the colonial era to the modern.

Physical and human environments also influenced behavior. A case in point is the experience of some of the Spanish explorers who were absorbed into indigenous communities. Anthropologists tell of creoles in the Andes who, after living for some time among the Indians, adopted their customs and ways of behaving and thinking and became so much like them that only their beards and light skin color distinguished them. The earliest Spanish chroniclers reported similar instances. Thus Bernal Díaz del Castillo, in *Verdadera historia de la conquista de la Nueva España,* wrote of the soldier-conqueror Gonzalo Guerrero, who became an Indian cacique in Yucatán. The explorer Alvar Núñez Cabeza de Vaca wrote in his *Naufragios* that when his companions rescued him on the Florida coast they hardly recognized him because his physical appearance had changed so greatly.

Geography, race, and culture are, of course, organically interrelated, but human dynamism is more influential than the physical environment in determining social physiognomy. Man has used his energy and inventiveness to transform his environment; only rarely has it overwhelmed him. Thus, despite the differences in the development of the Hispanic and Anglo-Saxon Americas, during the early colonial era the settlers of the two Americas shared certain characteristics of civilization. Both Americas were rich in resources for improving primitive conditions and creating a better life. How those resources were utilized depended on the collective dynamism of the particular ethnocultural group. For example, the creole region of the River Plate has made generally positive economic progress. By contrast, the indigenous communities of the Andean region have lagged behind. Progress in mestizo regions of Hispanic America has been uneven. The Anglo-American socioeconomic achievements are, for the most part, impressive, owing to motivation and systematization of work within the environment. From the beginning Anglo-Americans were determined to better themselves, and their endeavors provided them with the means to establish a mercantile capitalism later reinforced by industrial capitalism. Such developments, considerably improving economic and social conditions, in turn promoted a cultural and educational life. Consequently, Anglo-Americans were able to transform the frontier civilization into a modern one. Hispanic Americans, through the efforts of the educated minority, achieved notable cultural advances and a measure of urban sophistication but neglected the socioeconomic development of the masses and consequently the general progess of the Hispanic American civilization. They did make notable strides, in human terms, in the problem of equality—through *mestizaje*. But colonial ownership of land and economic and social paternalism retarded progress. Today Hispanic America remains in a state of transition, at a stage between frontier and modern civilization.

The Enlightenment and its rationalist philosophy advanced the principles of human rights and political liberty not only in Europe but in America as well. In the New World the political crystallization of these principles was achieved in the English colonies earlier (1776) than in the Spanish (1810).

The Anglo-American ideology of independence derived chiefly from John Locke's philosophy, which defined freedom as political autonomy not by one person's option but by the general popular will. Locke also advocated freedom of speech and thought and opposed the doctrine of the divine right of monarchs. The ideas about the rights of man and society promulgated by Jean Jacques Rousseau and Charles de Montesquieu also inspired the Anglo-Americans. The Encyclopedists also enlightened the process of Hispanic American independence. Among their works, which reached the Spanish colonies from France and the United States, Rousseau's pamphlet, *Discourse on the Origin and Bases of Inequality Among Men*, was especially influential. It was printed in Spanish in Charleston in 1803 and introduced into Hispanic America clandestinely. Various patriots took part in the contraband traffic in revolutionary ideas. Their efforts, bolstered by the success of the American and French revolutions, bore fruit in the victorious war against Spain during the Napoleonic occupation. The achievement of political independence in the New World ended three centuries of colonial rule in Hispanic America and 170 years in the United States. The era of national sovereign life had begun.

A panoramic view of Avenida 9 de Julio, in the center of Buenos Aires, Argentina. Courtesy Braniff Airways.

An Argentine gaucho. Courtesy Moore-McCormick.

Carlos Ponce Sanjines (left) and the author seated by a monolithic statue representative of the civilization of Tiahuanaco, Bolivia.

An Indian of the Uru tribe seated in a *balsa*, a reed boat, on Lake Titicaca, Bolivia. Courtesy Organization of American States.

Quechua Indians during Holy Week at Las Penas, Bolivia. The wool caps and ponchos protect these natives from the inclement climate of the high Andes. Courtesy Organization of American States.

Quechua Indian pageant in front of the Sun Gate at Tiahuanaco, Bolivia.
Courtesy Hamilton Wright.

Giant stone head on Easter Island, off the Chilean coast in the South Pacific. Courtesy Organization of American States.

Juan Fernández Island, also known as Robinson Crusoe Island, Chile.
Courtesy Organization of American States.

Two Chilean navy ships at anchor in the Strait of Magellan. Courtesy Organization of American States.

Christ of the Andes, high in the Andes of Chile near the Argentina border.
Courtesy Organization of American States.

An unusual cathedral made entirely of salt, deep within a salt mine at
Zipaquira, Chile. Courtesy Colombia Information Service.

A portion of San Felipe fortress at Cartagena, Colombia, built by the Spaniards in the sixteenth century. Courtesy Organization of American States.

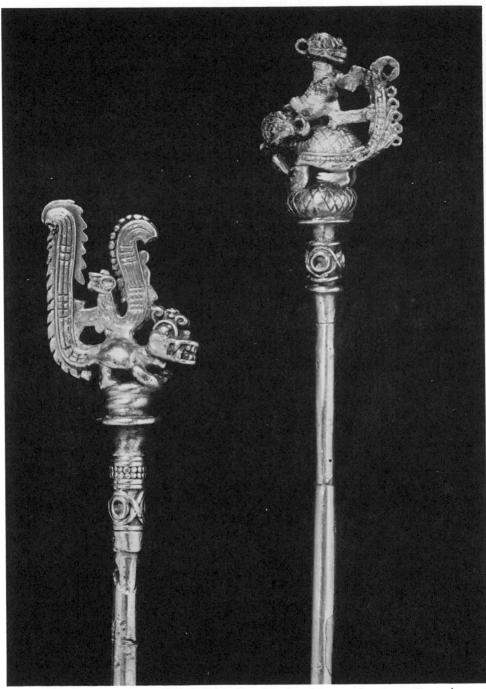

Quimbaya Indian gold shawl pins in the Museo de Oro, Bogotá, Colombia. Courtesy Organization of American States.

Pre-Columbian figures in the San Agustín Archaeological Park, Colombia.
Courtesy Organization of American States.

A Guajira Indian woman and her child in Riohacha, Colombia. Courtesy Asiatic Petroleum Corporation.

A Costa Rican criollo beside a gaily painted oxcart. Courtesy Organization of American States.

CHAPTER 5

INDIANS AND INDIGENISM IN HISPANIC AMERICA

The impressive Aztec and Inca civilizations disappeared when the Spanish conquerors imposed Western culture on them. By the time the Spaniards arrived, the most advanced civilization, that of the Mayas, was already in decay, its previously flourishing centers mostly abandoned. None of these native civilizations, or less-well-developed ones, such as Chibcha, Araucanian, and Tupí-Guarani, had had any previous contact with Spanish civilization. As the latter gradually absorbed various native traits, the evolving civilization, no longer Spanish, became what is designated Hispanic American or Indo-Hispanic American civilization. The most substantial native contributions to this new civilization were the influences of languages and customs, as well as some physical features resulting from racial mixture. In some Hispanic American countries, pre-Columbian elements are a strong influence in the current renaissance of indigenous literature and art.

The indigenous traits incorporated into the physiognomy of the new Hispanic American ethnic community are apparent as a biological phenomenon that is accompanied by distinct features. This phenomenon is called *mestizaje*, and offspring or descendants of Spaniards and Indians are called *mestizos*. *Mestizaje* does not necessarily imply acculturation, a complete cultural penetration of one group by the other. In the Spanish-Indian union the degree of penetration involved mostly the Indians' adoption of the Spanish language and the Christian faith. The result was an uneven level of cultural symbiosis. Thus we still find both Hispanized mestizos and Indians with insignificant mestizo traits, a circumstance supporting theories of the relativity of transculturation. Many mestizos have only superficial "Western" features. In their hearts they are Indian, even though they may speak Spanish. Those who are superficially Hispanized and others living in the remote interior of their countries were and are for the most part on the social periphery. In the words of López y Fuentes, these Indians are "motionless wanderers in the land of their ancestors, neglected and forgotten."

The early Spanish and Hispanic American chronicles contain descriptions of indigenous life—its social and political organizations, its customs and culture—before, during, and after the Conquest. Some of the important works are *Historia general de las cosas de Nueva España*, by Bernardino de Sahagún; *Historia verdadera de la conquista de la Nueva España*, by Bernal Díaz del Castillo; *Brevísima relación de la destrucción de las Indias*, by Bartolomé de las Casas; *Relación de las cosas de Yucatán*, by Diego de Landa; *Nueva crónica y buen gobierno*, by Felipe Guamán Poma de Ayala; *Comentarios reales de los Incas*, by Garcilaso de la Vega; *Crónica mexicana*, by Fernando de Alva Ixtlilxóchitl; and *Historia general del Reyno de Chile*, by Diego de Rosales.

In the demographic amalgamation resulting from racial mixture, the Hispanic element must be recognized as the major unifying force. The indigenous majority absorbed through *mestizaje* became a significant ethnic and social support of colonial society. During that westernizing process Hispanic American civilization established itself in such places as Mexico, Bolivia, and Peru, where the Indian is still preponderant, especially in the rural regions. This process helped mold a new spirit and was responsible for the emerging mestizo character. The Indians, meanwhile, continued in their traditions, particularly in Mexico.

Even in countries with a large native population the indigenes still do not share equally in the national life. Countries such as Bolivia, Ecuador, Guatemala, and Peru, whose literature abounds in works on Indian themes, reflect very little "native" influence culturally, economically, or socially, because the various ethnic groups tend to live apart from each other. Certainly physical apartness is a deterrent to either cultural or social integration. In some Andean countries, difficult local circumstances have resulted in instances of retrogression to the biological indigenous status by some mestizo groups, and even by creoles. Communities almost entirely indigenous that are separated from modern civilization cannot easily exert or experience influences that might transform their ancient lifeways and attitudes. Such Indians live simply, much as their ancestors lived centuries ago—and they number in the millions.

In recent times there has been some effort to draw the Indian into modern civilization. This effort has taken a number of forms, such as training the Indian in more productive agricultural methods, meanwhile trying to preserve the indigenous tongues and traditions. Scientific and folklore investigations have frequently inspired creative work by artists and writers. The term *indigenism*, or *Indianism*, is applied to such efforts. A useful distinction is made between *social indigenism*, which seeks a general acculturation by efforts to help the Indian raise his standard of living with modern resources and techniques, and *intellectual indigenism*, which uses literary and artistic means to arouse interest in the Indian. Anthropological, sociological, ethnological, and linguistic research is providing documentary reconstruction of the pre-Columbian civilizations, as well as broader knowledge of the Indian of today. Parallel studies continue, of course, in Anglo-America.

Opinions concerning the role of ancient indigenous culture in Western civilization range from frank admiration to cautious reservation. No one, however, denies the Indians' significant contributions to the advancement of the human spirit, as shown by the following representative opinions of Latin American and Anglo-American scholars. Hubert J. Spinden, the North American anthropologist, assumed a historic-esthetic attitude in comparing the ancient cultures of the New World and the Old:

> A remarkably close analogy may be drawn between the Mayas and Aztecs in the New World and the Greeks and Romans in the Old, as regards character, achievements, and relations to one another. The Mayas, like the Greeks, were an artistic and intellectual people who developed sculpture, painting, architecture, astronomy, and other arts and sciences to a high plane. Politically, both were divided into communities or city-states that fought among themselves for power. There were temporary alliances between some city-states, but real unity only against a common enemy. . . . To be sure, the religion of the Mayas was much more barbaric than that of the Greeks, but in each case its worship was idealized and beautified in art.
> The Aztecs, like the Romans, were a brusque and warlike people who

built upon the ruins of an earlier civilization that fell before the force of their arms and who made their most notable contributions to organization and government. The Toltecs, who were the historic vanguard of the Aztecs, may appropriately be compared to the Etruscans.[1]

Colombian author Gonzalo Restrepo Jaramillo, in comparing Indian civilization with the modern, offered the following opinion:

> The Indian peoples of pre-Columbian America did not know the wheel, and therefore their civilization advanced very little in practical achievements. On the other hand, it can be asserted that all the mechanical progress of western civilization depends on the utilization of this seemingly small discovery; and as the process of its application had to produce first the press and later the steamship, and the influence of one and the other is transcendental for the progress of the spirit, we can deduce that the development of the mechanical is of enormous benefit for the advancement of thought. The suppression of the wheel would bring about the recession of the world to full barbarism.[2]

Another significant observation comes from Mexican archaeologist Alfonso Caso. In analyzing the pre-Columbian cultures, he contrasted their spirituality and their lack of technical inventiveness:

> When the Conquest took them by surprise, the Aztecs were still a semicivilized people who had not yet reached the cultural refinement of the Mayas, the Toltecs, the Totonacs, or the Mixtecs. The Aztecs were in the midst of a flourishing era, but the old indigenous cultures that had already disappeared are eloquent proof of the sterility in which those great civilizations finally ended. They had lacked a constantly progressive ideal that would have led them to conceive of life as something more than an invariable, meticulous repetition of ceremonies in honor of the gods.
>
> Among the great cultures of Mesoamerica, religion, in great part, took the place of technical invention. The fundamental belief was that man did not have to solve his own problems, but must implore the gods to solve them and take pity on mankind. For the Indians of Mesoamerica, sacrifice was the technical means that made the rain fall, the corn grow, an illness disappear, a father, husband, or son return safe

[1]Herbert J. Spinden, *Ancient Civilizations of Mexico and Central America*, pp. 201–203.
[2]Gonzalo Restrepo Jaramillo, "Norteamérica: Signos de Interpretación," *Revista Universidad Católica Bolivariana*, Vol. II (1938).

from an expedition of war or commerce, or a wife give birth to a strong, vigorous child. Man alone could do nothing; his technique was ineffectual. Only by sacrifice could he induce the gods to satisfy with benevolence the needs of mankind.[3]

The Indians' theocentric view of life was manifested in their fear of the supernatural and in various superstitions originating in unexpected changes of nature. The culturally advanced tribes transmitted that view in their architecture and other works of art, as well as in poetry and lengends, which have been handed down orally. Much of the oral material has been collected and published by the Inter-American Indigenist Institute.

The many pre-Columbian works of architecture and sculpture in Mesoamerica and the Andean region attest to the creative ability of the ancients. Outstanding examples are the pyramids and other pre-Columbian structures in San Juan Teotihuacán, Tula, Monte Albán, Mitla, Chichén Itzá, Palenque, Copán, Tikal, Chavin, Tiahuanaco, Cuzco, Machu Picchu, and Sacsahuamán. Ceramics made by the various groups are extraordinarily beautiful. The murals at Bonampak display impressive originality of composition, as do the carved stone stelae throughout the region of Mayan civilization. Pre-Columbian gold and silver work is evidence of the artistic skill of tribes from Mexico to Peru.

While the sculptures and bas-relief representations of plants and animals on Mexican pre-Columbian monuments display much originality, some of it also bears a resemblance to works of other cultures. Some archaeologists, for example, see a similarity in the serpents on the balustrades at Chichén Itzá to those on the friezes of the temple at Amaravati, India. A decorative similarity has been noted in the representations of plants on the monuments of Palenque and Cambodia. Such similarities have inevitably produced theories about transoceanic contact. The Asiatic origin of American Indians is almost universally accepted. But there are also widespread speculations about cultural connections between the New World and other continents many centuries before the Europeans discovered America.

The gigantic pre-Columbian stone structures erected without mortar have aroused much admiration. Examples are the Inca for-

[3]Alfonso Caso, *The Aztecs: People of the Sun*, p. 96.

tress Sacsahuamán and some buildings of imperial Cuzco (parts of which the Spaniards used in the construction of churches and other buildings, which they usually erected on top of the pyramids to help eradicate the "pagan" beliefs). Other impressive works are the Atlantean figures of the Toltecs in Tula and the enormous stone heads of the Olmecs in southern Mexico and Guatemala. The Indians were also accomplished engineers, as demonstrated by stone roadways and hanging bridges, remains of which are preserved in the Inca region. They also devised systems for irrigation and for drinking water for the larger cities, such as Tenochtitlán, the ancient capital of the Aztecs, which, according to Jacques Soustelle, had about 100,000 inhabitants in its golden era.[4]

Various tribes developed pictographic writing for recording significant events. Examples are the Mayan stelae and the Aztec codices, the latter written on paper made from the maguey plant. Knowledge of mathematics and use of the concept of zero enabled some Mexican tribes to set up a double calendrical system: ritual-agricultural and annual. The precise calendrical calculations of the Indians are noteworthy, for their annual calendar antedated by many centuries the Gregorian calendar, which the Spaniards brought to the New World. In the field of medicine the Indians' knowledge of surgery, including trepanning of the skull, was remarkably well developed. They made false teeth and inlays of semiprecious stones. They used medicinal herbs, such as quinine, many of which were afterward incorporated into both the colonial and the modern pharmacopoeia.

Some Indian tribes developed structured political organizations, such as the Aztec confederacy, the Mayan city-states, and, especially, the Inca empire. That empire included extensive areas along the Pacific Coast of South America and had a well-defined social and political structure. Although that structure included subjugation of neighboring tribes, the empire allowed local autonomy and religious liberty. Owing to effective civil discipline, it became, in its time, the best organized indigenous state of the New World. Communal property ownership anticipated socialism, while its government structure was somewhat like that of a dynastic monarchy. Such features were different from the military regimen of the Aztec confederacy, with

---

[4]Jacques Soustelle, *La vie quotidienne des Aztèques à la veille de la conquête espagnole.*

its political absolutism and strict tributary system. The Aztec warrior-conqueror spirit was a contrast to the theocratic state of the Mayas, who were more interested in the sciences, the arts, and religious ceremonies than in war. On the Peruvian coast the Mochica and Nazca cultures were like the Inca culture, well organized socially but also creative in the arts.

Among the Indians continuity between past and present has been maintained in many survivals, which are as apparent in customs and beliefs as in communal concepts and artistic capacities. Among them is the ancient Indian community system generally called *ayllu*, which has survived until today under one name or another in various groups. Ancient Andean customs, such as the *minga*, the *huasipungo*, and the *pongaje*, are forms of forced labor that are still practiced among the Quechuas and the Aymaras. Peonage, which originated in colonial days, is still widespread in Hispanic America. That it persists in modern times is an indication of the age-old acceptance of servility first to the tribal hierarchy and, after the Conquest, to the landowners. Once the Conquest was complete, the Indians' ingrained obedience to authority enabled the conquistadors to extend Spanish dominion over the Aztec and Inca empires with relative ease.

In Mesoamerica, as well as in the Andes, certain pagan pre-Columbian beliefs and superstitions, curiously mixed with Christian rites, were preserved. In some areas of Guatemala, for example, the Indians still take their idols to the Catholic churches and pay homage to them with candles and incense as they do to God and the saints. This intermingling of pagan and Christian ideas, called religious syncretism, is one proof that the acculturation process among the Amerindians was never completely carried out. Throughout almost all of the New World native dances, often accompanied by music, have been preserved. The exceptional artistry of the Indians, which could no longer find expression in monumental works, is manifested today in the manufacture of serapes, ponchos, blankets, baskets, beads, sandals, pottery, gold and silver work, and other decorative objects. The aggregate gives a colorful aspect to the various regions. The Hispanic American and the North American Indian mythologies also display an imaginative richness, with legends providing a wealth of literary and artistic themes.

Indians are still victims of prejudice and abuse in Hispanic

America. Part of the reason lies in the social stratification that was established in colonial times, first by race and later increasingly by degree of economic well-being. Today on the social ladder the creoles stand on the top rung. They are followed by the mestizos, ranging from the wealthy to the lower middle class. The Indians, because of their poverty, stand at the bottom. The differences among these strata, which seem to preserve their old ethnic character, are clearly visible, and are frequently reflected in the attitudes of one group toward another.

This problem was discussed by the Mexican anthropologist Juan Comas in *Relaciones interraciales en América Latina: 1940–1960.* There he characterized the relationships among various ethnic groups from the Río Grande to Tierra del Fuego. Comas did not deny the existence of discrimination in Hispanic America, especially in countries with preponderant Indian populations. He classified attitudes, however, as social, cultural, and economic prejudice rather than racial prejudice as such. These attitudes persist despite various inter-American resolutions censuring racism and ethnic prejudices against Indians. He listed derogatory nicknames, such as *"indio,"* *"indiote,"* and *"naco,"* which clearly imply racism, though sometimes subtly camouflaged. Of similar opinion are various Anglo-American and European Americanists. In "The Racial Problem in Latin America," anthropologists Alfred Métraux wrote:

> In no region of Spanish-speaking America do racial relations appear with the inhuman rigidity with which one associates the notion of racism. But it would be erroneous to affirm, as frequently happens, that in countries with a strong percentage of indigenous population some forms of prejudice and discrimination of racist character do not exist.[5]

Métraux is probably correct in claiming that prejudices in Spanish America are less intense than those in Anglo-America. The intensity of such attitudes varies from country to country, depending on the ethnic structure. Of course, in every country there is a dominant sector whose behavior indicates that it believes it has the right to subjugate ethnic or national minorities. That attitude invariably causes discrimination in its various forms, whenever it may occur.

[5]*Courrier de l'Unesco* (Paris), 1960.

In the historic view, it must be remembered that Indians of both continents suffered from the time of their first contact with Europeans. According to the Peninsular chroniclers, such as Las Casas and Fernández de Oviedo, during the Spanish conquest of the Caribbean hundreds of thousands of aborigines perished. They were completely eliminated from Hispaniola, Cuba, and Puerto Rico, which then became staging areas for Spain's expansion from the islands toward the mainland. Later, during the colonial era, there were instances of "pacification," as, for example, the suppression of the Inca uprising by Tupac Amaru in 1780 and the campaigns against the Indians in the English colonies during the seventeenth and eighteenth centuries. However, the greatest losses suffered by the Indians in Hispanic America and in Anglo-America as well occurred during the era of independence, which was also marked by a few Indian uprisings, such as that of the Yaquis in Sonora in 1873, of the Mayas in Yucatán at the beginning of this century, and of the Plains Indians in the United States.

In the nineteenth century the Argentinian army, with the help of the gauchos, annihilated much of the large Indian population of the River Plate region, as a result of which the "indigenous problem" in Argentina and Uruguay ceased to exist. No less cruel acts were committed in the United States in the same century, during the Indian Wars and the Anglo-Americans' drive westward. On both continents such campaigns were invariably staged on the pretext of military pacification that, in fact, decimated the Indians.

The Argentinians and the North Americans sometimes took steps toward peaceful coexistence with their Indian neighbors and even concluded peace treaties with them. Unfortunately, such treaties did not last, and mutual distrust intensified. The Argentinians as well as the Americans frequently placed the responsibility for such negotiations on military commanders, who tended to resolve conflicts by military means. Even when they acted in good faith, they were often overruled by political orders from their governments, with tragic consequences for the Indians. In contrast, in Canada the resolution of Indian-white disputes was entrusted mostly to civilians, among whom were Christian missionaries. They assumed the more conciliatory role of intermediaries, even to the extent of becoming spokesmen for the natives. Thus in Canada disputes were settled by treaties. At times the Indians were drawn into the colonial power struggle between the British and the French, but over all Indian-white relations have been less troubled in Canada than in the United States. Neither country, however, has yet shed its paternalistic attitude toward its indigenous minority.

One fact that sometimes goes unnoticed is the dependency of the Indians on the ecology and climate of their region. Time after time in the colonial era Amerindians perished because they never adapted to the difficult labor in the mines, nor did the mountain Indians ever adjust to toiling on the plains. The ecological and climatic differences inflicted physical suffering on them almost to the point of annihilation. Many fell during the Chaco War between Bolivia and Paraguay (1932–35) mainly because the mountain-bred soldiers were not accustomed to jungle conditions. No less tragic was the forced removal of the Cherokee Indians from their homes in Georgia, North Carolina, and Tennessee to Indian Territory (Oklahoma) in the 1830's, during which many of the tribe perished. During the construction of the Trans-Andean Highway between Lima and the Amazon jungle, a massive transplant of Quechuas, who are mountain Indians, to the tropical areas was planned. Fortunately the plan was canceled; the results would have been tragic. Many years ago in Colombia a similar project on a smaller scale was also unsuccessful. Recruits from the mountains of Ecuador and Peru felt uprooted when they were taken to the coast and escaped to the mountains at the first opportunity. In still earlier times the Inca rulers periodically tried to transfer the Quechua and Aymara Indians to remote parts of the empire with climates unlike those of their homelands. After dramatic consequences those attempts were usually halted.

The most frequently mentioned factors complicating the Indians' integration into the national life of their respective countries are government inertia, society's relative indolence, and the resistance of Spanish American property owners to agrarian reform, which could alleviate the hunger for land among the dispossessed Indians. Among the difficulties that impede the Indians' acculturation are their own apathy toward adapting themselves to modern civilization and lack of education and consequently of ambition for economic betterment, as well as topographic and linguistic obstacles (at present more than five hundred indigenous languages and dialects are spoken in the countries of the New World). Indigenist movements in Hispanic America are relatively weak, and their actions have little effect, although, distinguished defenders of the indigenous cause occasionally make their voices heard.

It is interesting to note the attitude of some leading Hispanic American authors on the Indian problem. Germán Arciniegas and Luis Alberto Sánchez base their pro-Indian views on humanist and social grounds and racial pride—and, possibly, political considerations. José Vasconcelos and Pedro Henríquez Ureña assume a rather arbitrary cultural paternalism toward the Indians in which one senses intellectual insincerity. Ricardo Rojas uses Indian themes for his theoretical speculation. Domingo F. Sarmiento, Francisco García Calderón, José Ingenieros, and Carlos Bunge are openly racist as a consequence of their creole and European ideologies. Manual González Prada, José Carlos Mariátegui, and Victor Haya de la Torre defend the indigenous cause, emphasizing the social injustice. Mexican indigenism, highly developed and dynamic, counts among its promoters Manuel Gamio, Alfonso Caso, Ángel Garibay, Juan Comas, Miguel León-Portilla, and Gonzalo Aguirre Beltrán. Their counterparts in other countries are the Venezuelan Miguel Acosta Saignes, the Ecuadorians Aníbal Buitrón and Gonzalo Rubio Orbe, and the Peruvians Luis Valcárcel, Federico Kauffman Doig, and Manuel M. Valle.

Among the New World nations the indigenous consciousness is most deeply rooted in Mexico, although it is also evident in certain social groups in Peru, Ecuador, Bolivia, and Guatemala. Mexico is perhaps the one country that can take pride in its progress in indigenist activites, although they do not yet include all of the Indian population. (Owing to the initiative of Mexican indigenists, since 1940, April 19 has been commemorated as the Day of the American Indian.) Mexican anthropologist Antonio Caso once declared that "the indigenous problem in Mexico is not a racial but a cultural problem." It seems doubtful, however, that the same attitude prevails in other Latin American nations, judging by the alarming news about indigenist action presented by various Indianists at the International Congresses of Americanists between 1962 and 1974.

Almost all the reports indicated flagrant negligence by the government authorities and also by the Indians themselves.

It is true that in the twentieth century the incorporation of indigenous elements in some revolutionary activities in Hispanic America has raised the Indians from the historic abyss, as in the previous century they were freed from literary oblivion. These activities, however, served the ambitions of some political leaders more than they visibly improved the lot of the Indians. The Indians of Mexico and Bolivia have received land, but in the rest of Hispanic America the agrarian problem is still more involved with political phraseology than with practical solutions. The destitute Indians continue to feel alienated from their countrymen and lack a national consciousness.

Many Hispanic American novels deal with the conditions in which Indians live in the twentieth century. Among the most significant are *Raza de bronce* (1919), by Alcides Arguedas; *El indio* (1935), by Gregorio López y Fuentes; *Huasipungo* (1934), by Jorge Icaza; *El resplandor* (1937), by Mauricio Magdaleno; *Sumag Allpa* (1940), by Gonzalo Humberto Mata; *El mundo es ancho y ajeno* (1941), by Ciro Alegría; *Tungsteno* (1948), by César Vallejo; *Entre la piedra y cruz* (1948), by Mario Monteforte Toledo; *Hombres de maíz* (1949), by Miguel Ángel Asturias; *Juan Pérez Jolote* (1952), by Ricardo Pozas; *No se suicidan los muertos* (1957), by Esteban Pavletich; and *Los ríos profundos* (1958), by José María Arguedas. A few outstanding recent works of this genre are *Oficio de tinieblas* (1962), by Rosario Castellanos; *El Titán de bronce* (1964), by Isabel Centellas; *Madre milpa* (1965), by Carlos Samoya Chinchilla; and *Sangre del maíz* (1966), by José M. López Valdizón. The Indianist novel also began to receive the attention of literary critics, among whom Concha Meléndez, Gerald E. Wade, Aida Comette Manzoni, María José de Queiroz, and Antonio Sacoto are outstanding.

The indigenous problems in the United States have taken a different direction, usually varying from extreme policies of isolation and assimilation. After long and dramatic struggles that reduced the number of Indians, many of them were assigned to isolation on reservations. The reservations have now become autonomous and are administered by tribal councils with the help of government representatives. This arrangement has a double purpose: it protects the Indians from possible abuse and exploitation by outsiders, and it allows them to maintain their traditional ways of living. They are, however, provided with many facilities for voluntary cultural integration.

Ancestral tradition founded on close family relations within the tribal community is sacred to United States Indians. In Arizona in recent years, to avoid separating Navajo youths from the roots of their civilization, schools have been established where the language as well as the history of the Navajos is taught. The growing attendance at these schools seems to indicate a gradual improvement in an educational system that was previously carried on almost exclusively in English. This measure has encouraged other tribes, such as the Chippewas of Minnesota and the Pueblos of New Mexico, to establish schools of higher education similar to the Navajo Community College (founded in 1969), which are controlled by tribal authorities, though they receive government financial support. It is hoped that the Indians will be able, by means of education, to benefit from Anglo-American civilization while maintaining their own.

The decimation of the United States Indians in the nineteenth century, in some ways comparable to the annihilation of the indigenous peoples of Argentina, nevertheless laid the foundation for their rehabilitation. The United States government signed treaties with various Indian tribes providing for certain annual payments as indemnification. Indigenous communities were organized as cooperatives. Some of these have prospered; others, because of unsuitable land or climate, have been less successful. The discovery of oil in Oklahoma made a few Indians millionaires, but the condition of the Indians as a whole is not good, and many remain in difficult circumstances, dependant upon government assistance. One-half of the Indians of the United States receive federal aid, though they possess extensive communal land. Beginning in 1933, as part of the government program of social action—the "New Deal"—begun by President Franklin D. Roosevelt, efforts have been made to improve their condition. Schools, hospitals, and technical-agricultural vocational centers, which aid in the acculturation of the inhabitants while guaranteeing them their community and protecting their ethnic individuality, have been built on the reservations at government expense.

The process of integration of reservation Indians into Anglo-American civilization has had a different fate, partly because of psychological resistance and partly because of the Indians' desire to preserve their racial and cultural identity. Many of them, especially the reservation Indians, follow their "Indian soul" and thus remain separated from the Anglo-American social environment. (These attitudes are less common in Oklahoma, where, with the termination of the reservation system, the Indians were less isolated and gradually began to be assimilated into white culture. They do, however, seek to maintain cultural contact with their past and to preserve some aspects of their ancestors' lifeways.)

The attitude of North American Indians toward their white neighbors has historical foundations. Though they lost the wars, the Indians never lost their strong sense of racial dignity. Their deep-rooted consciousness of ethnic community, sense of justice, and veneration for nature were often poorly understood by the whites, who frequently broke the peace treaties. Perhaps those violations produced a greater degree of bitterness and distrust than that felt by the Hispanic American Indians, who, through several centuries of servitude to the Spaniards, had adopted an attitude of humility and resignation. The North American Indians have never served anyone, and they preserve their dignity and individuality. They prefer their own lifeways and remain, in large part, separated from Western civilization.

The Indians' attitude of indifference toward Anglo-Americans is almost reciprocal, a consequence of the state of war that existed for a long time between the two groups. Organized into loose and temporary military federations, some tribes effectively slowed the advance of settlers across the continent. The frustration of the former because they were unable to defend their land and the eagerness of the latter to occupy the land in order to cultivate it brought about a mutual distrust and antagonism. It became impossible to "Westernize" the aborigines, an effort that the Anglo-Americans, in contrast to the Spaniards, did not attempt to undertake by force of arms. Thus the two groups lived their own lives side by side. Cultural penetration was originally insignificant, even after some of the

Indians had been converted to Christianity, and the early settlers maintained only commercial exchange with them. The whites recalled the Indians' bravery with respect, and therefore white prejudices against the Indians were less pronounced than were those toward blacks.

An extensive literature describes the frontier wars, as well as the Indians' customs and beliefs. The idealization of the Indians in the novels of James Fenimore Cooper, Washington Irving, and Joaquin Miller, as well as the romantic "naturalism" of William Gilmore Simms, was balanced by a degree of veracity in the more factual accounts of Lewis H. Garrard, John C. Frémont, and Francis Parkman. The Indian theme acquired a greater significance in literature early in the twentieth century in the works of Mary Hunter Austin, Adolph Francis Bandelier, Hamlin Garland, Bret Harte, Oliver La Farge, and others. A genre of cheap fiction (the "dime novels") tended to create in the public mind the image of the Plains Indian as the typical Indian, and to identify him as a bloodthirsty savage, but that fiction has been replaced by much more sophisticated works, in both nonfiction and fiction, in which the Indian emerges as a human being. This current of intellectual indigenism continues the same humanitarian and folklore tradition that brought support to the Indian cause from government, civic, and religious groups. The Indian theme achieved international popularity through Hollywood films, many of which were unfortunately characterized by inaccurate if not downright irresponsible interpretations.

The United States Bureau of Indian Affairs is in charge of matters relating to the Indians. Owing to political pressures and sometimes regional economic interests, the bureau has rarely been able to provide satisfactory solutions. The Indians have always had more support from anthropologists than from bureaucrats. This is the impression given by John Collier, author of *Indians of the Americas* (1947). An anthropologist and Commissioner for Indian Affairs, Collier made observations about the North American Indians, particularly the Navajos, whom he especially admired. Collier observed the following traits among the Indians: an intense community spirit; a propensity to meditation, truthfulness, and artistic inclination; a sense of rhythm; ethnic-tribal unity that was always intensified in time of danger; and a sense of the intimate relation between man and nature. Those traits, Collier emphasized, involving both custom and spiritual heritage, are much more deep rooted than white society thinks. That is also true of the ancient democratic tradition, which explains the cooperative spirit at the tribal level. These traits have enabled the North American Indians to retain at least some of their heritage.

Although the condition of the North American Indians leaves much to be desired, it seems less tragic than that of the Indians of Hispanic America, who live on the edges of the economy. In that regard it is interesting to record the statement made by Miguel León-Portilla during the Twenty-fifth International Congress of Americanists in Mexico (1962). Referring to the expenditures of American nations for the rehabilitation of their indigenous peoples, he said, "If the countries of Latin America with indigenous populations combined their budgets for a period of twenty years, they would not reach the amount the United States spends in twelve months."

Various criteria are used in Hispanic America to determine the present-day population of the Indians of the Americas. Some census figures combine both full bloods and mixed bloods in the same group. According to the Peruvian Indianist Luis Valcárcel, the estimated number of Indians on the two American continents is twenty-five to thirty million. There are about ten million in Mexico, including those who speak only indigenous languages and also those with Indian cultural characteristics. About one million live in the United States and Canada, including the Eskimos and the Aleuts. Approximately three million live in Central American countries, principally in Guatemala. Almost two million are in Ecuador, Colombia, and Venezuela. Between nine and ten million live in the mountain and jungle regions of the Andean countries of Bolivia and Peru. In the rest of South America there are about one million, including the Indians of the jungles of Brazil, Paraguay, and the Guianas, as well as those of Argentina and Uruguay.

Compare the figures above with the pre-Columbian population of the Americas. According to the estimates of the Argentine Americanist Ángel Rosenblat, when the Europeans discovered the New World, approximately thirteen and one-half million Amerindians were living there. Approximately one million made their homes north of the Río Grande, and twelve and one-half million inhabited territories comprising Hispanic America. According to the North American anthropologist Herbert J. Spinden, the indigenous population from Alaska to Tierra del Fuego could have reached around sixty million. California historians Sherburne F. Cook and Woodrow Borah believe that, on the basis of regional demographic calculations, pre-Columbian Mexico alone had a population of more than thirty million. Thus the pre-Columbian native population of the New World could have been as large as one hundred million.

CHAPTER 6

THE MESTIZOS IN HISPANIC AMERICA

The Iberian conquest of the New World brought a confrontation between two races and cultures. The consequences were apparent in *mestizaje*. In Andean countries the mestizos are customarily called *cholos*; in Central American countries, *ladinos*. The North American traveler E. G. Squier, who visited Hispanic America in the middle of the nineteenth century, described mestizos as people of dark complexion and medium height, well proportioned and robust. He also observed that "it is difficult to say whether the whites have been more assimilated into the Indian way of life or the Indians into that of the whites." He seemed to indicate that the somatic features in *mestizaje* were perhaps less important than cultural assimilation.

As a consequence of the extensive mixing of Spaniards and Indians, which continues among their descendants today, mestizos now constitute the main body of the Hispanic American population. The Creoles are a minority in Hispanic America as a whole, though Uruguay and Argentina are populated principally by creoles and descendants of white immigrants (and consequently are called "creole countries"). In Chile and Costa Rica it is difficult to find traces of *mestizaje*, though large numbers of Indians lived in Chile in colonial times.

It is worth mentioning here that, while anthropologists define *mestizaje* as the cross between white and Indian races, the term has sometimes been loosely applied to any racial mixture. For example, Felix F. Pallavicini uses the term mestizos not only for Hispanic Americans but also for Anglo-Americans, inasmuch as he considers all of them products of various ethnic mixtures.

The United States racial mixture within the ethnic conglomerate seems somewhat like the Hispanic American *mestizaje*, but there are important differences. The ethnic structure of the United States is, of course, different from that of Hispanic America. In the United

States whites who have intermarried with similar ethnic groups and their descendants are dominant. Nevertheless, racial mixture also occurs among them, and also among the several United States minorities, though perhaps less extensively than in Hispanic America. This mixture includes people from Europe, Latin America, Africa, and Asia, making the United States a "melting pot" indeed. What is unique in the United States is not so much the ethnic and racial mixture as the ideological symbiosis from the blending of cultures and ideologies of various countries. The ideological melting pot is the result of the process of leveling and adjusting to the constant evolution of society. In those terms I believe that the ideological melting pot in the United States is more important than the racial one, although sometimes the two phenomena are inseparable.

Simón Bolívar, "the Liberator," described the mestizos in 1819: "We are not Europeans, we are not Indians, but we are rather halfway between the aborigines and the Spaniards." The Spanish colonial attitude toward the Indians as racially inferior has never been completely overcome, as shown, for example, in Arthur de Gobineau's pernicious racial doctrines of "Nordic supremacy." The developing mestizo civilization, however, forged its own consciousness and claimed its rights to "cultural citizenship."

The Colombian essayist Germán Arciniegas considered mestizos as much European as American, pointing to the fact that the Old World itself was a world "where men of Asia, Africa, and Europe gathered and fused." Thus he considered the Europe of the era of discoveries a "continent of mestizos, a triangle of races and cultures." Arciniegas' opinion, of course, should be understood as focusing on Iberians, whose geographic discoveries and colonization of certain parts of Africa and Asia before their discovery of the New World had been accompanied by interracial mingling. He also believed that the presence of different blood streams in the *peninsulares* endowed them with an imaginative and creative force that was conveyed to Hispanic Americans.

Arciniegas carefully examined the Hispanic American mestizo nature. He attributed to mestizos, among other traits, ingenuity and the creative urge, as well as a dual personality beset by internal stress. He saw the duality as a virtue resulting from the racial mixture, which had the advantages of enriching the individual psychically and opening new horizons in his spiritual development. Arciniegas also saw the mestizo as suffering from indecision, self-deception, and instability. The inevitable conflicts seemed to him to be counteracted by high intelligence and an enormous potential.[1]

Arciniegas was convinced that Hispanic Americans display a more developed "Faustian spirit" than Europeans because the natural desire to progress is enhanced by a desire to emulate the achievements of the Europeans. The result is a certain degree of mestizo vitality, though the rhythm of life in mestizo America is generally slow.

A fervent admirer of pre-Columbian Americans, Arciniegas believed that the achievements of the indigenous civilization in the New World were superior to those in Spain during the Conquest. His proindigenist attitude, though sometimes overemotional, is understandable. With a certain mestizo-Americanist pride Arciniegas expressed his admiration for the grandeur of the old Aztec and Inca capitals and for the monuments of indigenous art. His comparison of the artistry of the pyramids of Teotihuacán and Chichén Itzá with the Gothic Cathedral of Burgos and the plateresque façade of the University of Salamanca is, however, very much open to question. The monuments have very different styles and characteristics. But his originality in analyzing the complexity of *mestizaje*, in which pride is interwoven with the American consciousness and the deeply rooted feeling for the land, cannot be denied.

As pointed out earlier, the mestizo constitutes the ethnic trunk of Hispanic America, and consequently the destiny of many countries rests on him. Yet only a few Hispanic American writers are attracted to the difficult theme of *mestizaje*. More than thirty years ago the Peruvian essayist Luis Alberto Sánchez studied the ethnocultural transformation within the complex Hispanic American personality.[2] In analyzing the mestizo spiritual dualism, he assumed an attitude that is best described as wavering between indigenism and creolism. He emphasized that "the mestizo is biologically close to the Indian but intellectually close to the European. Sánchez' thesis seems logical, but it does not necessarily hold true for all Hispanic American

[1]Germán Arciniegas, *America: Tierra firme*, pp. 46–48.
[2]Luis Alberto Sánchez, *¿Existe América Latina?*

mestizos. In Colombia and Venezuela, for example, the mestizos seem more creole than Indian.

Because of the deep-rooted Spanish tradition, Colombian *mestizaje* tends to identify itself with the creole more in the intellectual sense than in the ethnic one. But, as the Colombian Fernando González has written, many South Americans conceal their Indian (or Negro) antecedents. González wrote: "In reality, that mixture is good; but in our consciences we have the feeling of having sinned. We live, work, and feel the complex of illegitimacy."[3] That sense leads many South Americans to simulate the Europeans. The reverse is the case in the Mesoamerican countries, especially in Mexico, where mestizo consciousness is evident and many Mexicans are proud of their indigenous origin or extraction.

As already mentioned, the Andean mestizo is popularly called cholo. The Peruvian José Varallanos in his work *El cholo y el Perú* shed interesting light on the term, which he traced to the eighteenth-century author Concolorcorvo, who, in *El Lazarillo de ciegos caminantes*, identified the cholo with the mestizo. Varallanos, however, considered cholos a separate race and assigned them a unique place in the multiracial highland society. While reaffirming the cholos' Spanish-Indian duality, this writer, himself a cholo, attributed to them considerable cultural and social ability, which he claimed they inherited from their Iberian ancestors. He also ascribed to the latter all their psychological defects, minimizing indigenous influences on their personality. Varallanos' apologetic, though proindigenous, work does not take sufficient note of the Indian heritage in the spiritual makeup of the cholo. It does, however, contain extensive information on the past and present attitudes of other ethnic groups toward Indians and cholos. Of a polemic nature and with anti-Spanish and anticlerical overtones, Varallanos' exposition is one in a chain of contemporary Peruvian writings that tend to reinforce the mestizo's pride in his indigenous ancestry. It is a contribution to the effort at "social rehabilitation" initiated by Manuel González Prada and followed by José C. Mariategui, Haya de la Torre, and others.

Great discrepanices still exist in the terminology applied to the

---

[3] Fernando González, *Los Negroides: Ensayo sobre la Gran Colombia.*

mestizo. In the broadest usage a mestizo is any mixture of European with nonwhite American whether Indian or Negro. Apparently that usage gained a fair degree of currency in some South American regions. The Chilean scholar Rolando Mellafe has introduced two new terms: *euromestizo*, to denote union of Europeans (Spaniards) with creoles or predominantly white mestizos, and *afromestizo*, to denote a racial mixture in which African blood predominates. Those terms, though differing from scientifically accepted anthropological terms, seem comprehensible and useful since they suggest the specific preponderant bloodlines.

Sánchez considered race a product of geography and an ethnically unifying factor that would influence first the Indian, then the Spaniard, then the Negro, and finally the mestizo, who is a synthesis of all the races. His concept of *mestizaje* meshed better with the free "intellectual" interpretation than with the rigid anthropological concept. In discussing ethnic transformations, Sánchez made certain observations about the unequal degree of racial mixture, the results of which are noted first in the "Indianization" of the white and then in the "whitening" of the Indian. Sometimes such phenomena complicate the matter of determining how much the characteristics of the *peninsulares* influenced the indigenes and to what degree indigenous traits have entered the personality of predominantly Spanish descendants. Not only biological symbiosis but, to an even greater degree, certain characteristics of personality are concerned. Similar considerations lead to distinctions between thoroughly Hispanized mestizos and Indians who are somewhat "mestizoized." At times it is difficult for the observer to penetrate the internal motivations of either, which can only be discerned through behavior.

Sánchez considers that the mestizo has not yet achieved his historic dimensions:

> He still lacks a clarification of his emotional position, difficult to determine because of his present lack of adaptation. . . . The lack of support of his many traditions and the suffering he has endured because of them have been tremendous influences from which stem, in part, his grandeur and his misery.

The forming of the mestizo personality has been a complex process. According to Sánchez, while the Indian tried to absorb everything Spanish that could be assimilated, the white *peninsular* held himself aloof from the Indian. Spanish motivation was based more on concupiscence than on a will to engender new spiritual values. The creation of such values required a cultural level not yet achieved by most of the Spanish colonists, and a gulf inevitably separated the two peoples. Sánchez pointed out that the gap was not bridged through the mestizo, for the contradictions resided more in his soul than in his blood. This perceptive deduction seems to confirm the existence of a psychic dualism in the mestizo personality. The racial mixture, whatever its biological or physiognomic advantages or disadvantages, carried with it economic discrimination that during the colonial era and afterward became social prejudices and class distinctions.

Sánchez discussed those social inequities vigorously and honestly, dating them from the pre-Columbian period. Prejudice already existed among the Aztecs and Incas, who, considering themselves superior to other tribes, married only within their own clans. White racism arrived with the Spaniards. (Sánchez considered Bartolomé de las Casas the first Spanish New World racist. Though he tried to help the Indians, Las Casas was unjust to the Negro slaves.) Abuse of Indians and Negroes during the colonial era was widespread, and mestizos were relegated to inferior posts and subjected to other forms of discrimination. Sánchez believed that the Spaniard, in his eagerness to legitimatize his conquest, perpetuated a racial myth that has effectively retarded the formation of a distinctive mestizo personality. Unlike some scholars, who prefer to ignore or minimize racism in Hispanic America, Sánchez stated forthrightly that "the problem of racism implicit and explicit in Latin America must be considered as primary."

Very interesting observations about *mestizaje* may be derived from studies undertaken in Mexico, where the racial mixture seems the most balanced in all of Hispanic America. The Mexican ethnohistorian Wigberto Jiménez Moreno, in his work *El mestizaje y la transculturación en Mexiamérica*, carefully examined the process of ethnic mixture in various parts of Mexico, the southwestern United States, and Central America. He studied the matter in agricultural regions largely populated by indigenes, as well as urban areas in which the mestizo population was increasing. In Yucatán, he reported, for a considerable time the settlers of Spanish origin remained very determined in their apartness from the Indian, exhibiting the "cohesion and aggressiveness that minorities display when they are confronted by a majority, which included developing attitudes that were somewhat racist and, predictably, discriminatory." Instances were also cited of strong Hispanization in various isolated regions of New Mexico where people, proud of their Iberian descent, had forgotten that their ancestors arrived from New Spain—that is, from Mexico—and did not come directly from Spain. It should be emphasized that Hispanic pride is typical of mestizo civilization.

The role of mestizos has become apparent since the War of Independence. Outstanding mestizo *caudillos* (guerrilla leaders) in Mexico as José María Morelos and Vicente Guerrero drew support from the Indians. From 1910 on, Indians and mestizos became increasingly important elements in the military forces. Although the revolutionary command was staffed with creoles and mestizos, there were also important peasant leaders, such as Emiliano Zapata and Pancho Villa. President Lázaro Cárdenas, of predominantly Indian origin, did a great deal for the indigenous cause through agricultural reform. Jiménez Moreno claimed that since that time "the indigenous element is one of the factors that have given Mexico an unmistakable physiognomy, and Mexico is, at this time (1961) one of the most balanced mestizo countries of the American continent."

The dramatic participation of the mestizos and Indians in building modern Mexico is described in a realistic manner in the large body of works commonly classified as the novels of the Mexican Revolution. Notable examples are *Los de abajo* (1915), by Mariano Azuela; *El águila y la serpiente* (1928), by Martín Luis Guzmán; *¡Vámonos con Pancho Villa!* (1931), by Rafael F. Muñoz; *Tierra* (1932), by Gregorio López y Fuentes; *Cartucho* (1931), by Nellie Campobello; *La asonada* (1931), by José Mancisidor; and *Mi caballo, mi perro y mi rifle* (1936), by José Rubén Romero. An antirevolutionary reaction was later manifested in such works as *El luto humano* (1943), by José Revueltas; *Al filo del agua* (1947), by Agustín Yáñez; and *La región más transparente* (1958), by Carlos Fuentes.

There is no doubt that the Mexican Revolution in its initial stage (1910–17), as the first authentic act of protest on the continent in the twentieth century, influenced the awakening of mestizo consciousness in other Hispanic American countries. And it later fostered an intellectual and political rebellion.

The Colombian novels of violence, which describe the tragic events of the undeclared civil war in Colombia that began in 1948, display a remarkable similarity to the Mexican narratives. Examples are *El Cristo de espaldas* (1951) and *Manuel Pacho* (1966) by Eduardo Caballero Calderón; *El alzamiento* (1960), by Luis Castellanos; *Balas de la ley* (1953), by Alfonso Hilarión Sánchez; *Tierra sin Dios* (1954), by Julio Ortiz Márquez; *La calle 10* (1960), by Manuel Zapata Olivella; *Quien dijo miedo* (1960), by Jaime Sanín Echeverri; *La mala hora* (1962), by Gabriel García Márquez; and *Las bestias de agosto* (1964), by Enrique Posada.

The Cuban revolutionary novels take the same ideological direction in narrating the rebellion of Fidel Castro in 1958 and describing the anatomy of his revolution. Examples are *Mañana es 26* (1960), by Hilda Perera; *No hay problema* (1961), by Edmundo Desnoes; *Maestra voluntaria* (1962), by Daura Olema García; *Los muertos andan solos* (1962), by Juan Arcocha; *Pequeñas maniobras* (1963), by Virgilio Piñera; *Vivir en Candonga* (1966), by Ezequiel Vieta; and *La vida en dos* (1967), by Luis Agüero. Then, of course, there are the many memoirs of exiles opposed to the Cuban revolution.

In addition to the revolutionary and regional novels that enrich mestizo literature, no less important are the novels of social protest.[4] A popular format is the narrative of so-called "magic realism," combining reality, fantasy, and myth with a distortion of time and space. This genre has always been present to some degree in Hispanic American literature, nourished by the varied environment and the multiplicity of customs and native legends that has always furnished writers with rich topics. The first writers who raised the form to an art were the Guatemalan Rafael Arévalo Martínez, whose novel *El hombre que parecía un caballo* (1915) is a curious psychozoological concoction of fantastic characters, and the Ecuadorian Demetrio Aguilera-Malta, whose *Don Goyo* (1933) was the first novel of magic realism from the tropics.

The writers who follow this literary trend have been influenced by

---

[4]This theme also runs through the poetry of the times. See Ramiro Lagos, *Mester de rebeldía de la poesía Hispanoamericana.*

European and North American writers (such as Joyce, Michaux, Faulkner, Gombrowicz, and Ionesco), but their work is rooted in the folklore and culture of the New World. Examples are *Juyungo* (1943), by the Ecuadorian Adalberto Ortiz; *Confabulario* (1952), by the Mexican Juan José Arreola; *Los pasos perdidos* (1953) and *Guerra del tiempo* (1958), by the Cuban Alejo Carpentier; *Pedro Páramo* (1955), by the Mexican Juan Rulfo; *En Chimá nace un santo* (1964), by the Colombian Manuel Zapata Olivella; *Cien años de soledad* (1967), by another Colombian, Gabriel García Márquez; and *La casa verde* (1968), by the Peruvian Mario Vargas Llosa. Such writers as Miguel Ángel Asturias, Rómulo Gallegos, and Arturo Uslar-Pietri not infrequently employ native magic and mythical elements in their works.

The gradual improvement in attitudes of the various ethnic groups within the mestizo is unquestionably a result of the enormous progress of mestizos in literature, the arts, and science. Another unifying element is the mestizos' attachment to the land, inherited from their ancestors and clearly revealed in their literature. That element is much less apparent in creole literature, especially that of the Río de la Plata region. Other literary elements that seem to derive from the Indian ancestry are gentleness, artistic perceptivity, and a certain languid air. The marked contemplative tone is as much a heritage from the *peninsulares* as it is from the indigenes. The Spanish heritage is expressed in unbridled imagination, aesthetic sensibility, and emotional exuberance, traits that are common in both mestizo and creole writing. The speculative, spiritual tone is a universal characteristic of Hispanic American literature.

Dating from the time of Garcilaso and Alva Ixtlilxochitl to the modern era, a long list of distinguished mestizo men of letters and artists could be compiled. Such a list would include Rubén Darío, Amado Nervo, José Santos Chocano, Jorge Isaacs, Ricardo Jaime Freyre, Manuel Altamirano, Ricardo Palma, César Vallejo, Ciro Alegría, Diego Rivera, José Clemente Orozco, José Sabogal, Oswaldo Guayasamín, and Carlos Chávez. Miguel Ángel Asturias achieved international fame as a winner of the Nobel Prize (1967).

The cultural and artistic contribution to modern civilization of these and other artists is so well known that it need not be belabored here. In Hispanic America they are distinguished not as mestizos but as creators of works that transcend race. It is perhaps for that very reason that few literary critics give adequate attention to the mestizo contribution as such. It is curious to note that the very term *mestizo*, widely used in anthropological literature, is seldom applied in the arts. One sees vague references to "our mestizo continent," but the theme is seldom elaborated upon. An example is the work by the talented Uruguayan critic Mario Benedetti, who in *Letras del continente mestizo* (Montevideo, 1967) writes about various luminaries of mestizo letters, analyzing their work but failing to identify it with their ethnocultural background. Despite the title of the book, Benedetti, a creole, has almost nothing to say about the inward nature of "cultural *mestizaje*." This and similar creole works betray either a lack of comprehension of the mestizo nature or an unwillingness to try to deal with its complexities. The task is left to a few mestizo intellectuals themselves, who have sometimes approached the task with ingenuity.

Efforts are made from time to time to define the aspirations of *mestizaje* in intellectual terms. The Venezuelan essayist Arturo Uslar-Pietri has written that "so bewitchingly enslaving is the vocation of *mestizaje* and of pursuit of its historical basis that it is still manifested, even in those instances in which thoughtful men attempt to react intellectually against the tradition and heritage of the past and establish a new course."[5] Uslar-Pietri was referring to the focus of mestizo authors on American matters, possibly in reaction to the creoles' lack of interest in it as thematic material. It is a legitimate aim, which at the same time illustrates the progressive withdrawal of Hispanic America from Iberian peninsular affairs. Though it does not signify a break in all cultural ties between Hispanic America and Spain, it is logical that Hispanic American society progressively concentrates on its own vital problems, for its future depends on their solution. *Mestizaje* occupies a place of principal interest obviously because mestizo society constitutes the trunk of Hispanic American population.

The tendency to reject Peninsular roots is reinforced among some Hispanic Americans who blame Spain for the repressions and social

[5]Arturo Uslar-Pietri, "El mestizaje en el Nuevo Mundo," *Revista de Occidente*, No. 49 (1967), pp. 24–25.

misfortunes Hispanic Americans, especially Indians and mestizos, suffered under its colonial tutelage and afterward. As the Mexican scholar Leopoldo Zea points out, although Hispanic America won political emancipation from Spain at the beginning of the nineteenth century, it did not then achieve mental emancipation. Hispanic Americans continued to be Spaniards after they were separated from Spain and displayed the same virtues and the same defects as the *peninsulares*.[6]

Thus, after independence, Hispanic American republican despotism, with its "caudillism," absolutism, paternalism, "latifundism," and other isms, replaced the Spanish colonial despotism. These attitudes are still present in many Hispanic Americans, though they may be unaware of them. Spain and Hispanic America remain inseparable psychologically, as they are linguistically and religiously, even though they have for some time followed their own paths of cultural development. Interaction of the "old" inherited features with those acquired later complicates the mestizo personality to the point that Hispanic Americans scorn certain peninsular customs and attitudes that they themselves cultivate.

These considerations make it even more difficult to analyze mestizo personality. The diversity of attitudes and motivations, some logical and some contradictory, make rational interpretations or generalizations all but impossible. Trying to penetrate the mestizo's psychology is like coming near the well of his experiences but finding ourselves unable to draw from it. The discrepancy between the real and the imaginative makes mestizo literature thematically attractive, however. It offers a tremendous ideological and anecdotal variety, demonstrating a high degree of intelligence.

The Mexican essayist and thinker Octavio Paz has provided a wealth of insight into the nature of mestizo conduct and attitudes. In *El laberinto de la soledad* he analyzed conflicts that arise in the mestizo consciousness. Among them he pointed out egocentrism, a recourse to violence, the abuse of authority by the powerful, skepticism, and, in the commonfolk, resignation to postrevolutionary disillusionment. Although Paz referred specifically to Mexican mestizos, his analysis can also be applied in varying degrees to other Hispanic

[6]Leopoldo Zea, *Dos etapas del pensamiento en Hispanoamérica*, pp. 74–85.

American mestizos. Paz attributed the servile manner to the misery and the oppressive social inequities that have humiliated the people (but on occasion have also roused them to rebellion). Paz attributed some inner turmoil to the ethnic clash between the Spaniards and the Indians at the beginning of the Conquest. An example is the attitude toward the union of Hernán Cortés with the Indian woman Malinche (also called Doña Marina). Her role as his mistress has been considered a form of treason to the Indians and, therefore, to Mexican dignity. Today the terms *malinchismo* is used to describe those who are "infected" by "foreign contagions" and are therefore enemies of the people. It should be noted that Mexico is the only state of the original Spanish colonies that has never erected a monument to its conqueror, Cortés. The other nations have honored their conquerors, Pizarro, Jiménez de Quesada, Valdivia, Mendoza, Cabeza de Vaca, Orellena, and Martínez de Irala. The Mexican rejection of the Hispanic tradition is undoubtedly motivated as much by pride as by a profound nationalistic sentiment, which Paz described as "an aggregation of gestures, attitudes, and tendencies in which it is difficult to distinguish what is Spanish and what is Indian." As Paz saw it, the Mexican does not want to be either Indian or Spanish. He wants to break with the colonial past that produced *mestizaje*. He denies himself as a mestizo because he does not see his destiny clearly. That denial thrusts him into personal and historical solitude. Though Paz did not deny the Spanish cultural impact, as he made clear, many Mexicans "live by excluding the past." This conflict does not greatly concern the Indians. Paz wrote, "The Indians have never paid the least attention to indigenist propaganda, which is sustained by fanatical mestizos and creoles."

Now and then Paz deplored the tragedy resulting from uprooting the past: "It is astounding that a country that has such a vigorous past, profoundly traditional, tied to its roots, rich in ancient legend, if poor in modern history, may only conceive itself a negation of its origin." With regard to the Mexican mestizos' racial attitude the thesis of Paz, and of Jiménez Moreno, does not differ from Sánchez' thesis about the Peruvian mestizos. All contradict the excessive optimism of Arciniegas' thesis about Colombia *mestizaje*. It should be remembered that Peru, Mexico, Bolivia, and Ecuador have large indigenous populations, while their numbers are insignificant in Venezuela and Colombia, though all these countries are fundamentally mestizo countries.

If the mestizo's attitude with regard to origin sometimes exalts the value of what is indigenous, contrary attitudes are occasionally manifested by Hispanophiles who disproportionately praise everything Spanish. In this respect mestizo pride knows no national frontiers, since intellectual pride is one of the basic features of the Hispanic mind.

In recent times mestizo consciousness has experimented with a reevaluation of its emotional and historic ties with its mother country. The Hispanic American seems to have become increasingly aware that the ties with Spain, although positive in cultural influence, were negative in their influence on the social structure and in their predominance in the political and ecclesiastical hierarchies of the colonies. As mentioned previously, exclusion of mestizos and other ethnic groups from colonial administration prevented them from inheriting a tradition of the sort that developed in the English colonies of the New World. After Hispanic America became independent, there was no government model for the new republics.

Spain cannot be blamed for the political backwardness of the succeeding decades, however. In 160 years of independence strides could have been made to develop a political and social system that would meet the aspirations and needs of the republics. Yet there remains in the mestizo mentality an unconscious reproach toward Spain, even in countries whose indigenous population was little or not at all affected by Hispanic influences.

It is, therefore, understandable that some mestizo leaders and writers, moved by pride in the past, have played down the Spanish-creole role in shaping the social texture of Hispanic America. In so doing they have elevated Indian nativism. Among the writers whose works reflect this emphasis are the Colombian Arciniegas, the Peruvians Sánchez and Haya de la Torre, the Mexican Paz, and the Ecuadorian Gonzalo Humberto Mata. While not denying Spain's cultural contribution, they have condemned its colonial, socially stratified structure with all its effects, which are still present in the mestizo mind. They have tarnished the image of the "Latin" makeup of the New World, sometimes even to the point of denying its validity. The purpose is reasonably clear: to unify a diverse, culturally and racially heterogeneous people.

Efforts to emphasize the Indian heritage in Hispanic America have been reinforced by anthropologists, who have contributed the terms Indo-America and Indo-Ibero-America, which attempt to reflect the preponderance of the indigenous peoples of the Andean region and elsewhere whose lifeways and mentality have little or nothing in common with the peninsular "Latinity." (It should be repeated here that the term Latin America is a nineteenth-century invention of the French, coined for political, not ethnic, purposes. It is still widely used on both sides of the Atlantic Ocean, though for the reaons stated before it seems inappropriate.)

Mestizo civilization has become a subject of serious research, which includes studies of various aspects of Hispanic American life. Anthropology makes a clear distinction between *biological mestizaje*, that is, mixture of blood, and *cultural mestizaje*, the transfer of cultural elements, also often termed *social acculturation*. In the acculturation process it is necessary to take into account the degree of transferrence of cultural values from one group to another and the latter's capacity to absorb them. Biological *mestizaje* has little or no relation to acculturation, since the latter requires intellectual assimilation. Social acculturation, the absorption of certain customs and features of a social character, occurs in mestizo countries rather frequently. Perhaps the most important aspect of Americanist studies to date is the close tie between *mestizaje* and interracial attitudes.

A notable event in the study of *mestizaje* was an international symposium held in 1960 by the Institute of Ibero-American Studies in Stockholm. The meeting, organized under the aegis of the Pan-American Institute of Geography and History and attended by European, Hispanic American, and United States scholars, discussed *mestizaje* primarily from the historical perspective. It prompted a work, *El mestizaje en la historia de Iberoamérica* (Stockholm, 1950), edited by Magnus Mörner. This subject has been more extensively treated by Marvin Harris in *Pattern of Race in the Americas* (New York, 1964) and by Charles Wagley in *Minorities in the New World* (New York, 1964), as well as in occasional papers presented at various International Congresses of Americanists. A relevant study is *Acul-*

turación de los indios de México (Warsaw, 1970), by the Polish ethnologist Maria Frankowska, which includes a study of religious syncretism.

The major contribution to the field of race relations is that of the Spanish-Mexican anthropologist Juan Comas. His *Relaciones interraciales en América Latina: 1940–1960* (sponsored by UNESCO), is a panoramic study of ethnic groups from the Río Grande to Tierra del Fuego. Its significance is further enhanced by its allusions to racial problems in Anglo-America. Using authentic data and field reports of various regional investigations in Hispanic America, Comas confirmed the existence of racial discrimination, especially in countries with a preponderant indigenous population. He, however, saw such discrimination as proceeding from social, cultural, and economic prejudices rather than from specific racial attitudes among the various strata of the population. According to Comas, "Such a state of things—by deed though not by right—motivates great sectors of the population that have not been integrated into the respective nationalities of their countries."

Comas' view coincides with that of European Americanists, especially anthropologist Alfred Metraux. In his *Problema racial en América Latina,* Métraux wrote:

> In no part of America where Spanish is spoken are racial relations characterized by the inhuman rigidity that is associated with the idea of racism. But it would be erroneous to assert, as has frequently been done, that certain forms of prejudice and discrimination of a racist character in the countries with a large percentage of indigenous population do not exist.

There is no doubt that prejudice is subtly camouflaged, and in spite of such assertions it can be debated that racial prejudices are less intense in Hispanic America than in Anglo-America.

Life continues its march and carries with it changes that are reflected in the social transformation of the mestizos. In recent times mestizos have achieved "respectability." The belated rise of the middle class is closely related to the current social revolution. Among the observers of those changes perhaps the most impartial and authoritative is the North American social anthropologist John Gillin. In *The Social Transformation of the Mestizos* he wrote that during the preceding fifty years the old prejudices against racial mixture and the mestizos gradually began disappearing from many sections of Hispanic America. He believed that Hispanic America had begun experimenting with a fundamental revision of its social structure in which the role of genealogy and the physical attributes of race were beginning to diminish in importance.

Gillin saw the rise of a "new aristocracy" that is striving to attain power and influence in business, politics, and intellectual life. In various countries the members of this new group are obviously the mestizos. Those who are able to rise in the social scale by their own efforts tend to have little respect for nobility of ancestry and racial "purity." Gillin emphasized that in the process of change dynamism and individual abilities surpass ethnic considerations. Gillin's observations are very encouraging, because they portray the mestizo as gradually filling a purposive role in history. His intelligence and social dynamism will help him in the process, which can unfold even within the compass of his spiritual anxieties.

In concluding these reflections, it is necessary to repeat that racial mixture was experienced in Spain long before the colonization of the New World. Invasions, conquests, and occupations by a multitude of people—from Tartessians, Celts, Iberians, Phoenicians, Carthaginians, Greeks, Romans, and Arabs—made the Spanish people a race of many bloods. Features of many civilizations and ethnic idiosyncrasies were blended in them. The Spanish people had antecedents of Afro-European *mestizaje*, a mixture they brought to America. Through their commercial, maritime, and colonizing experiences the Portuguese settlers who went to Brazil took with them European, African, and Asiatic elements. They too extended *mestizaje* through mixture with Indians and Negroes.

Some Iberian writers avoid the term *mestizaje*, but its historic implication is clear. It is reflected in the work of the illustrious Hispanist Américo Castro, *España en su historia*, whose subtitle, *Christians, Moors, and Jews*, is very significant. It was those religious and ethnic groups who established the three principal branches of Spanish culture long before Columbus' time. Their influence in spiritual matters survives today. The Spaniards who began the New World *mestizaje* and enriched it with their knowledge and cultural values also produced a complex, often contradictory society that awaits a thoroughgoing analysis of its motivations, its weaknesses, and its greatness.

It is worthwhile to add a few observations about the approximately ten million United States citizens of Mexican descent who live principally in Texas, New Mexico, Arizona, and California. Exposed to "Anglo-Americanization," they try to preserve their ethnic identity by speaking the Spanish language and following the Mexican customs of the days before their homelands were incorporated into the United States. Many Mexican-Americans are bilingual, but the great majority are attached to their ancestral culture. While they conform to some unimportant Anglo customs, they do not show marked acculturation in that environment, where they live largely as they wish. This voluntary alienation has been accompanied by social and economic disadvantages and has produced a psychological conflict. That conflict is manifested on the one hand by their resistance to the acceptance of Anglo-American civilization, which seems spiritually foreign to them, and, on the other hand, owing to limited contacts with their mother country, a lack of identification with authentic Mexican cultural values.

A melancholy dualism emanates from the mestizo spirit, and there is no easy remedy in the complexity of modern life. A similar spiritual restlessness appears to afflict the half-million Cuban exiles in the United States who took refuge there from Castro's revolution. The children of these exiles show themselves to be much more adaptable, as so do other Hispanic American immigrants who do not live in dense ethnic groups surrounded by but isolated from Anglo-Americans. The voluntary withdrawal of minorities into their own ghettos limits their opportunities in the new environment. It does permit them, however, to preserve their spiritual patrimony, which is diluted in contact with the Anglo majority.

Happily, in recent years interracial relations in the United States have undergone a positive change that permits social identification of the various minority groups. Convinced that they were denied their civil rights or alienated from the majority, they began to claim a greater participation in the life of the nation. As a result of their often militant attitude they now receive recognition of their ethnic and spiritual patrimony, where previously only the value of their labor was recognized. Now there is increasing attention to ethnic studies of varous minority groups, especially blacks, Chicanos, and Puerto Ricans.[7] Various schools provide bilingual teaching in English and Spanish. Universities and colleges have introduced Chicano studies, which include Spanish-language courses in the history, demography, and literature of the Southwest, as well as courses in dialectics and Mexican-American folklore. The dominant tone of the few books on Chicano literature is race in the ancestral, indigenous, and mestizo sense. That literature is a re-creation of legends, *corridos*, folk tales, and works exalting popular Mexican heroes and Chicano leaders. Its purpose is to inspire ethnic pride in the readers.

It is useful also to note that, among the many languages spoken in the United States, Spanish is second only to English. About twelve million United States citizens speak it daily. The United States occupies fifth place among the nations of the world with a Spanish-speaking population, surpassed only by Spain, Mexico, Argentina, and Colombia.[8] Parenthethically it may be added that more than 300,000 North American students enroll in Spanish classes each year, testimony to the widespread comprehension of the language among United States citizens.

[7]Although the exact etymological origin of *Chicano* is unknown, it is believed that it comes from the word *chico*, meaning "boy." The term has acquired great popularity and has even entered the political vocabulary. According to Luis Leal, it is used to designate United States citizens of Mexican origin, an improvement over *Mexican-American*, which implies that one is neither Mexican nor American. Luis Leal, *México: Civilizaciones y culturas*, p. 152.

[8]*Américas*, Vol. XXIV, No. 1 (1972).

CHAPTER 7

CREOLES AND CREOLISM IN HISPANIC AMERICA

In most of Hispanic America creoles are an ethnic minority, although in the River Plate region, Chile, and Costa Rica, they constitute the majority. Because River Plate creolism has distinctive traits, it is discussed separately (Chapter 8). Here I am concerned principally with the cultural and social characteristics of the creoles in Mestizo America whose activites are closely linked with her lifeways. My purpose is to show the development of creolism and its general and historic features as ingredients of Hispanic American civilization.

Ethnic creolism deals with racial origin, while cultural creolism has a literary connotation. According to the anthropological definition, creoles are descendants of Spaniards born in America who never mixed with other races. In the intellectual sense, two somewhat contradictory definitions arise. According to one, creoles are persons born of Spanish parents in the New World. According to the other, creoles are persons born in America without designated ethnic ancestors. In colonial days the latter definition grew out of the more or less free use of terms by chroniclers and writers from whom later lexicographers have borrowed. The Antillean scholar José Juan Arrom, alluding to that phenomenon in his *Criollo: Definición y matices de un concepto*, wrote: "It was not pigmentation of the skin or social condition that characterized the creole, but the fact of his having been born in the New World of parents who were not indigenous, whether European or African." Arrom traced the etymology of the word *criollo* from the Portuguese *crioulo*, *criadeiro*, and *criadouro*, which refer to one born or reared in a specific region—in this instance, the New World. According to the Brazilian philologist Leite de Vasconcellos, *criollo* is a derivative of *criadouro* corrupted by Negro pronunciation. It is thus a linguistic borrowing from the Portuguese language that is accepted as a part of Spanish colonial vocabulary.

In general historical usage creoles were basically the "American people," the "new men" of the New World. The historian Bernardino de Sahagún and the geographer Juan López de Velasco described the creoles and attributed to them various traits that distinguished them from the "native-born Spaniards," the *peninsulares*. Among the traits mentioned were those having to do with spirit and behavior rather than physical ones. The writers attributed differentiating characteristics to "the climate and the atmosphere of the land" and also noted those characteristics to some degree in *peninsulares* who remained in the colonies for many years. It is likely that these and other writers of the colonial epoch did not always distinguish between creoles and mestizos.

In his work *Apologético en favor de don Luis de Góngora* (1662), Peruvian-born Juan de Espinosa Medrano alluded to himself as a creole and made it clear that as a creole he should rightfully be considered a member of the upper level of colonial Peruvian society. Use of the term *creole* to signify place of birth, rather than race, was common and led to ambiguities in differentiation. Another prominent Peruvian writer, Garcilaso de la Vega, who was himself a mestizo, reported in *Comentarios reales de los Incas* (1609), a book written in Spain:

> They call the children of Spaniards born in America creoles because they are born in the Indies. The Negroes coined the word, a fact that usage indicates. Among them it means a Negro born in the Indies; they coined it to differentiate between those who are born in Guinea and go to the Indies and those born in the Indies because they think they the former are more reputable and of higher quality for having been born in the mother country. The Spaniards, similarly, have introduced the term creoles into their language to designate those born in Spain. Thus they call the native-born Spaniard and the native-born Guinean creoles.

Archival documents in Cuba, Puerto Rico, and Santo Domingo confirm that these terminological peculiarities were common in Caribbean America. African influence on the population was considerable from the beginning of colonization. In other parts of the Spanish colonies, however, Negroes were a minority or were partly absorbed by the natives. Ultimately the term creole came to mean whites born in America as distinguished from white colonists from Spain and later from other European countries. The confusion surrounding the term disappeared with the passage of time, when social and economic stratification in colonial society became fixed and ethnic and cultural differentiation was intensified.

In the eighteenth century, with the dawn of the Age of Enlightenment and the upsurge in social and political consciousness, the term creole became closely identified with American aspirations. At the beginning of the nineteenth century it was under creole leadership that the Spanish freed themselves from the mother country. Undoubtedly that action was motivated by a deep-rooted New World community spirit, but it also reflected the material interests and amtitions of the creole aristocracy and their resentment at their exclusion from political and ecclesiastical power. After independence the creoles continued to exercise leadership in politics, economics, and social life.

The creoles, the new ruling class, continued most of the political and cultural practices of the *peninsulares* with whom they had lived. They emulated *peninsulares* in manners, and even exaggerated them, assuming an affected gallantry that bordered on pomposity. Many of them spoke a florid and rebundant Spanish that had baroque overtones. But there were differences. Regionalisms salted their language and reflected New World influences. Creoles contributed greatly to Hispanic American linguistic enrichment.

Similar traits were also displayed by the *indianos—peninsulares* who had resided for a long time in America, finally coming to resemble the creoles so closely that it was difficult to distinguish one from the other. From the beginning creole cultural life felt the impact of a colonial upbringing. Creoles lived in an environment in which military rigidity, a legalistic spirit, and an evangelizing ardor went arm in arm with chivalry, passion, and skill in subjugating the Indians. They largely assimilated those traits, perpetuating Peninsular traditions. They are credited, along with the *peninsulares*, with enforcing Spanish authoritarianism in the colonial society. "However," wrote Sánchez, "they lived unadapted to their milieu, creating a heterogeneous ambience that was not conducive to social unity."[1] Sánchez considered that to be their greatest defect, because as a result the Conquest was not fully consummated in the ethnic sense, and

[1]Sánchez, *¿Existe América Latina?* p. 123.

cultural assimilation was not fully effected. The Indians, the mestizos, and the Negroes never identified themselves with the idea of *Hispanidad*, the authority of the "few selected ones, or even Roman Catholicism, all of which were embraced by the creoles. In these remarks Sánchez' Hispanophobia (shared by other writers) was in evidence, though he credited creoles with mental flexibility and other intellectual endowments.

As a consequence of their contact with the natural environment of the New World, the creoles acquired distinctive characteristics. They reacted toward nature in a way little understood by Spaniards who had not spent some time in America. The grandeur of the landscape, the lushness of the flora, the abundance of the fauna, the mosaic of the peoples, and the mysterious forces that they saw as ruling their destinies opened wide horizons to the creoles' imagination. They took in all they saw, and they felt it with extraordinary intensity. The real mixed with the magical, the lyric interwoven with the epic molded their concept of the world. Without discarding metaphysical elements of Peninsular derivation, they based their vision as much on untamable force as on real nature. To them the American cosmos was different from the classic idyl and other Spanish poetic forms, whose cadences they imitated with astonishing fidelity. For this reason the creole writers enjoyed almost the same degree of respect as that accorded the Peninsular intellectuals, especially those of the viceroyalties of New Spain (Mexico), Peru, and New Granada (Colombia and Ecuador).

The unlimited liberty of the physical surroundings produced a sharp individualism in the creoles and inspired them with self-confidence. They manifested that confidence in an authoritative posture derived from Spanish individualism. *Peninsulares*, however, owing to their deep-rooted eqalitarian tradition and in the *fueros* (privileges granted by kings to Spanish provinces or cities), sometimes displayed a more democratic attitude than that of the creoles. The latter occasionally exceeded the former in imposing their will on the Indians and the mestizos. They were apparently supported by the belief not so much in the glory of their distant mother country as in their own national future. That faith reinforced the creoles in a certain independence of reason and judgment.

The creoles' attitude affected to some degree the behavior of the colonial *peninsulares* who were commissioned by the crown. Those officials, removed much of the time from direct imperial control, did not always respect the royal orders to the letter. The Colombian essayist Eduardo Caballero Calderón, in his work *Americanos y europeos*, wrote: "When the New World fell into the hands of routine bureaucrats, already much influenced by America, they wrote in bold letters in the margin of royal orders that they did not intend to carry out, 'Noted but not executed.'" That attitude seems to indicate that the officials were concerned more with the creoles' interest than with the crown's. A kind of hidden political dissidence gradually moved the creoles to a psychological disjunction from their mother country and determination upon their own conduct, which was, however, often ambiguous. History shows, for example, that the Peruvian creoles frequently displayed more devotion to the crown than did their Mexican counterparts.

Their conduct took various forms, depending on the circumstances. Their manner toward the *peninsulares* differed from that toward the mestizos and Indians. To protect their latifundias, the creoles were respectful to the colonial authorities. They displayed no such behavior in their treatment of the subjugated classes, from whom they demanded blind obedience. In this dichotomy were the complexities of Hispanic American society rooted.

The outstanding characteristic of the creole aristocracy today is its conservatism with regard to landholding. The evidence is in its frequent opposition to agrarian reform that has been proposed as a base for the economic and social transformation of Mestizo America. In defense of its ancient privileges in landholding, the creole aristocracy utilizes paternalism not only in its own dominions but in public life as well, and with extraordinary subtlety. It displays great flexibility in political matters, but always maintaining control over them directly or indirectly. It almost invariably identifies itself with American roots, both regionally and nationally.

Many creoles are still deeply attached to traditional customs and social practices, but most of them fit into the current social and political scene and are in no way distinguishable from mestizos. Associated with mestizos in various enterprises in daily life, they demonstrate considerable practical sense, flexibility, and astuteness, combined with persuasiveness and a willingness to compromise. To these characteristics must be added a certain epicureanism and an ability to imitate and adapt that enables them to survive in the turbulence of Hispanic American life.

In Mestizo America the attractions of *Hispanidad* incline some creoles to loyalty to Spain. As a political tendency directed toward Madrid, *Hispanidad* aspires to tighten the bonds between Spain and the nations in which Spanish is spoken. But recently it has placed emphasis on greater ethnocultural unity. Some mestizos participate in programs of cultural cooperation even when they do not share Spanish political ideology. In such instances national pride is shared alike by creoles, mestizos, and *peninsulares*.

As a counterpart of *Hispanidad*, the concept of *Latinidad* has sometimes been influential in various Hispanic American nations. Its basic idea is the preservation and defense of Hispanic America's common socioeconomic interests. The political cohesion is embodied in the doctrine of Panamericanism and in the unitarian ideology championed by the Organization of American States. Although the essence of *Latinidad* has been so far only vaguely formulated, its general ideological premises seem to imply a unified destiny for Hispanic America and to exclude involvement in Peninsular affairs.

The Creoles are a passionate and sometimes melancholy people, and they are also endowed with an extraordinary propensity for metaphysical speculation. They inherited these traits from their Peninsular ancestors and seem to have developed them even further, exposed as they have been to a mysterious, frequently hostile natural environment. That intimacy with nature has inspired in them a preoccupation with the tragic, the sensual, and the fantastic. Those traits produce an individualism that seems intellectually dogmatic and at times arrogant, religiously conservative, spiritually somber, proudly passionate, often capricious, and not infrequently fatalistic.

There are distinguishing traits in the landholders and the intellectuals. The landholding aristocrats are reactionary, obstinate—often intransigent—while the cultured creoles of the cities are for the most part more adaptable, progressive, and conciliatory. The latter, who function in public life as intellectuals, officials, businessmen, professionals, and artists, have a creative dynamism whose impact continues to be felt in the mestizo environment. Saturated with community and patriotic spirit, these creoles frequently become spokesmen for important national problems, thus sharing the aspirations of the mestizo intellectuals. It is not surprising that some of the better twentieth-century novels of social, indigenist, and even Negro protest have come from the pens of creole or mestizo writers. Their preoccupation with the critical problems of everyday reality shows that these creole intellectuals of Mestizo America feel a community of spirit with it. Their works reflect the beat of the New World pulse even when their interpretations of its diversity are at variance with the mestizos'. Very different is the attitude of the creoles of the River Plate region, especially of the *porteños*—the residents of Buenos Aires—who are so concerned with cultural cosmopolitanism that they stay aloof from national problems.

In Mestizo America some creoles who through assimilation have taken on mestizo traits frequently share similar ideological preoccupations, particularly as regards national identity. The creoles have close and emotional bonds with their homelands. But in their political manipulations the creoles often oppose the well-being of their fellow citizens. Psychologically, it goes without saying, the creoles are decidedly varied and complex.

Studies of creoles, other than those of the River Plate region, are extremely scarce. The few that have appeared in Venezuela, Peru, and Chile are therefore important guides. Sometimes the creole is discussed from almost the same psychological perspective—that of his "interior world"—as that of the mestizo, and consequently creole nuances cannot always be precisely identified. The Venezuelan critic Arturo Uslar-Pietri commented that the first creole literary expressions manifested a resistance to the transplantation of many Spanish forms, some of which were rejected outright, while others were greatly modified.[2]

Born into a physical environment far different from that of Spain, creoles have been affected by nature in an extraordinary manner. They dwell on its measureless and latently destructive force. They have made nature more than a setting; it is the center of their literary subject matter. Nature often becomes a protagonist in their novels, an idiosyncrasy not only of the creole but also of the Hispanic American in general.

[2]Arturo Uslar-Pietri, *Breve historia de la novela hispanoamericana*, pp.155–72.

That approach is characterized by a primitive realism with magical elements, a tendency toward the mythical and symbolic, and the predominance of intuition—traits that, according to Uslar-Pietri, distinguish Hispanic American literature from Spanish literature. Out of that realism arose the primitive epic with its hero struggling against destiny in a hostile and mysterious environment. Uslar-Pietri saw nature and those associated with it as protagonists in the struggle. Following this guideline, Uslar-Pietri saw moral cruelty and psychological abnormality as characteristic of creole literature. He considered them in the light of the creole inclination toward complicated and artificial literary forms even when the subject matter itself is realistic. Among the other characteristics he mentioned are absorption in horror, in the emotional, and in cruelty, which, by producing a morbid psychological complexity, serve as a basis for tragic conflicts. All this produces an anguished tone in Hispanic American literature. A significant characteristic of the creole spirit is the view of life as a crusade and a catastrophe, a concept that helps create an exalted, almost apocalyptic ambience.

According to Uslar-Pietri, unchecked individuality and conceptual originality are other characteristics of creole literature, as shown by the presence of social themes, educational problems, and political and reformist subject matter. Those subjects by their essence not only involve active participation but also provoke polemics. That persistence of political themes—pedagogical and revisionist, in my view—gives to the writings of creole authors a heavy combative and defensive stamp. These elements are frequently present in Hispanic American essays. Uslar-Pietri believed that Hispanic American literature is rooted in the land and people of its world. Thus the creole works at "becoming mestizo" ideologically and thematically, an inevitable phenomenon in a multiracial society.

Other qualities of creole writing are a deep lyricism and plentiful imagination. Whatever the form of expression, aesthetic taste is prevalent: "The most esteemed novelists in Hispanic America are those who employ the most harmonious and poetic language." Another common feature is the baroque style, which creole and mestizo writers share to such a degree that it has become a common characteristic of Hispanic American literature.

Many of these traits, in differing degrees and variations, are found in the creole works that illuminate Hispanic American culture from the colonial era to the present. Their impact on the literary epic of Hispanic America has continued from Juan Ruiz de Alarcón y Mendoza to Florencio Sánchez, from Carlos de Sigüenza y Góngora to Rómulo Gallegos, from Sor Juana Inés de la Cruz and Rafael Landivar to Gabriela Mistral and Pablo Neruda, from Andrés Bello and José Martí to Alfonso Reyes and Gonzalo Zaldumbide, from Manuel González Prada and Baldomero Sanín Cano to Horacio Quiroga and José Eustasio Rivera, to mention only a few representatives of Hispanic American letters. It must not be forgotten, moreover, that four of the Hispanic American winners of the Nobel Prize were creoles: Gabriela Mistral (1945) and Pablo Neruda (1971), Chilean poets; and Dr. Bernardo Houssay (1947) and Dr. Luis Federico Leloir (1970), Argentinian scientists.

At the end of the nineteenth century the term *literary creolism* came to be applied to a specific type of literature characterized by a rural or nativist theme embellished with local color and flavor. In contrast to urban and sometimes cosmopolitan subject matter, this type of literature dealt with the regional scene and with Hispanic American customs. The tendency to exalt the common elements flourished during the romantic period, but was weakened when the social and urban themes, with their depiction of upper-and middle-class life, gained popularity. Chronologically literary creolism is almost parallel with Modernism, which, because of its aesthetic excesses and a certain thematic artificiality, had perhaps less importance in the novel than in poetry, although it produced several noteworthy novels. Literary creolism with its descriptive realism appealed to a much more extensive reading public than the less-comprehensible modernist works. It signified a return to the vernacular regionalism, which avoided universal elements but described concerns of the provinces, their humble people, and the scenes that surrounded them.

Literary creolism had its origin in the naturalism and realism that the regional European novel had developed earlier. As a literary current creolism flowed into not only the narrative writing but also the poetry and the theater of various Hispanic American countries. Literary creolism largely developed in Mestizo America. The Venezuelan review *El Cojo Ilustrado* (published from 1892 to 1915) was distinguished among its promoters. Its initiators in the novel were the Venezuelans Vicente Romero García, Miguel Eduardo Pardo, and Gonzalo Picón-Febres. Chilean creolism owes its major literary achievement to Mariano Latorre, the author of the novel *Zurzulita* (1920), and a much-acclaimed master of the creolism school of that country. Literary creolism is generally lacking in ethnic significance. Its significance lies rather in its regional, social, and even nationalistic identification. In Chile, a dominant creole country, literary creolism, through its extensive thematic treatment of the middle and lower classes, made an enduring impact on the national mind, though its popularity lasted only a few decades. It penetrated the urban creole class only superficially.

Literary creolism as a thematic identification with the masses showed perhaps more authenticity and anecdotal intimacy in Mestizo American letters than in those of Creole America. Concentrating on the reproduction of ordinary daily and local reality, it had no consciously aesthetic features, though some of the gaucho novels had artistic merit. If we try to identify creolism with regionalism on a grand scale, creolism would include a large body of Hispanic American literature with a rural setting. There is evidence of creolism in the works of various regions of Mestizo America, particularly Mexico and Colombia. Examples are the Mexican novels of the last third of the nineteenth century, in which romantic regionalism is mingled with local customs and rural settings. Rural scenes with unmistakably realistic themes are also seen in the novels of the Mexican Revolution that began appearing in print about 1920. A combination of rural setting and civil-war theme is also apparent in the Colombian novels about "the Violence" that have been appearing since about 1950. Although the plots of these novels are political and social rather than folklore, their stamp of regionalism, depiction of local customs, and concern with the physical setting are justification for labeling them creole. Many Bolivian, Ecuadorian, Peruvian, and Cuban novels that deal with rural affairs can be placed in the same category.

Chilean creolism of the twentieth century includes no less than two generations of nationally known creole writers, among them Eduardo Barrios, Daniel Belmar, Luis Durand, Rafael Maluenda, and Manuel Rojas. Some of these and others, after starting out in that genre, later became absorbed in the fantastic, the psychological, the metaphysical, the aesthetic, producing a crisis in the Chilean novel. Fernando Alegría has pointed out that María L. Bombal, in her novel *La última niebla* (1935), dealt the first blow to creolist regionalism, while Manual Rojas, in his picaresque novel *Hijo de ladrón* (1951), gave it the *coup de grâce*. A good example of the ideological crisis that arose in connection with the nativist current was provided by *El Criollismo* (Santiago, 1956), which contains critical expositions by Ricardo Latcham, Ernesto Montenegro, and Manuel Vega. They discussed the ups and downs of Chilean creolism as a national trend and compared it with the River Plate and United States creolism. The literary concepts they describe are of general interest and merit attention.

According to Latcham, Chilean literary creolism enriched the language and symbolized the race in such popular characters as cowboys, muleteers, rural peasants, bandits, smugglers, coastal seamen, nomads, *rotos* ("broken ones") of the cities, peasant tenants, peons, and capital residents. Creolism described provincials in detail and also dealt with such problems as sexual anxieties and the tragedy of the middle and lower classes. In that respect creolism was faced with the limitations of historical time and setting. It dwelt overmuch on descriptive details, neglecting plot and action.

Montenegro proposed injecting more vigor and aggressiveness into creolism and also varying the narrative technique, though without drawing away from the folklore tradition. He criticized the almost photographic presentation of scenes, preferring more sensitivity and intimacy in setting. Vega explained that the position adopted by the Chilean creole writer coincided with the attraction the Spanish landscape held for the poets and writers of the Generation of Ninety-eight. He observed that those mysterious and interwoven relations between man and the land he inhabits were also foreshadowed in Chilean novels. Vega attributed great importance to Chilean writers' "psychological and historic understanding and appreciation of human elements." That comment proved overly optimistic, because it was precisely the lack of close union of man with the land, as well as the parochialism and provincialism of many creole novels, that contributed to the decline of creolism in Chile.

There are some analogies in the literary creolism of Hispanic America and of Anglo-America. The United States and Canada are predominantly "white" nations, but their civilizations owe their origins to both European and non-European sources, while Hispanic American creolism has predominantly a New World base. The ethnic and cultural variety of the United States is manifested in diversified folklore elements. Therefore, literary creolism as defined by Hispanic American literary historians is also present in United States literature, with its emphasis on authentic rural and urban backgrounds.

Some Hispanic American critics consider Mark Twain's *The Adventures of Huckleberry Finn* a work of "pure" creolism, combining folklore with ethnic diversity in a regional setting. Another work that also involves a regional setting is *Old Creole Days*, by George W. Cable. Earlier writers whose works fit in this genre are James Fenimore Cooper, Washington Irving, and William Gilmore Simms, whose Indian stories of a romantic stamp also present settlers and trappers of various origins. The same folklore and multiethnic trend is evident in the frontier narratives of the nineteenth and twentieth centuries. They are characterized by the presence of whites, Indians, and blacks, and immigrants from many other countries. Their protagonists vary from cowboy adventurers and horse thieves to cattle ranchers and bootleggers.

Contemporary United States literature includes many books that can be compared with Hispanic American creole fiction. Prominent writers of this form of narrative are Erskine Caldwell, Sinclair Lewis, William Faulkner, John Steinbeck, and Tennessee Williams. Their themes revolve around regional socioeconomic problems and are usually accompanied by vivid descriptions of customs and attitudes almost always presented in a folklore vein. The more recent novels often depict such groups as migrant farm workers, factory workers, prostitutes, homosexuals, lesbians, marijuana peddlers, and various counterculture groups. Perhaps the greatest merit of these novels lies in their characterizations, which are generally better than those of Hispanic American creole narratives. The latter, with a few notable exceptions, traditionally pay more attention to setting and plot and less to the development of the characters.

Carving on a stela at Bonampak, Mexico. Courtesy United Fruit Company.

Catharsis, mural painting by José Clemente Orozco in the Palace of Fine Arts, Mexico City. Courtesy Mexican Embassy, Washington, D.C.

Paricutín volcano, which last erupted in the early 1940's and destroyed the town of Parangaricutiro, Mexico. Only the church tower remains. Courtesy Aeronaves de México.

A section of the temple of Quetzalcoatl at Teotihuacán, Mexico. Courtesy Mexican Government Tourist Department.

A representation of Coatlicue, Aztec earth goddess, Mexico. Courtesy Organization of American States.

Library of the National University of Mexico, Mexico City, decorated with frescoes by Juan O'Gorman. Courtesy Mexican Government Tourist Department.

Bullfight in Mexico City. Courtesy Mexican Government Tourist Department.

Zapotec ruins of Monte Albán, state of Oaxaca, Mexico. Courtesy Mexican Government Tourist Department.

A gold pendant representing the universe, found at Monte Albán, Mexico. Top to bottom: The nocturnal heavens, portrayed by two gods playing ball; the sun; the moon and a butterfly; the earth—the head of a monster giving birth to man and then devouring him. Courtesy Mexican Government Tourist Department.

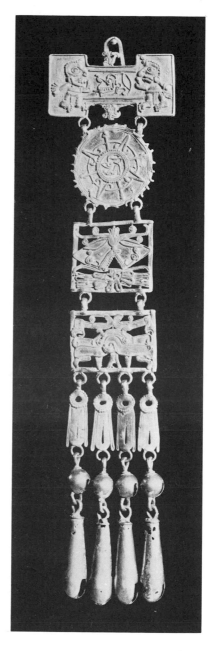

Zapotec funerary urn with a front sculpture of the Corn God, found at Monte Albán, Mexico. Photograph by the author.

Indian fishermen on an island in Lake Pátzcuaro, Mexico. Courtesy Canadian Pacific Railway.

Mexican *charros* in a rodeo at Rancho San Isidro, Mexico. Courtesy
Organization of American States.

A Tarahumara Indian from the state of Chihuahua, Mexico. Courtesy Organization of American States.

El Castillo, at the restored Mayan center of Chichén Itzá, Yucatán, Mexico. Courtesy Mexican Government Tourist Department.

Monument to Rubén Darío at Managua, Nicaragua, overlooking Lake Managua.

Scene along the Panama Canal. Courtesy Braniff International.

CHAPTER 8

CREOLES OF THE RIVER PLATE REGION

The civilization of the River Plate (Río de la Plata) region, which includes Argentina and Uruguay, is very different from that of the rest of Hispanic America and even from that of the other "creole countries," Chile and Costa Rica. Argentina, with the largest concentration of whites, has two distinctive features, the pampas (plains) and the *porteños* (the inhabitants of the port city Buenos Aires). The one a natural feature, the other a human phenomenon, together they produced a deep-rooted social complex of national dimension.

During the period of the viceroyalty the destiny of the River Plate region took a course different from that of the rest of the Spanish colonies. Since it had no precious metals, the area was little affected by Peninsular immigration. People were scarce. *Mestizaje* was always insignificant, and the Indians were rejected to the point of annihilation. Spanish influences diminished following independence, and especially after 1880, when Argentina opened its doors to European immigrants of non-Iberian origin. The relaxation of the connection with Spain produced a social uprooting. It also created an ethnocultural vacuum gradually filled by the cosmopolitanism of the new inhabitants, who brought their own customs and ideologies, which were frequently alien to Hispanic traditions. These Old World ideologies brought to, or imitated in, the New World had little or nothing to do with the hemispheric situation and thus placed the River Plate civilization in a marginal position with respect to the rest of Hispanic America. It was an artificial ethnocultural transplant. Argentinian oral linguistic peculiarities, which were first manifested in the gaucho slang, are noted today in the use of *lunfardo* in Buenos Aires and also in the peculiar Spanish pronunciation of the *porteños*. The literary language continues to be Spanish.

It is not easy to discuss the cultural enigma of the River Plate solely within the framework of the creole mind, because creolism

197

manifests itself in many and varied ways. Except for a historical and ethnic spiritual communion, there are visible differences among the creole nations of Hispanic America. Chilean creolism, for example, is distinguished by its deep-rooted collective good citizenship and high percentage of educated citizens. Costa Rica is the only nation in the New World that has no army but instead has a legion of teachers. Costa Rica is today the only true creole antimilitary democracy, a role it shared for several decades with Chile and Uruguay. Chile and Costa Rica seem to have more emotional traits in common with the rest of Hispanic America than do Argentina and Uruguay. The latter countries strongly tend toward cosmopolitanism and thus draw away from the spiritual community of the New World.

Argentina, with the discrepancy between its enormous economic potential and its unequal social structure, has a high educational level and an extraordinary literary and artistic production. That nation, however, given too much to mimesis, metaphysics, and the esoteric and too little to local matters, has made but a weak effort to establish what could be called a national culture. State interference in public and social life, combined with Europeanized spiritual and political tendencies, ties the Argentinians more to the European mind than to the spirit of the mestizo American peoples. The social and cultural differences between the capital and the Argentine provinces, with the psychological contradictions that arise from the diversity of the population, make Argentinian creolism decidedly different from the creolism of other parts of the New World.

The cultural and geographic division of Argentina between *porteños* and provincials—for the most part gauchos—set forth by Sarmiento in *Facundo* (1845) in relation to his concepts of "civilization" and "barbarism," later underwent modification through the influence of immigration. From the end of the nineteenth century that immigration has been predominantly Italian, with some Spanish, French, English, Slavic, German, and oriental components. The multifaceted nature of the population continues to delay the formation of a defined Argentinian national culture despite the nation's well-defined political entity. Creole civilization of the River Plate continues its evolution in two sectors: the urban, led by Buenos Aires, and the provincial, from which the gauchos were eliminated by European peasant immigrants and the local creoles.

This sociocultural dualism was intensified by the unfortunate geographic distribution of the population, half of which resides in the province of Buenos Aires and the other half in the vast interior. The two distinct influences have produced lively repercussions in Argentinian culture and many studies of its complexities, beginning in 1928 under the inspiration of the writings of José Ortega y Gasset. Among the early students of Argentinian life and manners were Raúl Scalabrini Ortiz and Ezequiel Martínez Estrada. They were succeeded by Eduardo Mallea, Julio Mafud, Ernesto Sábato, Juan José Sebreli, Emilio de Matteis, Rodolfo Kusch, and others. My purpose is to present Argentine realities through their self-analysis, to which I shall add my own observations made during travels in that region.

Among writers who visited the country in the first half of the twentieth century were the North American Waldo Frank, the German Otto Keyserling, and the Spaniard Ortega y Gasset. The last, who visited a number of times, left his meditations in "Intimidades" (1929), an essay forming part of his book *El espectador*. Ortega's observations about Argentina are sociological and philosophical in nature. He spoke of Buenos Aires as a "harsh city" and of creole life as a "broken limb." Argentina, he said, was an agency—or, better, an "emporium"—inhabited by a society divided into two parts: a nationalized nucleus and around it a periphery of recent immigrants not yet assimilated into the national spirit. The two components were in very different stages of evolution. According to Ortega, the European immigrant, whom he called the "abstract man," dominated the native creole, the "historic man." History had not given the country enough time to digest that Atlantic "inundation." Consequently, Argentina had to endure for a considerable time a "historic indigestion." The duality of the collective body would not end until Argentina ceased being an emporium so that it could convert itself into a true nation like the rest, with a defined sociocultural personality.

Ortega pointed out a number of distinctive traits in the Argentinians. The first was a dualism of the soul that impeded direct communication of thought, detracted from social acceptance, and hampered the development of the courage to face their destiny with anything more than a willingness to endure it. In that they differed from Europeans, who submitted to life and to destiny and made destiny their very lives, considering it their goal. The Argentinians were admirably given to individualism because they gave themselves to nothing, much less to the service of something different from themselves. But if they were indeed egocentric, they were not egotistical, Ortega believed. Otherwise they could not have made the progress they had made in only a century. The typical Argentinian was involved not in reality but in an image of himself. Seeing himself reflected always in his own imagination, he became narcissistic and conceited. As an illustration of the narcissistic Argentinian, Ortega pointed to Martin Fierro, who in his monologue talked with his image and complained that others did not recognize it. Ortega said that almost all young Argentinians saw themselves as potential great writers.

Among positive traits, Ortega pointed out the flexibility, frankness, and impetuosity that characterize all youthful national life. They explained the Argentinian's interest in the outside world, his restlessness, and his universal curiosity. The Argentinian's dynamism led Ortega to prophesy for Argentina "the possibility of an iminent history and optimum humanity." For Ortega the essential in Argentinian life was its presentation of itself as a nation-in-promise. He did not, however, see that promise in the pampas. Its immensity oppressed him but failed to move him spiritually because it was scantily populated and its life unremarkable. However, he acknowledged the Argentinians' hopes for a great future for the pampas (like the hope of the Brazilians for the Amazon region). Ortega identified these aspirations with the Argentinians' concept that he called "futurismo concreto," a way of nourishing themselves on their illusions as though they were already reality. That trait was important in Ortega's observations, for he extended it to the Argentinian personality.

According to Ortega, this "futurism" was not a common ideal or utopia but a psychological state. It was a projection toward an imaginary future, a sort of mixture of the real with the abstract. It arose from a lack of internal security, since "the creole soul is full of inherited promises and suffers greatly from a divine discontent." Another trait he observed was the "hermetic" condition of the Argentinian soul as opposed to his conventional exterior. Internal insecurity inclined him to adopt a conventional attitude in order to convince himself and others of what he was not. Thus the word and the attitude served him only for external use. They provided a mask to hide the lack of authenticity. The Buenos Aires citizen was always on the defensive, a circumstance that, Ortega said, explains "that defensive preoccupation which restrains and paralyzes his spontaneity and leaves standing only his conventional personality." The constant danger from foreigners hungering for his riches, his social position, and his public standing provided some justification for his defensiveness.

Ortega attributed the Argentinian's psychic dualism in part to the pressure of immigrants who were exclusively concerned with making a fortune and whose dynamism threatened the native creoles. Ortega thought that another source of that conduct was the excessive intervention and authoritarianism of the state, which had no social spontaneity. Consequently, the Argentinian played a double role: one as an authentic person in himself and another as a social person with an artificial exterior. In Ortega's view the Argentinian public structure encouraged this dualism of the soul and explained the imbalance between social reality and an idea of the state that did not correspond to that reality. Apart from the internal political tangle, Ortega considered the function of the Argentinian state advanced because it ruled the people as an incipient nation.

Intentionally or not, Ortega failed to distinguish between *porteños* and provincials. His observations applied principally to the people of Buenos Aires, whom he knew better. He scarcely mentioned the people of the pampas, and thus his analysis was wise but incomplete. By touching on fundamental problems, he stimulated some Argentinian essayists to examine more closely the mind and social conduct of the people of the River Plate region. The respect that Ortega paid to the political structure of Argentina was not shared by many of his Argentinian followers. Some did, however, accept in varying degrees his sober conclusions about the sociopsychological disjunction of creole society.

Chronologically, those nearest Ortega are the *porteño* Scalabrini Ortiz and the provincial Martínez Estrada. Their pioneer works about the Argentinian personality opened the way for later similar essays by Mallea, Sebreli, Mafud, Sábato, Matteis, Kusch, and others.

Raúl Scalabrini Ortiz dedicated his work *El hombre que está solo y espera* (1931) to *porteño* life and personality, which he presented candidly in all its ups and downs. In vivid and journalistic style he described the average man of Corrientes and Esmeralda streets in the Argentinian capital. He called his hero Adán (Adam) Buenos Aires (the same name appeared in 1948 in a *porteño* novel by the poet Leopoldo Marechal). The "man" of Scalabrini Ortiz' work was not an intellectual but an individual of the middle class with simple mentality and few economic ambitions. The great metropolis was hostile. The cosmopolitan conglomerate, to which he was only gradually becoming accustomed, was still somewhat strange to him and had prevented him from developing his own personality. He could not, moreover, be expected to have a community of spirit or a national consciousness.

According to Scalabrini Ortiz, the *porteño* was "a chemical combination of the races that nourished his birth." His ethnic amalgamation, although of the creole stamp, as well as the physical environment surrounding him, was responsible for a peculiar mentality that impelled him to assume a cautious and artificial behavior. Moroseness and skepticism were mixed with eagerness for something unknown but hoped for. Solitude and fear of social isolation led him to maintain a friendship that he esteemed more than money and was perhaps one of his few spontaneous sentiments. Unlike European friendship, which was expressed through personal relationship, a *porteño*'s friendship was more an egocentric "game," permitting him to forget his selfishness and taking him out of the impersonality of the metropolitan masses. He hated solitude because he did not want to be alone. He respected social class more than he did the individual.

Scalabrini Ortiz accorded the *porteño* a certain degree of ingenuity, not in the intellectual sense but rather as a sort of alertness. That quality permitted him to manage his affairs by means of an

> intrepid individualism that confronts fatality with a free attitude that recognizes no limit to his independence, tramples and overturns all the principles of European society, and squanders his vital force in futilities and pastimes without material utility, deepening the abyss between father and son.

Moroseness blunted his intellectual faculties. He did not read. He did not plan ahead but acted on sudden intuition. Since he was not ambitious, he did not feel the need to suppress his spontaneity, for that would be contrary to his closed mind and almost taciturn character. He was a resigned being because he believed in nothing and nobody, withdrawn as though he were in a cave. He was bad-humored but not severe, and he was almost irresponsible. He was resentful. He asked nothing, for he conceded nothing. In spite of his moderate worldly appetites, his greatest pleasure was to pass the day drinking maté and eating beef while engaging in carefree chatter with his friends.

Toward strangers the man of Corrientes and Esmeralda streets displayed an odd attitude that could be reduced to the injunction, "Don't meddle." Scalabrini Ortiz thought that to be the true standard of the *porteño*, since it concerned intervention not so much in personal affairs as in those belonging to the state. The attitude seems to indicate passivity in political matters, even though the *porteños* argued about them as much as they did other problems, on the corner or in their favorite cafés. The café meeting and the encounter on the corner assumed the status of institutions in *porteño* life, serving as pastimes as in other Hispanic American countries. The *porteño* did not wish to judge the man; he approved or disapproved the act, not the actor. That distinguished the *porteño* from other Hispanic Americans, who readily censured their rulers. The average man of the street in Buenos Aires was not interested in political programs or in oratory, which rarely produced any results. He foresaw the events; he trembled and hoped to see them realized in the leaders, but he did not have faith in them. The *porteño* did not think; he felt. He was sad and insecure, with the result that he was contemplative although not naturally reflective. European morality, which was still influential in the city, hindered him with its censure of inaction and negligence.

It seemed to him that city life went from hazard to hazard in unexpected episodes to which he surrendered the fatalism. "Tradition, progress, humanity, family, and honor are trifles which the *porteño* feels are useless; therefore he laughs at them." He destroyed illusions. He had the character of the man of the pampas; he was idle, taciturn, patient, and haughty.

Scalabrini Ortiz wrote that "Buenos Aires . . . became the capital of the countryside." He was referring to the phenomenon that began about 1930, when peasants began migrating to the capital in such numbers that they permeated the *porteño* environment. The social "proleterization" that ensued could not fail to affect the middle and lower classes. Consequently Buenos Aires came to be called the "great village"—which obviously did not please capital residents.

The character delineation Scalabrini Ortiz gave of the *porteños* could not be applied to the provincial intellectuals. He found them intelligent, courteous, and polished, a characterization I learned to be accurate during my sojourn in Argentina.

According to Scalabrini Ortiz, the essential of *porteño* life was an immateriality covered and mixed with European modes. That affected cultural life more than anything else. The author characterized the *porteño* intellectual thus: "Cut off from the town from which he came, the ambitious man is enclosed in his own ambition. He distills in his study not unpolished, everyday truth but the filtered material that he extracts from his European books." As a result most *porteño* writers ignored Argentine reality but considered literature an "empty cloud of words." Scalabrini Ortiz qualified their attitude as a form of intellectual apostasy. He did not fail to mention, however, that among the new writers of his day there was a zeal for what was typically *porteño*. Undoubtedly he was referring to the work of renewal by the Generation of Twenty-Two and others. It should be added that the authors of the Generation of Forty and, above all, *"los enojados"* ("the Angry Ones") of 1950 to 1965, despite their biased standards and pessimistic outlook, began to mobilize the Argentinian national conscience. One of their idols was Martínez Estrada, to be discussed later.

Scalabrini Ortiz' bitterest observation was that "the writer in general does not listen to the spirit of the land"; that is, he lacked a sense of belonging to the land. Scalabrini Ortiz agreed in that respect with Ortega y Gasset, who also noted little Argentine spirit in Argentine letters but much vanity, ardent lyricism, and feverish idealism. As a *porteño* Scalabrini Ortiz faced the complexity of life in Buenos Aires with valor and insight. He did not, however, give enough attention to creole astuteness in the manner of Martínez Estrada and especially of Julio Mafud.

Ezequiel Martínez Estrada, the cultivated provincial essayist, was more universal and also more passionate than Scalabrini Ortiz. Preoccupied with the future of his country, he made a rigorous examination of the enigmatic Argentine in *Radiografía de la pampa* (1933) and especially in *La cabeza de Goliat* (1940), which bore the subtitle *Microscopia de Buenos Aires*. He made a dramatic presentation of the River Plate that combined history with sociology and ecology with psychology. His aim was to show the swift and unplanned growth of Buenos Aires with its centralized political and administrative power and monopoly of the business produced from the wealth of the interior. He contrasted the constant enrichment of the capital with the progressive economic and cultural impoverishment of the Argentinian provinces. He compared Buenos Aires with the head of Goliath, in an original metaphor as a monstrous octopus strangling its victim, the interior of the country. His judgment of Argentina's political and territorial structure was severe and bitter; so too was his judgment of the Argentinian nature, especially that of the women of the capital.

As a man of the interior, Martínez Estrada was an excellent interpreter of the pampas, whose characteristics were sometimes excessively idealized in gaucho literature. He believed that the natural forces of the pampas had no positive effect on their inhabitants. Rather, those forces enslaved and stupefied men through their solitude, immensity, and monotony. They deprived him of his will, subdued his voice, and blurred his vision. The physical vacuum of the plains was transformed into a human psychic vacuum. "The man of the pampas has a restricted conception of the world, being a captive in the cage formed by his horizon." The primitive forces of nature infected his thought and conduct. Isolation turned him into a strange being. Man worked the land in order to live, but he did not love it. He was performing a sacrifice. The illusion of hope alienated him from the land. He did not feel happy; therefore, he lost any sense of the land. He became as somber and taciturn as his environment. Struggling against it, "the man of the pampas becomes unstable and insecure, which by reflection he transmits to his surroundings." Not surprisingly, Martínez Estrada affirmed that "the illusion of the countryside and the poetics of gold lose their hypnotic force and repel the immigrant." That, in my view, explains the exodus of many inhabitants from the pampas to the cities and the infiltration of their "antiland" psychology into the *porteño* population.

In view of these circumstances, I have asked myself for the explanation of the lyrically magnificent presentations of the pampas by gaucho authors from José Hernández to Ricardo Güiraldes. Undoubtedly the plains do have their enchantment, which overwhelmed the gauchos and fascinated the writers. It must not be forgotten that, for the gauchos, the pampas were a very convenient region, abounding in wild cattle that they appropriated for food and trade without having to work. The region also afforded them refuge from justice and from a civilization that contrasted with the gaucho "barbarism" revealed in the gaucho literature itself. That literature displays an ideological variety in those indomitable and picturesque sons of the pampas. Early poetic manifestations, which arose during the war of independence and the civil war against Juan Manuel de Rosas and later, exalted the gaucho for romantic and patriotic reasons. Such motives are apparent in the works of Echeverría, Hidalgo, Ascasubi, and Hernández. Domingo F. Sarmiento, Acevedo Díaz, De Viana, and even Reyles describe the gaucho in a realistic manner. The exaltation lingered, but artistically it ended with *Don Segundo Sombra* (1926), by Güiraldes, a farewell to a gaucho world that had already vanished. The gauchos of Benito Lynch and Florencio Sánchez are not properly gauchos but are peons tied to work on the fenced and "civilized" *estancias* (large country estates). Even so, the Argentinian-Uruguayan gaucho literature and the dramas of Sánchez are the most original contributions of Hispanic American letters. They are similar to Modernism, the novels of the Mexican Revolution, the Afro-Antillean poetry, and the indigenous narratives that constitute a valuable literary contribution by Mestizo America.

Martínez Estrada had a particular vision of Argentinian reality. His most serious concern was not the pampas but the profound difference between Buenos Aires and the interior—that is, between the *porteños* and the provincials—which he attributed to the process by which the nation was formed. He believed that not two political parties but two countries had long existed: the Buenos Aires of the Unitarians and the provinces of the Federalists. In that struggle the city-nation conquered the province-republic, and the monstrous growth of Buenos Aires prevented true federation, union, and progress. He concluded his analysis thus:

> A history of riotous mobs, of regional hatreds, of embezzlements, of systematic persecution of the intellectuals of good stock, the depreciation

of that which is not oriented toward pecuniary gain, the hegemony of the army as the only institution of law and order, the subjugation of teaching to politics demonstrate that in the course of a century a parenthesis is closed and that history has recovered its regular course.[1]

In dramatizing the preponderance of Buenos Aires, Martínez Estrada wrote, "Each skyscraper raised in the capital makes the piece of land far off in the provinces poorer, more backward, and less productive." The interior of the country no longer attracted the Argentinian as it had in the past, because that interior was without illusions: it was work, sickness, ignorance, and oblivion. For the *porteño*, to look toward the interior was to look outside, to the exterior. For him the interior was Europe. Ortega, Scalabrini Ortiz, and Mafud all subscribed to that thesis. Martínez Estrada noted the influence of foreign immigration on the Argentinian demographic structure. He saw it in the rural mentality displayed by many *porteños*, in the Italian-style *"chatura"* and in the dubious methods and tactics they brought with them from the plains. In my opinion that is evidence of the fusion of the *porteño* and the provincial in the complex creole nature.

Martínez Estrada described other *porteño* features: sadness, a pervasive solitude, anonymity, fear of life, cosmopolitanism, and lack of perception of reality. He considered as *porteño* infirmities a number of contradictory and therefore conflicting traits: excessive ambition, a mania for titles, hate, cunning, shame, snobbery, courage, fear, assumption of protective coloring, and abjection. *Porteños* made a game of reason and justice, while dignity was nowhere to be found in the city because the state had taken it away. Similarly, because of its arbitrary politics, the state had shed its citizens' "divinities of blood," shattered their faith, and put itself in their place. All *porteños* were alike in aggrandizing the city. The principal tone of Buenos Aires was its traditional mercantile spirit, accompanied by an elaborate state structure but relatively little culture.

In his criticism Martínez Estrada touched on many points that roused the *porteño* politicians and intellectuals. His work did not enhance his own popularity. Because he had wounded the pride of the rulers, his works brought on a prolonged dispute. Among the few

---

[1]Martínez Estrada was here comparing what had happened in Argentina during the tyranny of Rosas with the situation a hundred years later under Juan Perón's dictatorship.

Argentinian critics who have done justice to Martínez Estrada is Enrique Anderson Imbert, who evaluated *Radiografía de la pampa* with commendable impartiality. Imbert thought it "the most bitter book that has been written in Argentina and the first great literary testament of the frightful moral crisis that befell the country in 1930."

Faithful to his convictions and his independent criteria, Martínez Estrada had a clearer vision of his country than any of his compatriots had. At the same time he fervently—and, in my view, accurately—defended the interior regions of Argentina. To counter the depreciation of the provincials by the *porteños*, I should mention that some writers of the Argentinian interior, such as Alberdi, Sarmiento, Hernández, Lugones, Rojas, Gálvez, Eduardo Mallea, and Martínez Estrada, made brilliant contributions to the River Plate culture. Without them it would be difficult to imagine an Argentinian literature and particularly its natural and national spirit. Foreigners visiting among the provincials are struck by the care with which they speak and pronounce the Spanish language and their sincerity and friendliness. Indeed, all Argentinians, both capital and pampas residents, are welcoming and courteous to visitors.

In his essay *Historia de una pasión argentina* (1937), Eduardo Mallea pointed out the lack of harmony between the urban and rural sectors. He divided Argentina into the visible and the invisible—the first, the winner; the second, the long-suffering. He deplored the lack of conscience in the latter as much as in the former. Although he saw material progress, he failed to perceive progress in the national culture. He censured the men who directed public and academic life, classifying them as mediocre, torpid, plebeian, and individualistic, in contrast to the men of the first hours of Argentina's history. According to Mallea, they were the vague incarnation of vague "ideals." He said that in Argentina "work goes on without creative foresight and without animation; it is vegetative, tellurically obsessed by the immediate windfall," more for utilitarian ends than for humanistic or humanitarian ones. Mallea blamed that state of things upon the excessive wordiness of some and the silence of others. He trusted, however, that from that silence there would emerge a different Argentinian consciousness—moral, historic, intellectual, and human. Mallea's intellectual sensibility could not conceive a "national literature" without "nationalism," which in turn could not exist without a consciousness of history. Mallea's conclusions undoubtedly clashed with the declarations supported by the *porteños:* "We have much in our favor; we are rich; we are better than anybody else."

Mallea admired European culture, but, unlike most Argentinian writers of his time, he did not blindly imitate it. His essay is a sort of intellectual autobiography intermixed with profound meditations about Argentina from a universal perspective. He was a "provincial" who had become a *porteño*. He displayed a humanist fervor and an irreproachable patriotism that qualified him as a model Argentinian. Mallea felt spiritually exiled in his country: "We Argentinians are all exiled, exiled from the spirit, exiled from the civilization from which we came, from that ancestral association in which, different from us, men produced art, thought, philosophy." He lamented the "fundamental poverty" of Argentinian character. Mallea's observations were penetrating, but his vision of the Argentinian future was somewhat clouded by an idealism that viewed national problems as less complex than they really were. He was sincere in his intent to create an image of a new, more advanced, more authentic, and happier Argentina.

Mallea and Martínez Estrada—and Sarmiento before them—thanks to their attitude toward their native ground, are identified in Argentina with national feeling. Another author whose work reflects interest in the national character is Julio Mafud. In his essays *El desarraigo argentino* (1959) and *Psicología de la viveza criolla* (1965) he analyzed in greater detail the mind and social conduct of the people of the River Plate. Mafud belonged to the literary thrust of "los enojados" and, in accordance with ideological revisionism, cast new light on the old problems of Argentinian intellectual history. The advantage of his investigation is that he frankly and systematically exposed the emotional complexities of the Argentinian's mental processes. He was not, however, above making some intuitive speculations.

As a sociologist Mafud considered the Argentinian complex of problems from a general point of view; consequently, he did not separate *porteños* from provincials. He considered Argentinians an ethnic group with many common traits, although he recognized the local origin of their peculiarities. Owing to the complexity of the development of the Argentinian personality, Mafud had difficulty defining the "average" Argentinian as the "national being." The principal obstacle is the social dislocation that resulted when the modern community of the River Plate region was formed. According to Mafud, three groups contributed to the psychological formation of the Argentinian personality (and all to a certain degree are still latent in the Argentinian's conduct): the Indians, the gauchos, and the latter-day immigrants with their European influence. Each group produced its own life-style that was incompatible with the others'— and all were unacceptable to the creoles.

Mafud believed that the European life-style, artificially imposed, cut off the deeply ingrained influence of the Europeans' predecessors, the indigenes and the gauchos. That sociological thesis—the European "amputation" of the indigenous and gaucho influences in the Argentinian civilizing spectrum—is somewhat surprising. Actually, the creole Argentinian army with the cooperation of the gauchos annihilated the Indians, most of whom were nomadic, before or at the time of the great European immigration. What had happened was a nullification of the indigenous roots, chiefly by the creole natives themselves. It is necessary, however, to accept the second part of Mafud's thesis—that, as a result of the great influx of immigrants beginning about 1880, the free gauchos were reduced to peons and day laborers on the *estancias*.

According to his view, both the gauchos and the *porteños* were creoles, but on different social levels. Logically the immigrants would affect them, weakening cultural and social ties between Argentina and Spain. Since then the growing sociocultural cosmopolitanism in that region has loosened those ties even more. Leaving aside Mafud's thesis, one must ask what deep-seated influences the incipient Argentinian culture could expect from the vagabond gauchos. Whatever they may have been, we must recognize the reverberating echoes of the gaucho in Argentinian literature through the recollections of the frontier civilization. Nor can the emotional fervor that survived the era in the spirit of Martín Fierro be eliminated. As an expression of spiritual rebellion and solitude, it still nurtures some Argentinian literary and social concepts and is also reflected in a similar attitude in Uruguay.

Mafud attributed the Argentinians' social uprooting to occupation of the land, which was responsible for the psychological clash that also occurred in the capital and was expressed in the nostalgia of the immigrants for their native lands and the nostalgia of the creoles for their vanished past. The impact of current and previous immigration produced an alienation between the old and new inhabitants of Buenos Aires that established a new life-style. Creole astuteness then appeared as a reaction of creole natives to the more enterprising European immigrants, arising from the creoles' feelings of inferiority and their attitude toward economics. It became their defensive armor. It involved taking advantage of the foreigner through deceit and trickery and utilizing their keenness in every way their ingenuity could devise. Their acuity was not, however, like that of the rogue who serves various masters and under their protection takes satisfaction where he can find it. They were the selfish sort, men without scruples but with ambitions, economic anxieties, and surreptitious appetites that impelled them to any violation, always under the cloak of good intentions.

Creole astuteness is a degradation of values that is now ironically considered synonymous with manliness, virility, and *machismo*. In a chain reaction the immigrants adopted the attitude that served them best in "making themselves creole." It became a collective vice. It must be added that the development of that acuity marked the transition from rural to urban civilization in Argentina at the end of the nineteenth century and the beginning of the twentieth. It was achieved in the midst of social anarchy and bitter rivalry between people of the countryside and the merging petite bourgeoisie. An excellent account of the transformation of the descendants of the gauchos into bourgeois citizens is found in the picaresque novel *Divertidas aventuras del nieto de Juan Moreira* (1910), by Roberto J. Payró.

In a scrupulous sociological examination Mafud pointed to the following factors as contributing to the Argentinians' uprooting: antisocial individualism expressed in the emphasis on "I"; the lack of tradition (after rejection of indigenous and gaucho, as well as Spanish, tradition); ideological utopianism resulting from a lack of coordination in the process of continuity; incapacity for self-government; the absence of a structured social integration with a resulting marginality of the masses; the clash between the passive creole and the active immigrant; and the lack of psychological unity.

Because the ethnic structure is dominated by whites, it is obvious that creoles are the masters of the region. Of lesser importance, then, is the still-disputed question whether the gaucho, long ago absorbed into Argentinian society, was of creole or mestizo origin.

In my opinion, Argentina is a relatively young ethnic melting pot and consequently needs more time to reach its collective potential. Within the complex Argentinian personality there are promising traits, such as individual creativity, the cult of friendship, talent for improvisation, a high regard for courage, and an inclination to be always on the side of the persecuted and the fallen. In one or another form these traits balance the lack of roots and social indifference, the weak community spirit, the constant economic anxiety, the excessive politicization, and mimesis in culture and customs. These elements have not yet permitted the forging of a national spirit that is defined in the cultural sphere. Argentinian civilization remains in a precarious state of civilization in comparison with the mestizo civilization of Hispanic America. Argentinians do not lack intelligence or skill, but it seems that they suffer too much from esoteric concepts, regional pride, and fragmented goals difficult to plan for or reach. Mafud's statement that "Argentina is the country with the highest standard of living in Hispanic America, but one of the most rootless nations of the continent" seems entirely correct.

Some aspects of Argentinian civilization are incomprehensible to other Americans. One is the tendency toward fantasy, cultivated to excess by Argentinian writers. There is a significant scarcity of novels on regional and national topics that could bring the readers to grips with their world. Avoidance of such themes also slows the growth of popular culture. The preoccupation with fantasy further weakens the already insignificant Argentinian social consciousness. It is counterproductive to *Argentinidad*. According to the Uruguayan humanist Alberto zum Felde, Argentina's situation "fluctuates between the indecisive localist voice and palpitant intellectual cosmopolitanism."

With that said, it must be conceded that Argentinian writers have brought the fantasy to a pinnacle of excellence, particularly when it is interlaced with magic realism. The model was the unforgettable novel of the Amazon *The Green Mansions* (1904), by the Anglo-Argentinian author William Henry Hudson. Contemporary examples are the fantastic stories of Jorge Luis Borges, Adolfo Bioy Casares, and Silvina Ocampo. Of no less importance are such works as *Bestiario* (1951), by Julio Cortázar; *El grimorio* (1961), by Enrique Anderson Imbert; and the detective-type novel *Operación masacre* (1958), by Rodolfo Walsh, to mention only a few. Also popular are anthologies of fantasy and detective stories, which reveal the *porteños'* taste for this kind of fiction. It should be noted here that mystery novels, especially those classified as magic realism, are also popular to a degree in Mestizo America, though the vogue has considerably diminished. They continue to be extremely popular in the River Plate region.

Another weakness in River Plate literature is the proliferation of Argentinian and Uruguayan literary "generations." They not only confuse foreign Americanists but also produce discord among the River Plate literary critics and the writers themselves. It may be noted that perhaps the most balanced literary critics of this region are those who have lived abroad for some years. Their critical perceptions are made clearer by distance.

Owing to its multifarious roots in the past, Argentina is not lacking in folklore traditions in music and in the dance, notably the tango. Some Uruguayan folklorists believe that the tango has an African origin and was brought by runaway slaves to Argentina from Brazil by way of Uruguay. Ildefonso Pereda Valdés doubts that origin, since Negroes did not dance individually but in groups. Thanks to Argentinians, the tango became enormously popular in foreign lands. Curiously, although it was accepted as a ballroom dance in Europe and the Americas, in Argentina for some time it was considered an expression of sadness, discontent, and rancor. That certain movements of the tango suggest sexual intimacy convinced some researchers that it was a corruption of an older dance form. According to Ernesto Sábato, "There are erotic representations in the tango and a tortuous manifestation of inferiority." Consequently, it is less often danced in urban centers. But the tango is still popular. In other forms too the repertory of music and dance of Argentina and Uruguay is as rich as that of other nations.

Endowed with skill and creative imagination, the creoles of the River Plate region have produced an extensive and interesting literature. From the time of Esteban Echeverría and Domingo F. Sarmiento, River Plate letters have followed a brilliant course of development. Among the distinguished Argentinian authors are Del Campo, Obligado, Hernández, Cané, Payró, Lugones, Larreta, Storni, Banchs, Arlt, Güiraldes, Lynch, Martínez Estrada, Borges, Fernández, Mallea, Marechal, Molinari, Gálvez, Ocampo, Cortázar, and Sábato. Among Uruguayan authors the following stand forth: San Martín, Acevedo Díaz, De Viana, Herrera y Reissig, Agustini, Ibarbourou, Rodó, Quiroga, Sánchez, Reyles, Ercasty, Amorim, Onetti, and Benedetti. It is also significant that the only Nobel prizes in science with which Hispanic America has been honored were awarded to Argentinians: to the physiologist Bernardo Houssay (1947) and to the chemist Luis Federico Leloir (1970).

In concluding these reflections about the River Plate civilization, I should note that the creolism of that region is multifaceted and at times contradictory in thought and conduct. The cultural cosmopolitanism draws Argentinians and Uruguayans closer to European and even Anglo-American currents than to Hispanic American ones. But apart from some survivals of Old World customs and tastes, Argentina and Uruguay differ greatly from Europe in their economic and political structure. It is true that the River Plate peoples share with the mestizo countries of Hispanic America linguistic unity, religion, and various political habits, but they have little or nothing in common with them in the literary sphere, as seen in their lack of feeling for the land and community spirit, both of which abound in mestizo letters. Nonetheless, there are promising creole traits: dynamism and intelligence. Argentina publishes more books, produces more operas, and holds more art exhibits than any other Hispanic American country. All this is evidence of great promise.

Although the region is considered "developed," many of its problems seem generic to colonies that have not yet reached their maximum potential. The restless spirit of enterprise, comparable to that of the first colonists, who also long felt tied to Europe, confirms that interpretation. A somewhat analogous situation developed among Brazilian pioneers, vaguely expressed in *saudade* ("nostalgia"). It is hoped that the passage of time will produce in Argentina the spiritual fusion, already perceptible in many of her literary and artistic works, that will produce the great culture her people deserve.

CHAPTER 9

BLACKS IN THE AMERICAS

The Negro presence in the Americas is linked historically with slavery, an institution that has been practiced from remote times in various parts of the world. Slavery existed in Asia, Africa, Europe, and even pre-Columbian America, where it was practiced among indigenous tribes, who sometimes sacrificed their slaves to their gods. The slaves were captives of war or raids who were forced to serve the victor or sold to other tribes. Slavery was an accepted institution in the empires of Babylonia, Persia, Egypt, Greece, and Rome. African chieftains engaged in the practice.

When imperial Rome conquered European, African, or Asiatic countries, slaves of various races, adhering to different religions and speaking diverse languages, appeared in the Roman capital and countryside. Sometimes the slaves with a more advanced culture became the spiritual conquerors of the victors. A well-known instance is that of captive Greeks, who became the tutors of the less-civilized Romans. The Arabs, who dominated parts of Spain and Portugal for eight centuries (A.D. 711–1492), had some Negro blood. Mixing with the *peninsulares*, they introduced features of African culture (Miguel de Unamuno once said, "Spain is half-African"). Wars between the Spaniards and the Moors later brought slaves to both sides. One recalls that Cervantes, a Turkish slave in Algeria, was ransomed by missionaries. The Germanic tribes, extending their dominions over their Slavic neighbors, often captured and enslaved Lusatians and Serbs, "incorporating" them into their race. The most notorious instance in modern times was in World War II, when the Germans enslaved various European nations, subjecting the people to forced labor and in the process killing millions of Jews, Poles, Russians, and others. Genocide and slavery went hand in hand, both justified by theories of racial superiority. The Spaniards and Portuguese introduced Negro slavery into their American colonies in the sixteenth century, bringing slaves from Africa to substitute for the Indians, who were unable to endure the conditions in the mines and on the plantations. Black slave labor contributed in varying degrees to the economic development of the Hispanic American colonies. A century later the English colonists in North America, especially in the South, followed the practice of slavery. Although the great majority of the slaves were Africans, as Aquiles Escalante notes, both male and female white slaves were not rare, especially in the first half of the sixteenth century.

Both Latin and Anglo-Saxon nations pursued the "commerce in Negroes," that is, the slave trade. According to the Chilean scholar Rolando Mellafe (in *La esclavitud negra in Hispanoamérica*), the headquarters of the slave trade were in Guinea, Lisbon, and Seville. The principal Hispanic American ports of entry for the slave ships were Campeche, Veracruz, Havana, Cartagena, Portobello, Panama, and Caracas. The trade was carried on under the flags of Holland, Portugal, France, England, and, much later, the United States and some of the Hispanic American republics. During the colonial epoch slave ships had the protection of the Spanish convoys that accompanied the fleets engaged in commerce between Spain and America. Few slavers, and those only at the beginning, flew the Spanish flag, since Spain preferred to arrange concessions known as *asientos* with foreign countries, from whom it collected high duties. This practice satisfied the moral mandates against taking part in such commerce, which at times was the subject of theological controversy. Spanish religious convictions required, at least at the beginning, that slaves brought to America be baptized and remain for some time in the care of good Christians.

During the three centuries of the Negro slave trade more than fifteen million Africans were brought to the New World. Of that number about ten million went to Latin America, and approximately five million to what is now the United States.[1] The trade must have been as profitable to the slave merchants as it was to the planters, who benefited from slave labor for generations. Apparently the treatment of black slaves, except for noteworthy instances of creole and mestizo cruelty, was somewhat better than that of the equally enslaved Indi-

---

[1]Charles Wagley and Marvin Harris, *Minorities in the New World*, pp. 88, 120.

ans. Undoubtedly the size of the investment the landowners made in new laborers was an incentive to make the best possible use of them, which necessitated some concern for their physical (if not their emotional) health. According to the Colombian historian Sergio Arboleda:

> Enslaved Negroes during the colonial period were less unfortunate than many of the Indians who were called free. The interests of the master, who considered slaves part of his capital investment and knew that their descendants would belong to him, procured their preservation and increase.[2]

As a consequence of their superior physical condition and intelligence, blacks were often made overseers and were also called upon to punish the Indians. Instances are known of black *cimarrones* or *montuvios* (runaway slaves), who fled far into the jungle, taking with them food and sometimes Indian women. Such circumstances obviously adversely affected relations between Negroes and Indians, producing in the former a feeling of superiority and in the latter a sense of humiliation and inferiority. The echoes of those attitudes of the past are still heard in certain parts of Hispanic America, where, as Manuel Zapata Olivella states, blacks, because of their skills, are considered superior to the less-acculturated Indians.

In areas populated by both groups the offspring of Negroes and Indians are called *zambos*.[3] Persons of Negro and white parentage, called *mulattoes*, constitute a civilization that reflects interaction of the values, culture, and customs of the two races. Generally speaking, the Western influence dominates the African. As a result, Eduardo Caballero Calderón, writes, "The mulatto feels closer to Europe than to Africa." Mulatto civilization attained considerable importance in northern parts of South America and extended into Caribbean America and many regions of Brazil (all tropical areas). According to Fernando González, mulatto influences have even spread into regions that are only sparsely populated by blacks. In some regions of Colombia, Ecuador, and Venezuela the impact of the mulatto is seen in the way of life of the mestizos.

[2]Sergio Arboleda, *La colonía: Su situación políca y económica.*

[3]Recently the term Afro-mestizo has been introduced by writers specializing in the study of Negro influence in Hispanic America.

The development of the mulatto civilization followed a different course in the United States. In spite of their acculturation in the dense black population of the South, those of mixed race have not yet acquired all the benefits of Anglo-American civilization, which are more accessible to the less numerous but more dynamic groups of the North and Middle West. But in one way or another Negro impact on United States life continues to increase. By way of comparison, it can be said that there are many Hispanic American blacks who feel as "Latin" as the other sectors of Hispanic America. United States blacks display a much greater sense of equality to their white fellow citizens. As a result of educational and professional advantages many United States blacks are socially and economically far ahead of their Hispanic American brothers. The latter retain many more of the ancestral African traits than the former. The intensity of the movement to assimilate the Negro into Anglo-American culture is today part of the ongoing process to which all ethnic groups in the United States are subjected.

The colonial Spanish plantation economy favored slavery because it was based on tropical agriculture for export, which returned higher profits than any form of cultivation for domestic use. That system of slavery intensified the division in the colonial population by making a rigorous distinction between masters and servants. Essentially it was a form of regional paternalism that had political applications. It originated from "plantation mentality," which embraced human exploitation through unscrupulous means. That mentality fit into the Hispanic American colonial structure and was related to the slave system that later developed in the English colonies of the South. The system was inhuman and oppressed all who were its victims.

Even in that colonial economy—the economic dependence of many on a single *latifundista*—many slaves in Hispanic America achieved liberation through manumission. Some were given liberty for services rendered during the Conquest and afterward, sometimes as a reward for fidelity to master, and sometimes because an excess of laborers made the maintenance of slaves uneconomical. A slave could also obtain freedom by repaying the master the original amount of the purchase. Of course, this was possible only when the slave was permitted to own property. In such circumstances, according to Mellafe, some free Negroes gained sufficient funds to acquire Indian slaves for themselves. At times free Indians who had acquired wealth as artisans bought Negroes, becoming themselves masters of slaves.

In the colonies of the Americas voices were periodically raised in protest against the institution of slavery. Both Protestant and Roman Catholic churchmen spoke out against it. Particularly vocal were the Quakers, who would in the nineteenth century spearhead the abolitionist movement. Europeans too were distressed by the presence of slavery, particularly in North America, whose English colonies paid more than lip service to the concepts of freedom and the dignity of man. An interesting and little-known sidelight to history is one effort to alleviate slavery dating from the American Revolution. The Polish hero of that war, General Thaddeus Kosciuszko, was distressed by the sufferings of the Negroes. When he left the United States in 1789, he authorized his friend Thomas Jefferson to use the compensation the grateful Republic had offered him for his services

> to employ the whole thereof in purchasing Negroes from among his own or any others, and giving them liberty in my name; in giving them an education in trade or otherwise; in having them instructed for their new conditions in their duties of morality, which may make them good neighbors, good fathers and mothers, husbands and wives, in their duty as citizens; teaching them to be defenders of their liberty and country, of the good order of society, and in whatsoever may make them happy and useful.[4]

Jefferson, himself a slaveowner, had long opposed the practice. According to the black Colombian scholar Ramón Lozano Garcés, "Thomas Jefferson intended to condemn Negro slavery emphatically and clearly, but his noble purpose did not have the backing of the other signatories of the Declaration of Independence."[5]

For various reasons slavery in Hispanic America gradually began to lose ground. Decline in the export of sugar to Europe at the end of the seventeenth century reduced the advantage in owning slaves—their labor did not always produce the expected profits. Another cause was the increase in *mestizaje*, which made it possible to replace slaves with a wage-earning workforce. The mestizos' labor produced better

---

[4]Miecislaus Haiman, *Poland and the American Revolutionary War*, pp. 21–22.
[5]Ramón Lozano Garcés, "Dimensión universal del negro," *Revista Universidad de Antioquia*, No. 171 (1968).

economic results when the blacks and Indians participated in that *mestizaje* as peons or *inquilinos* (tenants).

Mellafe believes that *mestizaje* is one of the most important regional factors in the decline of Negro slavery in Hispanic America. Added to that was the impact of the eighteenth-century Enlightenment with its emphasis on equality and the rights of man. Undoubtedly it caused a breach in the colonial mentality and at the same time aroused the hope of eliminating the taxes Europe had been imposing on its American possessions. Finally, industrial capitalism, based on a system of wage earners and work efficiency that was lacking in the slave system, dealt slavery the final blow.

The United States inherited the slave system from the English and a similar system from the French when they acquired Louisiana in 1803. The practices of the southern planters, who derived their wealth from the cultivation of sugar, cotton, and tobacco with black slave labor, aroused much discontent in the industrialized North. Runaway slaves from the South took refuge there, and freedmen left to find better opportunities in the North. The northern abolitionist movement, in which humanitarian reasons were fused with economic ones, mobilized public opinion and became a powerful political force that largely brought on the Civil War. During the war, in 1863, President Abraham Lincoln declared the abolition of slavery.

In Hispanic America some of the new republican governments proclaimed emancipation a few years after achieving independence; others vacillated. Mexico, Central America, and Chile, where slavery had little economic importance, were the first to abolish it. Some nations, bowing to the influence of slaveowning landholders, passed laws providing for gradual emancipation. Venezuela, Colombia, Ecuador, and Peru abolished slavery in the 1850's.

Events in North America influenced the abolitionist sentiment in Brazil, where the emancipation of Negroes was achieved in 1888. The resulting discontent among conservatives, combined with other internal matters, precipitated the transformation the next year of the Empire of Brazil into a federal republic.

Interestingly, the British had outlawed the black slave trade in their colonies in 1807, following with abolition of slavery in 1834. France in 1848 and Holland in 1863 followed Britain's example. To put an end to the abominable business, the British crown signed treaties with American nations and European countries that had colonies in America. The Papal Bull of 1839, which not only condemned slavery but also threatened with excommunication those who devoted themselves to the Negro slave trade, had a great moral influence. It is believed that this dual intervention, together with the good will of the Hispanic American rulers, gave the final blow to the Negro traffic between Africa and America. Puerto Rico and Cuba, still under Spanish colonial dominion, achieved liberty for their black slaves in 1873 and 1886, respectively.

Unfortunately, emancipation did not resolve the problems as some emancipators had hoped. The economic interests of Hispanic and American planters were more powerful than the political idealism of their governments. According to Magnus Mörner, the consequences of the abolition of Negro slavery in Hispanic America were not very positive. The freedmen soon returned to the plantations as poorly paid day laborers. In southern Brazil the freedmen were in competition with European immigrants, although the latter avoided the plantations, preferring to colonize virgin land. For these and other reasons the blacks had a marginal existence.[6] Their return to the fields was almost a return to the slave tradition of the plantations. The same situation prevailed along the coast of Peru, and in the Caribbean and the Guianas, where the blacks were in competition with newly arrived immigrants from Asia—Indians from India and Chinese. A subsistence economy could be the only lot for the black people.

The situation of the blacks in the United States after abolition also changed very little. During the Reconstruction period they obtained congressional and local representation and some access to the judicial system. But on the whole they were not able to maintain these improvements for very long, especially in the Deep South, where they were exposed to the antagonism of their white neighbors. Thus the only beneficiaries were the blacks who moved to the industrialized North and Middle West. In those areas their assimilation into the American way of life followed a more normal pattern as they were absorbed into urban society.

Most of those who remained in the South became tenant farmers

[6]Magnus Mörner, "Proceso histórico del mestizaje y de la transculturación en América Latina," *Revista Aportes*, No. 14 (1969).

or returned to the plantations, where they performed their accustomed tasks under conditions that differed little from those of the days before emancipation. The doctrine advocating "the redemption of the South by the whites" prevailed, fomenting racial conflict. There were also considerable numbers of poor whites whose socioeconomic conditions were almost indistinguishable from those of the blacks. As agricultural tenants both occupied lands of low productivity and lived a marginal existence; the good land was in the hands of the plantation owners.

The industrial and commercial development of the United States required many laborers, and that demand prompted the exodus of the black population from the South to the North between World War I and World War II and immediately afterward. In that demographic movement blacks demonstrated mobility and initiative. The inevitable process of urbanization stimulated a considerable growth in the black middle class. The rural-to-urban transition was accompanied by a visible improvement in the black's economic and cultural status.

Though much of the United States Negro population still lives in segregated neighborhoods, the circumstances confining them to traditional occupations are gradually disappearing. Today blacks are working extensively in technical, professional, commercial, union, and other positions. Negro participation in local politics has had positive effects. In 1975 seven large North American cities, among them Washington, D.C., and Atlanta, Georgia, had black mayors. Since only three of those cities have a predominantly Negro population, that phenomenon seems to indicate a diminution of racial prejudice. Despite the continuing inequality of treatment and resulting violence, the general betterment of the black population of the United States continues on a fixed course and is slowly bringing positive results.

In Hispanic America unfavorable economic conditions in the rural areas cause a steady migration to the cities, principally of the Indians, whose numbers are greater than those of Negroes. The blacks, who live in dense communities in the cities as well as in the rural districts, are more conservative and economically less ambitious than the blacks of Anglo-America. The black sociologists Zapata Olivella and Caballero Salguedo believe that social consciousness has not yet awakened among them, although they show a strong sense of racial community. The Hispanic American blacks seem content with the little they have. Mobility and initiative are seen only among educated blacks—for example, teachers and doctors in Colombia, Venezuela, and the Caribbean who move to areas that offer better opportunities.

Black intellectuals, professionals, and politicians are few, but some are numbered among the writers and poets who have distinguished themselves in Hispanic American letters. In general those writers identify themselves proudly with the culture of their respective countries, even when their subject matter is related to *négritude*, to be discussed later in this chapter. Negro dynamism is extensively manifested in music and the dance. Although there are black Hispanic American landowners, most of the blacks are farmers, small merchants, artisans, laborers, fishermen, and so on. Their economic weight is limited to their own regions and has no national dimensions. Hispanic America lacks black millionaires, in contrast to the United States, which numbered about seventy black millionaires in 1970. A similar disparity prevails in education. While the United States now has more than one hundred Negro universities and colleges, led by Howard University, in Washington, D.C., none has yet been established in all of Latin America, including Brazil, whose black population is larger than that of the United States.

In Hispanic America all persons of mixed blood—mulattoes, mestizos, and *zambos*—are an integral part of the population of their respective countries, along with Indians, creoles, and blacks. As a result of centuries of ethnic crossing, the racial problem is not as acute in Latin America as it is in some parts of the United States, where a certain ethnic homogeneity prevails. The whites often look upon their ethnic minorities as "strange," especially if they have different customs and physical appearance. Anglo-Americans, with notable exceptions, prefer that the "other" citizens become like them and act like them. Though the developing United States cosmopolitanism of the last one hundred years makes that psychological attitude difficult to justify, it exists nevertheless. It seems to be a reaction of the "old" Anglo-Americans to a perceived threat to their way of life. It also appears to be the cause of more than a few prejudices, which exist side by side with intellectual and economic liberalism. Some sociologists believe that the lack of tolerance indicates that the racial conglomerate has not yet fused into one people and that each ethnic or cultural group tries to impose its own attitudes and customs on the rest. Periodic clashes are the inevitable result. Other societies also experience these conflicts, even societies whose traditions are much older than those of the United States.

Blacks have played an important role in the development of the United States. During recent decades the black community has attained a high degree of spiritual cohesion through its dynamic activism. There are increasing numbers of black lawyers, judges, doctors, teachers, artists, writers, architects, dentists, federal and local government officials, military officers, technicians, merchants, and small industrialists. Their numbers are growing in education, science, television, and the press, as well as in entertainment, sports, religious life, and politics. Sometimes these facts surprise foreigners, who are accustomed to hear only about the social disparities and the violence reported in the press. When I observed in a Hispanic American seminar on inter-American cultural problems that in the United States there are black bishops, generals, and millionaires, my Latin colleagues expressed amazement. They told me that such progress was unlikely any time soon in Hispanic America because of the Negroes' "passivity"—and other circumstances they preferred not to mention.

The evident progress of blacks does not mean that their situation in the United States is satisfactory (the same may be said of some sectors of the white population—a fact that is sometimes overlooked). Despite various federal programs, such as the war on poverty, urban renewal, equal employment opportunities, and other measures, inequalities remain. The greatest obstacle that black and other minority groups from rural areas have to overcome is the painful adjustment to modern life in the great cities and a satisfactory community adjustment.

Interracial relations in the New World are not what they ought to be. Prejudices against blacks persist in both Anglo-America and Hispanic America, although they differ in form and intensity. In 1961 the Hispanic American anthropologist Juan Comas examined these prejudices in a study based on research by various experts in the field.[7] The work sheds an interesting light on the social attitudes toward Negroes in Brazil, which has a larger black population than

[7]Juan Comas, *Relaciones inter-raciales en América Latina, 1940–1960*, pp. 29–31.

that of the rest of Hispanic America together. The research merits special attention because of the comparisons made with the attitudes toward blacks in the United States.

According to the Brazilian scholar Costa Pinto, a racial prejudice in Brazil differs from that observed in the United States only in being markedly less intense. Oracy Nogueira, an anthropologist of Rio de Janeiro, holds that it is a difference not in intensity but in quality. He thinks the prejudice observed in Brazil is prejudice of kind—that is, prejudice based on the physical appearance of the individual. He labels that observed in the United States as prejudice of origin—that is, prejudice based on the supposition that a person is descended from a specific ethnic group even if he displays marked physical differences from that group. Another anthropologist, D. Ribeiro, who has studied ethnic and socioeconomic conditions in northeastern Brazil, says that "prejudice against Negroes and mulattoes exists and is manifested by the middle and upper classes as being based on stereotypes of racially and culturally inferior Negroes and an expression of resistance to racial mixture."

According to Comas, in the Caribbean nations a strong consciousness of color exists among whites and blacks and among mulattoes and blacks, although in varying degrees of intensity. The mulatto-black conflict is especially serious in the black Republic of Haiti, where the depreciation of the mulatto by his Negro progenitors is apparent. In the British Antilles, according to the Chilean anthropologist Alejandro Lipschutz, "the bourgeois mulatto looks down on the Negro worker and attributes the same defects to him that the Indo-American mestizo sees in the Indian." In the Dominican Republic, which has a preponderant mulatto population, racial prejudice is said to be minimal.

Discrimination is directed against blacks as well as Indians but differs in intensity from country to country with local conditions. Apparently Hispanic American discriminatory practices are manifested in the form of paternalism and the conviction that the abilities of Negroes are limited to manual tasks and that they have only a limited sense of responsibility in executing even those tasks. The attitude is sometimes open, sometimes hidden. It is not displayed toward the few black intellectuals and professionals, who are accepted by the mestizos and creoles.

The United States race problem is a favorite theme in Hispanic America, where there are many critics of the "gringos." Curiously, however, the black and Indian race problem in Hispanic American countries receives little practical attention, almost as though it did not exist, though everyone knows that it does and that it is very grave. In contrast to the situation in the United States, little effort is made to solve it. The inertia in this respect makes one conclude that, in general, the economic and educational situation of most United States blacks is much better than that of most of the indigenes and blacks in Hispanic America, particularly in the Andean nations, where the Indians live on the margin of national life. In the various Hispanic American countries blacks engage in the work reserved for the lowest class and are thus prevented from improving their socioeconomic level. Most of them live in extreme poverty and resignation to that lot.

Many Hispanic American and Anglo-American novels have portrayed the black with commendable understanding. Their authors are often far more perceptive about racial inequalities than are their respective societies or governments. It appears that the power of the novel sometimes penetrates the human heart more easily than an official mandate, thus serving as a useful instrument for the psychological mobilization of the oppressed.

From the appearance of Harriet Beecher Stowe's *Uncle Tom's Cabin* in 1852, the black theme has become an important preoccupation of North American writers. One thinks of such novelists as William Faulkner, Harper Lee, Sinclair Lewis, Warren Miller, Robert Penn Warren, John Howard Griffin, Lillian Smith, and Sarah Patton Boyle. The complex human relationships among the races and sexes as well as the aspirations of blacks are presented with equal ability by black American writers, such as Ralph Ellison, Richard Wright, James Baldwin, Le Roi Jones, William Edward Du Bois, James Weldon Johnson, and William Melvin Kelly.

Hispanic American writers too have presented the conditions of black life. Among the mestizo and creole writers who introduced the Hispanic American Negro novel were the Ecuadorian Demetrio Aguilera-Malta, with *Don Goyo* (1933); the Cuban Alejo Carpentier, with *Ecué-Yamba-O* (1933); the Colombian Bernardo Arías Trujillo, with *Risaralda* (1935); the Venezuelan Rómulo Gallegos, with *Pobre negro* (1937); and the Ecuadorian Alfredo Pareja Diezcanseco, with *Baldomera* (1938). Negro motifs appeared in Hispanic American fiction as early as the middle of the nineteenth century. For the most part, however, they were fragmentary.

Among the novels of the few contemporary black writers, the following are distinguished: *Over* (1939), by the Dominican Ramón Marrero Aristy; *Juyungo* (1943), by the Ecuadorian Adalberto Ortiz; *Nochebuena negra* (1943), by the Venezuelan Juan Pablo Sojo; *Tierra mojada* (1947), by the Colombian Manuel Zapata Olivella; *Las estrellas son negras* (1949), by the Colombian Arnoldo Palacio Mosquera; *Cumboto* (1950), by the Venezuelan Ramón Díaz Sánchez; and *El paraíso* (1958), by the Ecuadorian Nelson Estupiñán Bass. Also significant are the novels of the Puerto Rican Enrique A. Laguerre, which deal with a variety of ethnic subjects. Some of the black novels are equal in narrative quality to those of major Hispanic American writers. They go to the heart of the racial complexities with great authenticity. Lamentably, because they are not readily accessible, those works are almost unknown outside their respective countries and sometimes even within them.

Some novels deal with the great influence that blacks have had on their surroundings in the course of the centuries they have lived in America. It is pertinent to remark here that African cultural traditions are much more extensive in Hispanic America than in the United States, for the blacks were able to preserve their traditions there with fewer obstacles. They could better maintain their culture where they lived in dense, homogeneous groups. The African heritage weakened in regions where Negroes were subject to more intense acculturation. Thus in the coastal areas of Hispanic America there are still many black communities where African culture is very evident, especially in Colombia, Ecuador, Venezuela, the Guianas, and the islands of the Caribbean. I learned there that their preference for living on tropical coasts was at first a manifestation of their longing to return to their countries of origin, a longing that subsided in the course of time.

Zapata Olivella, a noted black writer of Colombia, stresses the attitude the black assumed in the acculturation process. Dispossessed of his own models in religion, language, customs, geography, and society, he was compelled to accept new ones imposed by his masters and the society into which he was thrust. A dual attitude emerged: on the one hand, he assimilated, appropriated, and nourished himself with the culture of his new environment. On the other, he suffered the imposition of his masters' standards or those that had already been imposed on the mestizo. Choice was impossible; he had to submit. But the attitude was different when he began to reconstruct his own religious, cultural, and affective elements. According to Zapata Olivella, the Negro was then absolute master in his spiritual participation. His norm was to adopt the Hispanic factor and assimilate it to his African roots, which were distant in geography but not forgotten in temperament and emotion.[8]

Aquiles Escalante reports, in *El negro en Colombia* that African influences are manifested on the Colombian coast in "Afro-Colombianisms," in music, in carnival masks, in instruments, and in certain funerary practices that show parallelisms with those of western Africa. Black music is especially interesting. According to Zapata Olivella, its ancestral character is more evident on the Colombian Caribbean coast than on the Pacific coast, where it has been subject to Spanish influences. He also ascribes to African origin certain fishing customs and terms still prevalent among Colombian blacks. The Venezuelan ethnologist Miguel Acosta Saignes, in *Vida de los esclavos negros en Venezuela*, says that the Africans have always held onto their music and songs, which still enrich Venezuelan folklore. They perform them with great joyousness during Christian festivals. Peter Claver, "Apostle of the Negroes" of New Granada, is especially venerated by them. Acosta Saignes provides valuable information about black customs relating to marriage, festivals, agriculture, mining, and fishing, as well as the kinds of punishment that caused the slaves to run away and live as fugitives in the "*cumbas*" (hideouts in remote parts of the jungle).

The blacks never grew entirely away from their ancestors with respect to their spiritual cohesion and fraternity. These ties explain how they managed to survive the bitterness of slavery: since they could not trust other ethnic groups, they relied upon each other. They longed for their homelands and thought constantly of returning to them. On the other hand, depending on local circumstances, many

[8]Manuel Zapata Olivella, *El Hombre Colombiano*, p. 173.

blacks also succeeded in establishing their own way of life. Zapata Olivella made interesting observations on their behavior in Colombia:

> On the Pacific coast, where the association between the white and Indian was limited, the Negro tried to reinforce his own reactions, imposing his character on assimilated forms. Therefore, in this region we find many elements of material African civilization, such as polygamy, the patriarchal polarization of family, and the cult of physical strength. Thus the Negro assumed, spiritually and physically, a position of conqueror vis-à-vis the Indian, and in many totally Negro communities they reject the incorporation of elements alien to the African tradition. On the Atlantic coast, by contrast, the cultural contact has served to promote early biological and cultural mixing among the whites, Negroes, and Indians.

A preference for brightly colored clothing, linguistic peculiarities, an inclination toward magic (voodoo), and distinctive work habits characterize in part the blacks in French- and Spanish-speaking countries. Through the tasks imposed by slavery, blacks sometimes transplanted their African customs into their South American environment. They "conquered" colonial Brazil by means of food and the dance, which became part of Brazilian folklore. Myths are often mixed with their religious practices, especially in Brazil. Other African traits are the movements of the dance, the lyricism of their music and poetry, and their imaginative stories of fantasy.

Some of these traits are also preserved among North American blacks, who display an extraordinary feeling for music, dance, and song. Their inimitable blues and spirituals were incorporated into United States tradition, and black jazz attained international fame, as did its great performers, notably Louis Armstrong and Duke Ellington.

Negroes in the United States have made significant contributions in other fields. The agricultural scientist George Washington Carver derived various foods from peanuts and soybeans, making inexpensive food available for millions of people. Two well-known blacks were awarded the Nobel Prize for Peace: Ralph Bunche (1950), the highest-ranking United States official of the United Nations from 1957 until 1971, and the Reverend Martin Luther King, Jr. (1964), the great leader of the nonviolent struggle for Negro political rights, who has been compared with Gandhi. Considerable credit goes to Sterling Brown, Mercer Cook, and Frank M. Snowden, Jr., humanists of Howard University, who revived the black past and discussed its present potential. Negro speech has had a significant impact on the language of the whites, particularly in the South. Black religious leaders have led the fight for Negro rights. The Southern Christian Leadership Conference (founded in 1957) has been influential in this struggle.

Resentment is evident among Negro intellectuals when whites speak of Negro American culture as a subculture. In their view the Negro contribution is equal to that of other ethnic groups, confirmed by the Negro's integration into the Anglo-American culture. Negro-American history and culture have been brought together in a university-level discipline known as black studies. Many young black intellectuals have embraced the black-nationalism movement, which emphasizes their African roots, and call themselves Afro-Americans. They have adapted African hair styles and clothing, notably the dashiki. Some black groups, in their pursuit of "Africanism," have accepted the Muslim faith. Many of the bonds between American and African blacks are tenuous; the distance of centuries and continents and the differing life-styles set them considerably apart. But the establishment of black-ruled states in Africa has inspired American blacks with racial pride and encouraged their political ambitions in the United States.

Since World War II new black voices have been heard in Caribbean America. They have revealed a spiritual communion with Africa, expressed in what has been termed *négritude* ("Negroism"). Applied originally to popular Negro art of the French Antilles, *négritude* gradually evolved into a cultural and artistic doctrine. The word *négritude* was first used in 1939 by the Martinique poet Aimé Césaire in *Cahier d'un retour au pays natal*. Césaire, the Senegalese Séder Senghor, Haitians Jacques S. Aléxis and Jean Price-Mars, León Damas, of French Guiana, and others have elaborated on the doctrine. *Négritude* vindicates black artistic and folklore values in the face of the disinterest that white Western culture has displayed toward them. Its objective is the recognition of the black spirit in Antillean creative life.

According to G. R. Coulthard, it is not surprising that *négritude* was born in the Antilles, whose Negro and mulatto populations lived within European culture but separated from many of its concepts. It was a "psychic alienation" that required something more attractive to counterbalance the black's sense of inferiority, which had been imposed on him by colonial and neo-colonial rule. Various American and European countries have taken up the concept of *négritude* as primarily a racial one. Coulthard, however, sees it as similar to Hispanic American indigenism, for both movements have in common the effort to restore to those groups their historic and cultural heritage.[9] To judge from rising expectations everywhere, *négritude* accommodates well to those aspirations.

The new doctrine is gradually being reflected in the works of black writers in Hispanic America, especially in Colombia, Ecuador, and Venezuela. They do not hesitate to add to it certain regional modifications, however. Thus the Ecuadorian writer Adalberto Ortiz says that *négritude* (which he Hispanized as *negritud* or *negrez*) rejects the past because it carries the connotation of slavery and alienation. For him, *négritude* "is not a passing phenomenon, for it has restored to us the legitimacy of belonging to African culture, while at the same time we are part of the Hispano-American and Indo-American cultures." In *La negritud en la cultura latinoamericana* he writes that to live in reaction to great sufferings and degradation is a good incentive for the pursuit of such a concept; "To look at it without dogmatism, *négritude* for us who are Americans cannot be a 'return to Africa' nor an exaggerated apology for African culture but is rather a process of ethnic and cultural mixing in this continent." He adds that it can be appreciated "not only in the physical manifestations of mestizaje but also in certain literary currents and very powerfully in popular music and in the beliefs and superstitions of rural Negroes."

Various studies of blacks in the New World, some of continental scope, treat them in their historical, cultural, and sociological aspects. Among such works the following are particularly noteworthy: *Los negros esclavos* (1916), by Fernando Ortiz; *Las culturas negras en el Nuevo Mundo* (1937), by Arthur Ramos; *Casa Grande e Senzala*

---

[9]G. R. Coulthard, "Parallelisms and Divergencies Between 'Negritude' and 'Indigenismo,'" *Caribbean Studies*, Vol. 8, No. 1 (1968).

(1934), by Gilberte Freyre; *An American Dilemma: The Negro Problem and Modern Democracy* (1944), by Gunnar Myrdal; *Slave and Citizen: The Negro in the Americas* (1947), by Frank Tannenbaum; *Minorities in the New World* (1958), by Charles Wagley and Marvin Harris; *La esclavitud en Hispano-américa* (1964), by Rolando Mellafe; and *Race Mixture in the History of Latin America* (1967), by Magnus Mörner.

Owing to the extensive racial mixing that has taken place in different parts of the New World, it is difficult to determine the size of the Negro population. Some demographers employ the functional term *Negroid* to denote dominantly Negro peoples. Statistical studies of that population include Negroes and mulattoes and possibly those whom Mellafe calls Afro-mestizos. According to statistical tables used by Marvin Harris, the Negroid population in the United States makes up 10 percent or more of the total population. In Brazil it is between 31 and 40 percent; and in the Guianas, between 51 and 60 percent.[10] In Venezuela the Negroid population is 31 to 40 percent; in Columbia it ranges between 21 and 30 percent; and in Ecuador it is about 10 percent. Among the major islands of Antillean America, the percentage of Negroid population in Puerto Rico is between 41 and 50 percent; in Hispaniola (the Dominican Republic and Haiti), Jamaica, and the Bahamas, between 91 and 100 percent of the total. It is obvious that a "minority" of such size and influence must be reckoned a vital influence in the New World.

[10]Harris, *Pattern of Race in the Americas*, pp. 130–31.

CHAPTER 10

THE PEOPLE OF THE TWO AMERICAS

Hispanic America and Anglo-America are drawn together by their common hemispheric history, aspirations for individual and collective liberty, and profound individualism. They obviously differ in many other traits that reflect their origins and attitudes. Each group had its own ethnic and cultural roots and acquired others through experience and living conditions. The more or less stable characteristics reveal, through their Spanish and English beginnings, their undeniably European origins.

In the formation of the New World character, the period marked by the separation of the colonies from their mother countries had a great impact. That political break, dating from the eighteenth century in the United States and the beginning of the nineteenth in Hispanic America, made it possible for the new countries to blaze new trails in behavior and thought. A climate was created for the psychological transformation of attitudes. It is interesting, therefore, to examine the phases that followed to determine the degree to which the two Americas took advantage of their new opportunities.

From the beginning of their independence, the Anglo-Americans continued their economic and social development but for some time neglected the cultural aspects. The United States emerged as the economic empire of the New World. They achieved that role by systematically capitalizing on the Industrial Revolution and their extraordinary mechanical abilities. They achieved economic and social balance through a more or less equitable distribution of income among most of the people. Anglo-American industry and initiative were of decisive significance. There is little in modern history to compare with the North American experience. Economic success has always interested the people of the United States more than intellectual glory; and doctrines have engaged their attention far less than popular well-being.

By contrast, for most of the nineteenth century the Hispanic American nations occupied themselves with almost continuous internal conflicts that weakened and impoverished them. The persistent latifundia system and social stratification prevented socioeconomic integration. Nevertheless, Hispanic America was becoming emancipated culturally. The process involved a gradual literary transformation rather than a mental emancipation, since it had to struggle for a long time with Spanish, French, Italian, and other influences. From the artistic fusion of all these elements, and as a reaction against the functionalism of literature at the service of the political and social struggles, a current of Modernism emerged, led by that Hispanic American genius Rubén Darío, who utilized Modernism for the poetic renewal of the Hispanic world, including Spain. Political authoritarianism and structural and social conservatism, systems inherited from the *peninsulares*, have stood in the way of complete emancipation. Moreover, the Hispanic Americans blame the Spaniards for some traits that they themselves cultivate.

The differences in goals of the various ethnic and cultural groups partly explain these phenomena, as do the different ways people have of reacting to the experiences of life. Hispanic Americans are generally characterized as "passionate," doctrinaire, and contemplative, while Anglo-Americans are commonly described as pragmatic, dispassionate, and realistic. Hispanic Americans are called visionaries endowed with romantic and somewhat dogmatic philosophical and cultural concepts. Anglo-Americans are characterized by empiricism, rationalism, and positivism, which guide them toward concrete goals in the cultural, as well as the material, sphere. The Hispanic American posture is often intransigent, while the Anglo-American is more likely to be conciliatory. Hispanic Americans (especially the intellectuals) surpass Anglo-Americans in their inherent *humanism*, while the latter excel in *humanitarianism* and zeal for education.

As individuals Anglo-Americans are characterized by an exploring and expansionist spirit, an optimism that emanates from self-confidence and the will to self-fulfillment. A similar spirit is reflected also in collective efforts, whether civic or industrial—a possible reflection of the pioneer era, when close cooperation was necessary for survival. The interrelation between optimism and risk is obvious. As a basic trait in a traditionally immigrant society, risk stimulates man to achieve well-being and also self-reliance. This attitude also stems from the old Puritan belief that work makes man happy and that he can hope for redemption only through the work of his hands. The concept is still deeply ingrained in the Anglo-American conscience, where it has been gradually fixed as a kind of national axiom.

Hispanic American activities, as befit the slower tempo of their ambience, are distinguished by gentleness and contemplative deliberation. In general, Hispanic Americans lack enthusiasm for commerce, especially in economically conservative environments and in countries with a rigid social structure that instills a certain measure of pessimism. In industralized areas and the more advanced agricultural areas where there is promise of better profits and hope for the future, activities are more animated. As a consequence of traditional social and labor customs, old economic practices still seem stronger in much of Hispanic America than new technical and scientific methods.

Hispanic American intellectuals and professionals take an opposite attitude. Their dynamism not only contributes to creativity but also counters the relative passivity in other areas—except, of course, the always agitated area of politics.

Among New World traits are some that can be traced to profound differences in attitudes toward work and labor. Those attitudes, which arrived with the colonists, are still very evident and act as determinants of the conduct of both Hispanic Americans and Anglo-Americans. After the Spaniards had gained dominion over American lands and the Indians, they demanded blind obedience from them and from the African slaves. Their ambition to conquer quickly changed to a will to command, manifested in the well-known colonial institutions of *encomienda* and *repartimiento*. The conquistadors received *encomiendas* of land—and the Indians living on it—in exchange for caring for and converting the indigenes to Roman Catholicism. Entrusted for life to the *encomendero*, and sometimes to his heirs, the land was legally the property of the crown, which could turn it over to the Indians when it was convenient to do so. The *repartimiento* was a means of utilizing native labor; the Indians were divided among the haciendas to work in exchange for some benefits (theoretically pecuniary).

Those systems of forced labor left lasting scars on the American spirit. Descendants of the creole aristocracy, as modern-day *latifundistas*, inherit that imperious will either in its original or in a somewhat modified form. The clan of landowners was augmented by mestizo proprietors during the political upheavals of the independence era. The Hispanic American attitude of command persists today not only among the landowners but also among many who have posts of responsibility in other fields. This imperious posture, part of the Hispanic authoritarian concept, recognizes the hierarchial distinctions in the various levels of position and society.

Among the northern English settlers, whose ranks were made up of farmers and artisans, voluntary cooperation prevailed. They themselves had to cultivate the land and work in the shops. From time to time circumstances required mutual cooperation, which drew them together for the common good. Indentured servants were able to earn back their passage to America, which their masters had paid. Having discharged their commitments through their labor, they enjoyed the rights of the other colonists. The attitude of master-slave prevailed in the South. There the dependence of the blacks on their planter-masters was similar to that of Indians and Negroes on the Spaniards in colonial Hispanic America.

Since most of the labor force in northern Anglo-America was white, the spirit of mutual cooperation for the benefit of all spread rapidly. It was adopted by the subsequent waves of immigrants to the United States. The parallel concept of work as the cornerstone of all life is well developed in the United States and is less capricious than in other parts of the New World. Moreover, today the Anglo-American attitude is to make mutual concessions in order to assure the spirit of cooperation that is so indispensable in a highly industrialized society. That does not rule out disputes, since the various groups in the work force know how to protect their rights through the unions, which are more effective than those in Hispanic America.

What are the basic traits that distinguish the people of the two Americas? The Hispanic Americans' contemplative attitude, their tendency toward metaphysical speculation, and their doctrinal preoccupations make them at times overly theoretical. The Anglo-Americans' pragmatism, rationalism and preoccupation with social reality often make them seem too practical.

These differences can easily be demonstrated in various fields. A good example is law. The Constitution of the United States, framed in the eighteenth century and eminently realistic, has functioned with modification to the present time. In contrast, how many constitutions based on superb foreign models have been written and cast aside in Hispanic American countries. They did not lack merit— quite the contrary. Their idealistic contents did not correspond to the realities of the people's lives and did not meet the needs of the new governments. The short-term alternatives seem to be to promulgate laws that have a chance of enactment and enforcement.

It is also necessary to take into account the different legal criteria in the two Americas. In Anglo-America the legislative act does not normally remain hidden in the laws but undergoes a process of implementation. In Hispanic America a gap frequently exists between the law as enacted and its application, which demonstrates the disparity in basic legal concepts.

The Anglo-American juridical system tries to apply the same standards to all citizens without distinction. Since no society is perfect, the system is subject to error and shortcomings. The system provides recourse for this in the United States. By and large justice is administered in accordance with constitutional precepts by which laws are constantly measured. The Anglo-American mind is very practical as well as idealistic, and by and large the legal and judicial system, rooted in Anglo-Saxon principles, serves its people well.

Hispanic American legislation also has some European roots, though they have now largely been superseded by New World concepts, especially in the civil law. Something remains also of the *Derecho Indiano*. In general, the Hispanic American codes are based on sound philosophical concepts of law and on humanitarian considerations (a possible explanation for the absence of the death penalty in Hispanic America). In their litigations the courts apply various theoretical criteria, whose "flexibility" often seems to dilute their force. Hispanic American tribunals are theoretically independent, but, in contrast to those in the United States, are often tied closely to the government.

Hispanic America abounds in philosophical idealism, which is evident in its intellectual and educational life, particularly in the literature. An example is the essay *Ariel* (1900), by the Uruguayan

José Enrique Rodó. The protagonist, Ariel, who symbolizes the idealism of Hispanic American youth, is contrasted with Caliban, who personifies Yankee materialism. *Ariel* was followed by Rodó's masterpiece, *Motivos de Proteo* (1909), an expression of reformist doctrine. His famous credo, "To live is to change oneself for the better," could have inspired a creative surge in Hispanic American thought. Instead, however, an excess of "spirituality" prevailed, supported by the stylistic mannerisms of Modernism. Rodó's idealism remains only a notable moment in the history of literature.

The Mexican essayist José Vasconcelos offered, in *La raza cósmica* (1925), a utopian vision of a new American race conceived on the base of worldwide *mestizaje*. He blamed the uncertain direction of Ibero-American philosophy on the ideological "atheism" of Hispanic America, a theme he elaborated in *Indología* (1927). There he advocated a philosophical movement founded on emotion as more appropriate to the Latin ambience than the imitation of "foreign" philosophical systems. He reproached Hispanic American pragmatism, which he considered inferior to North American pragmatism because it had not been defined in a philosophical school as it had in the United States. Disgusted with the corruption and the vague idealism of his revolutionary milieu, Vasconcelos saw the only salvation in the triumph of Christianity. His thinking was frequently contradictory but sagacious over all, reflecting the revolutionary exigencies of his times, when militant Marxism was demonstrated as incompatible with orthodox Catholicism.

The Dominican Pedro Henríquez Ureña demonstrated a similar restlessness in *La utopía de América* (1925). Wavering between realistic and utopian concepts, he nevertheless could recognize in specific incidents the tyrannies that have traditionally harassed Hispanic America. He attributed an important role to Ibero-American intellectuals, whom he considered greater redeemers of the people than some of the liberators of the era of independence. He, like Vasconcelos and Reyes (discussed below) had the notion that Hispanic America, owing to its progress toward cultural maturity, was close to creating the universal man. In other words he revealed a faith in a coming spiritual regeneration that would require an intellectual rebellion that would take in all elements of Hispanic American cultures. He held that literary creolism and indigenism are genuine continental manifestations. He also believed that the cultural isolation of America was illusory and thought that the Europeanizing currents in Hispanic American letters were beneficial.

Idealism joined with an aesthetic sensibility found its major expression in the works of the Mexican Alfonso Reyes, who was perhaps the most universal and at the same time most "American" of Hispanic American writers. In *Ultima Tule* (1942) he exalted the "American intelligence," which he saw as a distinctively American view of life manifested through multifaceted artistic works. He saw this intelligence in the heterogeneous "ethnic tonality" of the New World, in the adaptation of the colonists to the environment, and in their cultural contributions. He therefore sympathized with the pride of the *"Indianos'* aristocracy," which has always been strong in the "Aztec lands." He also emphasized the external inspirations of Hispanic America, claiming that "our constitutional utopias combine the political philosophy of France with the presidential federalism of the United States." Reyes, though a literary genius, was a dreamer with a grandiose vision of America's destiny. He saw the New World as a place where "a more equal justice, a better understood liberty, and a more complete and better distributed felicity among men" was realized in "a dream republic, a utopia."

Of course, not all is idealistic and visionary in Hispanic American artistic life. Some writers on "brown America" have expressed in stark and unadorned style the reality that is seen and lived. They have lamented social wounds and the economic injustices inflicted on the Indians. González Prada, Picón-Salas, Uslar-Pietri, and Octavio Paz exemplify such writers.

As early as 1908, Manuel González Prada, in *Horas de lucha*, denounced not only the fate of the South American indigenes but also the attitude of some whites who believed they had the right to determine which races were destined to decline and which would be elevated to greatness. He considered that attitude an intellectual "verdict" designed to suppress the yellow and black races. He blamed the *peninsulares* and Hispanic Americans for the primitive state of the Amerindians. He also pointed out the low state to which Haiti and Santo Domingo had fallen, attributing that condition to the faults of the "Latin race." He indignantly predicted that "the final destiny of this half of America is regression to primitive barbarism." His was a dramatically different view of the New World from that of Hen-ríquez Ureña or Reyes.

González Prada also spoke of relations among the various races of Hispanic America:

> When an individual rises above the level of his social class, he customar-ily becomes its worst enemy. During Negro slavery, no overseers were more brutal than Negroes themselves; actually perhaps no oppressors are so harsh toward the indigenes as the *Hispanized indigenes* themselves who are invested with some authority.

González Prada had faith that the Indian would redeem himself, but through his own strength, not through the humanization of his oppressor.

Forty years later psychological dualism was the theme of *El laberinto de la soledad,* in which Octavio Paz examined the motivations of the mestizos. That dualism he saw manifested in the closed-off reactions of mestizos confronting the world or their fellow human beings. They avoid the risks of frank communication, hiding their feelings and inventing falsehoods. In the end they have deceived themselves more than they have deceived others and have become entangled in a psychological maze.

According to Paz, the lie has a decisive importance in daily life, in love, and in friendships, and is exteriorized in human masks. He says: "Our suspicion provokes the foreigner. If our courtesy attracts, our reserve chills, and the unexpected violences that rend us, the convulsive splendor or solemnity of our fiestas, the cult of the dead finally disconcert the stranger." The effect is an almost Oriental inscrutability.

The Venezuelan Mariano Picón-Salas has dealt with the search for a historic and cultural consciousness. In his *Europa-América: Pregun-tas a la esfinge de la cultura* (1947), he mentioned the intellectual nonconformity and the pessimism of Hispanic America, contrasting them with the social conformity and optimism of Anglo-America. On Hispanic America at midcentury he commented: "in Hispanic American life there is a spiritual complexity and an ideological and esthetic cosmopolitanism that evades and makes difficult any clear definition." This evasion apparently did not inspire him with op-timism. Some of the contemporary Hispanic American poets and fiction writers he considered radically "romantic"—belonging to the "New Romanticism," which he described as "the total dissolution where all flows into and loses itself in the current of cosmic anguish in which there is no fixed element to take hold of."

Picón-Salas pointed to the sensuality, the sadness, the discontent, and the psychic discontinuity as characteristics of the "new" romantic current, which found its most turbulent expression in the enormously popular art of Pablo Neruda. Other traits he ascribed to the movement are idealization of horror and an arduous search for the pathetic. He noted also in some South American indigenous narratives overly minute physiological portrayals of the protagonists—an "excessive" realism that produced the effect of unreality. He pleaded for a balance between the thematic-descriptive and the spiritual that would combine poetry and reality. He noted, too, that efforts to bring together the popular and local and the elegant and Europeanized had not succeeded. He believed that a fusion of the national and the universal was necessary to produce a synthesis, a convincing expression of the totality of the Hispanic American experience.

The enigmatic political and cultural scene is particularly attractive to Hispanic American writers. In *En busca del Nuevo Mundo* (1969) the Venezuelan Arturo Uslar-Pietri discussed the antiquated European notion of Anglo-Saxon racial superiority. That notion for a long time fostered a sense of inferiority in Hispanic American people (who, it may be said in passing, felt themselves superior to the Anglo-Americans). Foreign prejudice had stemmed from a lack of comprehension of Indo-Spanish *mestizaje*, which had been viewed as a dilution of the ethnic and cultural "purity" of the *peninsulares*. Uslar-Pietri effectively tied cultural *mestizaje* to the new Mexican consciousness. A number of Hispanic American literary works emphasize it, especially those of the Modernist school at its best. New World consciousness is also apparent in the fusion of certain features in notable contemporary novels: attachment to custom, realism, symbolism, romanticism, surrealism, epic form, and magical background.

Uslar-Pietri dwelt on the foreign influences that for many years have been apparent in Latin America, particularly that of the United States. Others, largely political, come from the socialist world, principally the Soviet Union and China. While Anglo-American influences consist mainly of Latin imitations of customs, commercial products, and the utilitarian standards of a bourgeois society, the impact of Russia, socialist Europe, China, and North Africa is seen principally in revolutionary ideas. Thus Hispanic America is constantly exposed to two ideological extremes, capitalism and Marxism.

Uslar-Pietri saw in this situation the danger that Hispanic Americans could become the "vassals" of one ideology or the other. Politicians and intellectuals are constantly tested as they try to keep these influences in balance. More, it forces an examination of the cultural values of Hispanic Americans who do not feel drawn to any system that would not reflect their own mode of living and governing themselves. This dilemma has no easy solution. Simply confronting it requires a great deal of courage. Uslar-Pietri does not suggest to us what option Hispanic America is likely to choose, nor even which one it should choose. He does not believe in the Russian Revolution, nor does he trust the American way of life. Either choice would be "trying to make reality the falsification of reality." Therefore, he encourages Hispanic America not to give up its own heritage. The Third World concept has been popular for some time in Hispanic America. Its leaders are opposed to economic imperialism and the institutionalization of certain political and cultural forms. A reform movement of leftist and nationalistic tendencies, it has drawn considerable numbers of intellectuals into its ranks.

Added to the traits of Hispanic American culture noted by its critics, the following are observable in contemporary works of art and literature: intellectual idealism, often expressed in a visionary utopianism that approaches an abstract or emotional philosophy; a creative aesthetic ability; a psychological dualism that combines a simulation of feeling, a sense of moral corruption and the hope of spiritual regeneration; an optimism concerning political affairs; fear of ideological vassalage in the imitation of Anglo-American customs and adoption of its ulititarian values; and a certain suspicion in the acceptance of European literary styles.

Other traits attributed to Hispanic Americans are Americanist pride coupled with an ambition for universalism; ethnic and cultural dissonances that cause intellectual and political restlessness; egocentric and emotional nonconformity that often hinders collective enterprises; the strong desire for social realization along with adherence to traditional ways of life and behavior; a tendency toward verbal preciosity, sensuality, sadness, and the search for the pathetic; an attachment to the epic and the marvelous and to romantic sentiment that provides escape from day-to-day reality; the idealization of horror and various forms of heightened realism that sometimes transform reality into unreality; courtesy and affability of manner coupled with irresponsibility; and individual capriciousness that hinders organized effort.

In contrast, Hispanic Americans (and other foreign observers) point out Anglo-American idiosyncrasies, expressed in mental, social, and cultural attitudes. These characteristics are practicality and optimism in carrying out any enterprise, a product of deeply ingrained pragmatism; technical and scientific specialization to the neglect of the humanities; educational proletarianism; idealization of work to a degree that approaches a social cult; the almost mystic faith in collective enterprise; and the resulting occupational and social pressures that produce neurotic behavior and cause physical ailments resulting from stress, particularly cardiac illness, high blood pressure, and ulcers.

Other well-defined Anglo-American traits are accelerated social mobility, racial restlessness and population fluctuations in the labor force caused by industrial competitiveness; a growing conformity of attitude resulting from the uniformity of the national information media; weakening of personal initiative with the formation of great trusts; neglect of cultural matters because of excessive absorption in social and economic issues; absence of an intellectual and artistic traditionalism, which facilitates flexibility and originality of literary and artistic expression; impatience, brusqueness, and conventionalism resulting from the automation of industry and the ceaseless demand for ever more domestic commodities; and a degree of naïveté in foreign relations occasioned not so much by lack of good will as by lack of understanding of the complexity of international affairs.

Still other basic traits decisively distinguish the two Americas. They have been well described by distinguished Hispanic American observers. One was the nineteenth-century Chilean José Victoriano Lastarría, who described the differences between Anglo-America and Hispanic America at the dawn of independence: "While the habits and customs inherited from England by the North Americans led them by natural evolution to their political independence, the habits and customs inherited from Spain by the Hispanic Americans led them to a new colonialism." He also pointed out that the wars of independence led by the *caudillo*-liberators were nothing more than the substitution of "republican" absolutism for colonial despotism.[1] The *caudillos*' personal ambitions were more important to them than their peoples' liberty. This attitude can still be found today in various Hispanic American nations.

The people of the United States also had to struggle for independence, but they chose a different form for their republican government. They shed authoritarian colonialism principle and substituted for it the democratic system, which better served their collective interests. In Hispanic America the will of the people did not count then any more than it does now. Once they had achieved independence, the people of the United States followed an evolutionary course in their political and social development that conformed with their ideal. Hispanic Americans, however, preferred to adopt the course of revolution, which is still the means used to change governments in many countries of Hispanic America.

In the middle of the nineteenth century the Argentinian Domingo Faustino Sarmiento, after a visit to the United States, where he observed a social, political, and educational structure more advanced than the Hispanic American one, offered this brief analysis:

> Yankee civilization was the work of the plow and the primer; the cross and sword destroyed South American civilization. There they learned how to work and to read; here, to be idle and to pray. There the conquering race introduced the virtue of work; here, it confined itself to vegetating in the bureauracracy or in parasitism.[2]

Perhaps all was not idleness and praying among the Hispanic Americans, just as not all Yankees were concerned with plow and primer. The people of both Americas had to pursue many activities. Sarmiento, however, judging the tree by its fruits, wanted to emphasize the contemplative and religious ambitions of Hispanic America by contrasting them with the socioeconomic and educational

[1]José Victoriano Lastarría, *Recuerdos literarios* (Santiago, 1885).
[2]Domingo Faustino Sarmiento, *Conflicto y armonía de las razas en América* (Buenos Aires, 1883).

ones of the Anglo-Americans. Since Sarmiento's time the Hispanic American bureaucratic inclinations have increased to a greater degree than among Anglo-Americans, for few Hispanic Americans pursue industry as the Anglo-Americans do. Sarmiento viewed the enormous progress of the United States as resulting from the flood of immigration. He pleaded for a similar demographic movement in Argentina, which since then has materialized in an influx of predominantly Latin Europeans of non-Hispanic stock.

Sarmiento's attitude and that of other Argentinian, Chilean, and Peruvian thinkers toward the United States were dubbed *nordomanía*, an admiration for the achievements reached by means of "Nordic"—that is, Anglo-Saxon—industriousness and homogeneity, particularly that of North America. Because of the inter-American political complexities of recent decades, *nordomanía* has lost its impact among Hispanic Americans, and for some time "anti-Yankeeism" has been the fashion.

Hispanic Americans, like Spaniards, are said to rely more on the heart than the mind, a circumstance that explains the emotionalism of their individual and collective reactions. It often takes them from one extreme to another, with resulting paradoxes. It also provokes extreme flights of imagination, notable as much in prose as in poetry, particularly in polemical writing. As a highly contemplative people, Hispanic Americans are inclined not only to mystical thought but also to every sort of abstract speculation, which gives them free rein to promote original attitudes and cultural and political concepts. Their idealism is frequently divorced from reality, from an awareness of the complexities of the human condition. The practical solutions they prefer to leave to the state. That attitude relaxes individual initiative and reinforces governmental authoritarianism.

Hispanic Americans often place more importance on political and cultural activities than on social improvement, which is an absorbing concern of Anglo-Americans. The dominance of the authoritarian principle, rooted in the intellectual absolutism inherited from the *peninsulares*, is apparent in many aspects of Hispanic American life. That almost dogmatic absolutism often hinders Hispanic Americans in their acceptance of changes that could lead them into a more rapid evolution. The Hispanic American attitude, retaining some of the traits of traditionalism and custom, at the same time shows a species of emotional nihilism, a curious mixture of frequently contradictory elements that often makes it difficult to arrive at important decisions.

The psychic inconsistencies that develop within the people are not infrequently responsible for the agony that is conducive to vacillation and promotes intellectual escapism. This phenomenon may arise from the frustrations of those who, considered mentors by their people, often find themselves caught in an ideological vortex. The only remedy left to them is to express their ideas in another form or suppress them completely. Of course, there are also those who are spiritually rebellious, reflecting the combativeness that is an almost universal trait.

Hispanic America today finds itself in a serious ideological crisis. On one side are various elements of cultural, economic, and religious traditionalism; on the other is a strong radical pressure, both socially and politically Marxist, that combats the status quo. Which of these tendencies is Hispanic American civilization going to follow?

The Anglo-American mind, perhaps less complex than the Hispanic American, is characterized by intellectual and theological liberalism inherited from the English and transformed into a uniquely New World philosophy. This liberalism provided for almost limitless investigation and invention that both fostered and nourished determinism and evolutionism. Anglo-Americans are little disposed to metaphysical abstractions, having adopted rationalism, the Puritan ethic, and pragmatism as their philosophical base. The philosophy of the pragmatist John Dewey also incorporates, however, aspects of idealism, notably in the advocacy of universal education and in concern for human well-being. In the course of time pragmatism has been adopted to serve and motivate progress in every activity, including business.

In their daily affairs Anglo-Americans are psychologically conditioned to a technological civilization resulting from the cultivation of the sciences and mechanical inventions. Projects are carefully calculated and carried out with confidence and initiative. North American dynamism is intimately related to a permanent industrial revolution that has been followed by social and cultural evolution. Standardization of the means of production and the way of life carries the danger, however, of social conformity, which weakens individuality. The utilitarianism of the United States varies in accord with the cultural level of individuals, and therefore the pecuniary concepts among them are unequal. A close connection exists between Protestantism and capitalist prosperity that had its beginnings in the Reformation. Rejecting certain dogmas, ecclesiastical hierarchy, and social norms, the Reformation opened the door to theological and intellectual liberalism. Protestantism, though not generally opposing the political structure, stimulated economic productivity, and gave attention to bettering the environment. It also, however, deprived society of no little joy of life and looked with suspicion on cultural activities. In the modern era that attitude has been modified.

The interdependence of various social sectors is rooted in the frontier ambience of cooperation and compromise, which facilitates the settlement of disagreements, especially in labor matters. In the 1960's and early 1970's the United States was the scene of upheavals in the areas of civil and human rights, particularly of blacks, women, and Indians, as well as an antiwar movement that had no parallel in the nation's history. Most of the conflict was expressed in peaceful demonstrations and court suits, but occasional riots and outbreaks of civil disobedience were evidence of the intensity of the movement. It is a struggle, in essence, to force change in "static" elements of Anglo-American society. It is likely to continue for decades, providing a series of stern tests of Anglo-American civilization and institutions.

CHAPTER 11

TWO CULTURAL ORIENTATIONS

The term *cultural orientation* applies both to intellectual and artistic life and to the educational system of the society. The cultural orientation of the colonial era was notably divergent in the two Americas.

In Hispanic America the upper-class Spaniards, the creoles, and a few mestizos early established an advanced culture, while the vast majority remained ignorant and unlettered. This condition—education and cultural advantages for the few—persisted beyond independence and is still evident to some degree in the countries of Hispanic America. The Anglo-Americans generally neglected cultural matters during the colonial era but did not abandon them entirely. Their concerns, especially in the northern colonies, tended to be religious rather than educational. In the nineteenth century, however, public education was established in the United States. The result was a cultural orientation that now includes most of the population.

While the Hispanic Americans generally favored the traditional education of elite groups, the Anglo-Americans undertook the education of the majority. The difference in objectives was reflected above all in primary education. The people of the two Americas are divergent in their views on whether it is preferable for the nation's masses to know how to read and write or to have a well-educated minority in the midst of millions of illiterates. Anglo-Americans have chosen the former course; Hispanic Americans, the latter. A much greater proportion of young people receive an education in Anglo-America than in Hispanic America. If we agree that education promotes the integration of the people into their culture, we must conclude that in Hispanic America education remains exclusive in the intellectual sense.

In the United States, in spite of racial inequalities, the law provides for public education for everyone without exception. Indeed, education is compulsory, and families that neglect to send their children to school are subject to fine and imprisonment. The opposite is true in many Hispanic American countries, where the available schools and teachers can provide education for only a limited number of school-age children. The rest remain unlettered. It is estimated that in some nations as much as 50 percent of the population does not know how to read or write.

In Hispanic America education both common and higher, is controlled by the government, which also controls other areas of cultural life. In the better-developed countries there are private institutions of learning, but these too cater to the upper classes. For the most part education depends on official support of one form or another. The same situation applies to the training of specialists and technicians in their own countries and abroad, as well as to inter-American scholarship exchanges. Examples are the scholarship program of the Organization of American States, programs of government scholarships that are offered in almost all countries, and the programs of the Conference of Buenos Aires, of UNESCO, and others. In many countries the publication of scholarly books depends on government subsidy, and cultural agencies designed to promote intellectual and artistic life also operate under government aegis or that of a semiofficial body.

In Anglo-America primary, secondary, and higher education is publicly maintained, though many independent schools operate through private support and tuition. Universities also have private and federal-government support for scientific and humanistic research. Private foundations such as Carnegie, Ford, and Guggenheim, which make multimillion-dollar donations to education, do not at the present time have counterparts in Hispanic America, where individuals who control vast fortunes display an indifferent attitude toward education. United States generosity is not limited to scholarships for its own citizens only but is extended to foreign scholars, including Hispanic Americans. The advancement of science, technology, and the arts receives a far greater stimulus in Anglo-America than in Hispanic America.

There are some basic differences between Hispanic American and Anglo-American universities. There are few career professors in Hispanic American universities, and only high university administrators are employed full time. Generally the teachers are prominent professionals, lawyers, physicians, engineers, dentists, writers, and journalists. They are real "cultural missionaries," considering their part-time teaching an honor and a patriotic duty. Because they are not well paid, they devote most of their time to their professions. In Anglo-America most professors are devoted exclusively to their university careers and are able to carry out full-time teaching and research programs. United States and Canadian universities often invite foreign teachers to serve on their faculties. Thus Hispanic professors play an important role in promoting knowledge of Peninsular and Hispanic American culture in the United States. Similarly, United States teachers hold visiting professorships in various Hispanic American universities.

University curricula differ in the two Americas. In addition to focusing on the traditional academic subjects in the humanities, Hispanic American universities are gradually adding modern science and even technical courses. United States universities, while offering traditional programs in the humanities, also specialize in science, technology, and business. Interest in international affairs is demonstrated in specialized studies of Hispanic America, Africa, Asia, and Europe. Hispanic American universities, in an effort to prepare their students for the complexities of modern life, favor the newer subjects in the social sciences, which complement humanistic and scientific courses of study.

Why have the universities in the two Americas taken different directions? It is well known that the launching of the Soviet Sputnik in 1957 accelerated the revision of programs in common schools, especially in mathematics in the United States. Revision at the university level was mainly in the sciences, but there was also unexpected support for the humanities as a key to understanding modern civilizations. That shift was an example of the intellectual flexibility of the United States. Although Anglo-American universities, like Hispanic American universities, are molded on European institutions, the new reforms bear little resemblance to the traditional European spirit.

Hispanic American universities want to keep abreast of new cultural and educational movements, and consequently interest has revived in modernizing academic programs. The interest in university reform is not new, however, but dates from the famous 1918 "manifesto" of the University of Córdoba, in Argentina. It supported not only academic freedom but especially the modernization of instruction through the inclusion in the curriculum of modern sciences and other subjects closely related to contemporary life. The Córdoba movement was not unique; similar proposals appeared in Mexico, Chile, Uruguay, Colombia, Ecuador, Venezuela, Peru, and Bolivia. All were manifestations of reformist intent, but the realization of that intent is sometimes hampered by complicated internal conditions. University instruction in both Americas has been for some time in a state of fluctuation because of social unrest.

The present tendency toward reforming academic programs to meet the needs of the nuclear age is evidence of a new direction in cultural orientation. Anglo-America arrived at its unique culture gradually, emphasizing social well-being. North Americans are able to provide their intellectual and artistic life with adequate possibilities for development. Though they may seem to be somewhat unselective, cultural influences are accessible to nearly all the people. Hispanic America chose a different road. There the cultural life has a much more personal nature. The literary world is an example. Though much of the Hispanic American literary production is brilliant, the quality is uneven. Writers write principally to satisfy their own ambitions, even though they consider their work a cultural mission, and many have to pay the cost of publishing their works. Such circumstances place Hispanic culture in such an exclusive and personal situation that it develops only within limited circles. Anglo-American writers, whose subject matter is varied, often deal with matters that awaken general interest. If they are "good," they are assured of publishers and readers. Composers have the same advantage. Many of them establish direct contact with the public, linking their work to an almost limitless cultural base.

It may be said, in essence, that Hispanic America displays a tendency toward cultural elitism while Anglo-America tends toward cultural egalitarianism. Thus Hispanic America boasts that it approaches an aesthetic culture that contrasts with the scientific and technological culture of the United States. The culture of each America bears its own indelible spiritual stamp.

Culture, in the purely intellectual and traditional sense, is the maximum expression of a civilization. The terms *culture* and *civilization* have a similar connotation and, by the definitions of cultural anthropology, include a number of spiritual and material elements. That plurality of ingredients makes it perhaps more appropriate to analyze civilization as a broad sociocultural phenomenon. If we accept the modern concept of civilization, with its inseparable moral, social, and technical elements, we may further inquire, What are the characteristics of the two great American civilizations in respect to their internal structure and intellectual mobility?

Hispanic American civilization may be considered a vertical civilization because of the stratified social structure with its economic and educational spread between the upper and lower classes. The well-educated minority easily assimilates the cultural values, which are scarcely comprehensible to the uncultivated masses, who look upon the educated minority as somewhat "magical." This intellectual distance constitutes a barrier to the expansion of civilization. There is thus a certain exclusivity in the Hispanic American culture. It inspires pride especially among the learned and among the artists, who feel superior to the common folk.

The presence of this cultural gap has not until recently stimulated the less privileged groups to try to close the gap. In recent decades a new cultural influence has been noted. It is exemplified in efforts to cut the ties that still link the Hispanic American present to its colonial past. Such circumstances have nothing to do with the creative vigor of Hispanic America. Witness the growing number of figures who have achieved international reputations, especially in letters and the arts. What Hispanic American culture lacks in popular appeal it more than makes up in ideological breadth and humanistic quality.

Anglo-American civilization has a horizontal character that is manifested in the more or less uniform public education of most members of the population and in the people's capacity for assimilating cultural values. Because of the unusual ethnic diversity and the incessant migratory movements of individuals and workforces, the process of social equalization still leaves much to be desired. But of the popular assimilation of the culture there is no question. Free from the traditionalist complex and endowed with an intense curiosity about diverse areas of human knowledge, Anglo-Americans absorb that knowledge as rapidly as their "ingestion" will allow. The procedure of drinking in knowledge from many sources is characterized by empiricism and, therefore, experimentation that yields many positive results.

In the search for new paths of progress an ideological transformation took place in Anglo-American creative vigor, social mobility, interest in science and technology, the "democratic sense," and absorption in international affairs. Utilitarian objectives are still more prevalent than humanistic ones. Apparently that is an inevitable phenomenon in a relatively young society that does not always revere the European roots from which it sprang. On the contrary, there is evident in all fields of activity an ideological revisionism that provides an element of mental freshness and adaptability. The availability of education aids in the transmission of the culture. What Anglo-American civilization lacks in humanistic refinement it makes up for in diffusion of that civilization among the people, in technological inventiveness, and in scientific planning.

These evaluations are not mine alone. In comparing Anglo-America with Hispanic America, the Cuban writer Jorge Mañach once said to North Americans: "You were born to dissension and invention; we, to tradition and convention. You possess a practical attitude toward life; we, a religious and aesthetic one. You are more technical, and we are more philosophical." The Argentinian writer Héctor Murena emphasized the neglect of science and technology in Hispanic America. At the same time he called attention to their development in the United States at the expense of the humanities. Murena related the infinite will for knowledge to a "Faustian civilization." The "Faustian" will of the United States lies in its insatiable scientific "thirst."

The most original and perhaps the most appropriate comment about the profiles of the two cultural groups came from the Mexican philosopher Leopoldo Zea. In his historical and philosophical analysis Zea concluded that "the Saxons are sons of modernity, and the Hispanic people of the Middle Ages." In other words, Anglo-Saxon concepts were transformed by the Anglo-American experience, while Hispanic Americans tend to cling to medieval patterns of thought and attitude.

A penetrating observation on the relationship between mechanical invention and the spiritual progress of the United States came from Colombia's Gonzalo Restrepo Jaramillo: "Exaggerated idealists have been accustomed to regard the mechanistic culture in which the North Americans excel as something of little worth; nevertheless, it exercises a capital influence on the destiny of a people without excluding the highest spiritual values." The author was referring specifically to the utilization of the printing press and of the steamboat in United States progress. He saw in the enormous progress of the United States and its growing civilizing influence on other peoples the embryo of a new universal culture. In his prophecy Restrepo Jaramillo anticipated by twenty years Jacques Maritain, who in his work *Reflections on America* made the same prediction. The Colombian called the new tendency "Anglo-Saxon culture," while the French philosopher called it "American Humanism." The similarity of the visions of these two intellectuals is surprising. I do not believe that the Anglo-Americans, with their intellectual modesty, have given serious attention to the suggestion. They are, however, aware of their technical and scientific advances.

Hispanic America achieved political emancipation before mental emancipation, with the result that it remains tied to a certain traditionalism in political and cultural matters. That is not to say that Hispanic Americans have lingered on the road to intellectual progress. Quite the contrary. Their progress is manifested in varieties of Romanticism, Positivism, Modernism, Realism, Existentialism, and other isms to be found in Hispanic American literary currents. Perhaps it is unimportant that those tendencies have European origins. It is important to note the Hispanic Americans' eagerness for cultural diversity, which favored spiritual change, that clashed with orthodoxy.

Preference for metaphysical speculation appears to provide Hispanic American intellectuals with moral force and psychic relief, but it separated them from the reality of daily affairs and allowed them to follow instead the road to intellectual perfection. Apparent at the same time is a revisionist tendency in educational and cultural mobility. Depending on external conditions, that mobility sometimes acquires the speed of revolution rather than spiritual evolution. Its reflections are also extended to the sphere of social transformation. It seems a poorly coordinated, even chaotic tendency, though it is a vigorous one, as shown by efforts to find new means of literary and artistic expression. This cultural renewal will contribute to mental emancipation and in turn the evolution of a truly modern Hispanic American civilization.

Anglo-America, partisan of egalitarian concepts, again followed a different road. Utilizing only a part of the English inheritance (largely moral concepts) and with a civilization that was basically anti-traditionalist, Anglo-America was disposed to accept heterodox ideas that gradually lessened its former insular character. It has accumulated many more concepts from the ethnic and cultural influx of the past one hundred years. Contemporary Anglo-American thought has been able to develop its own mode, which gave rise to the pragmatism that today guides almost all Anglo-American activities. Intellectual liberalism permits the people of the United States to absorb useful foreign ideas and adapt them to their own purposes.

The emancipation of the Anglo-American mind is an organic evolutionary process that is supported by frequently revolutionary methods employed in a more or less peaceful way and with the total cooperation of society. The egalitarian attitude also, however, led to uneven progress. Some brilliant achievements have tended to mask or overwhelm mediocre ones. The means and methods of communication that sometimes overpower the culture they transmit promote an almost anonymous civilization. That anonymity is manifested in the standardization of manners, of life-style, and even of literary models. The tendency is dangerous; it could lead to stagnation of the characteristic Anglo-American intellectual and social dynamism.

A comparison of the two cultures according to the influence of each in its own area is also an absorbing approach. In Hispanic America, which is distinguished more by the diversification of its culture than by its geography, it is difficult to make generalizations about the cultural standards shaped by ethnic structure and regional social conditions. Educational and cultural activities of the white nations of the River Plate, Chile, and Costa Rica often draw them close to the currents of Latin Europe. Through attachment to the land, the life of mestizo regions, such as Central America, Mexico, Ecuador, Peru, Bolivia, Colombia, Venezuela, and Paraguay, reflects a genuinely New World culture, an original "style." By and large the civilization of mestizo Hispanic America proceeds out of historic and current experience. Its art is produced by talented groups with similar literary and artistic aspirations. The high literary quality of their works has brought international recognition, including, for example, the prestigious Nobel Prize to Gabriela Mistral, Miguel Ángel Asturias, and Pablo Neruda.

Owing to individualism and the Hispanic temperament, cultural trends do not always concur; some reflect little or no popular feeling, while others, esoteric in nature, seem totally unrelated to reality. Outside the urban centers public education is still inadequate, and culture has not been popularized on a national scale. Hispanic American culture is still a limited culture. It is restricted principally to those who can read and write, excluding large sectors of the population, especially in the Andean countries. Hispanic American culture prides itself on its qualitative rather than quantitative values. Intellectual perfection does not have much to do with an average Hispanic American.

Also noticeable is the shifting of cultural trends in Hispanic America. Urbanization of the capitals of Mexico, Venezuela, Colombia, Peru, and Chile exerts not only a social but also a cultural impact. The influx of anonymous new migrant masses has caused demographic complexities and ensuing ideological confusions that have made it difficult to identify these drastically transformed capitals culturally. Some call it cultural anonymity. It appears that the cultural image of some of the larger countries is slowly shifting from the metropolitan areas to the provinces. The provincial areas are less deeply involved in ideological and demographic struggles, and their cultural development is therefore able to follow its own path with relatively little interference. Those areas have preserved more of the traditional traits. Also significant is the growing number of recognized writers and artists from the provincial areas. This trend of cultural radiation, whether temporary or not, may have the salutary effect of saving jeopardized national values. These observations refer, of course, to Mestizo America and not to the River Plate region, for Buenos Aires and Montevideo have long been the zealous self-appointed "custodians" of the creole culture of their respective nations.

What one notices in the United States at first glance is the almost continuous experimentation in education. Technology and scientific research bear the same experimental stamp. The extent of public education and "popular learning" is expressed in a conspicuous cultural proletarization that is unique in history. The typical United States citizen displays it in his compulsory public education, in his fondness for sports, and in his newspaper reading and television viewing. It cannot be denied that among the working masses are heard echoes of anti-intellectualism. That dates from pioneer times, when a strong arm counted for more than intellect. Many people who did not have the chance for a good education and are envious of the intellectuals send their children to colleges and universities. Their ambition thus promotes continual cultural betterment.

The Anglo-American professionals and intellectuals continue their expected growth with adequate or more than adequate remuneration, which also attracts the best foreign specialists to the country. Some intellectuals, for reasons of aethetics or cultural nonconformity, voluntarily remain in academic or personal isolation. The growing numbers of Anglo-American writers and, especially, scientists who have been awarded the Nobel Prize attest to the international recognition of the cultural achievements of the United States.

It is interesting to note the divergent attitudes taken by Hispanic Americans and Anglo-Americans toward their intellectuals, scientists, and artists. In Hispanic America, in spite of the gap between the cultivated minority and the unlettered masses, all levels of society render tribute to the learned, the erudite, and the artistic. In recognition of their individual or national merits, the people entrust them with administrative, educational, and diplomatic posts. Frequently they reward them with decorations. When they return to their countries after time abroad, ceremonies are held in their honor. When they die, state funerals may be held to render homage to their contributions to national life. In general, Hispanic American peoples of all classes treat their intellectuals with a certain admiration and affection. The fact remains, however, that some distinguished men of letters in Hispanic America have been victims of lamentable neglect and that it is still difficult for some to earn an adequate living with the pen. Many intellectuals, therefore, also take part in politics, a practice that differentiates them from their Anglo-American colleagues.

In Anglo-America the attitude toward intellectuals does not differ from that toward anybody else. Although some of them occupy important public posts, the learned and the artists enjoy a limited respect, and their reputations are largely confined to their own cultural circles. There is still a certain suspicion of them that borders on disparagement, an attitude held over from the pioneer era. The present lack of recognition of intellectuals is partly reflected in the scale of salaries, which is sometimes higher for laborers, craftsmen, and technicians than for university professors. In North America prestige is still a matter of income rather than intellectual achievement. In the United States technicians and scientists, motion-picture and television actors, athletes, industrialists, and preachers who run halfway around the world reviving the faith are the ones who enjoy the highest regard.

The attitude of both Americas toward their learned men is highly symptomatic. Hispanic American nations accord great respect to their artistic creators of culture, while designating only meager funds in their budgets for that same culture. Anglo-America, because of its material wealth, spends lavishly for educational and cultural objectives but displays less regard for the humanities, principally supporting the sciences. To repeat, the United States attitude toward cultural matters seems more humanitarian and less humanistic, while the Hispanic American posture seems more humanistic and less humanitarian. Although the validity of this thesis can be disputed, tendencies displayed by both cultures seem to confirm it. Meanwhile, pragmatic ideology is prevalent on one side, while on the other an excess of humanistic idealism predominates. We know that Anglo-America's preoccupations rest on economic matters while those of Hispanic America are based principally on political affairs. These circumstances explain the strange roads that culture takes in the greater part of the New World.

Because of the disparity in Hispanic America between urban and rural intellectual attainments, the limitation of academic education to select groups, and the strong regional ambitions and rivalries, Hispanic American civilization produces heterogeneous cultural manifestations that fail to hold society together. This Hispanic character presents a cultural tendency *sui generis*, colored by mental absolutism, possibly because of its Iberian heritage of religious dogmatism, its cultural exclusivity, and its political tradition of authoritarianism and revolution. It is a kind of idealism motivated by spiritual considerations and by a metaphysical thrust for intellectual perfectionism and aesthetic enjoyment within the aspirations of the elite. At times the idealism radiates outward, but because it lacks a genuine or relevant goal, it does not bring expected results. It simply withers. Idealism in the greater part of Hispanic America seems to have as its mission achieving the aspirations of small groups. It has an esoteric exclusivity. However, among these cultivated minorities appear at times a universal ideology and a sense of racial or continental destiny. It proceeds from ethnic pride and individual ambition. Frequently unpleasant reality is relegated to second place.

Though it has yet to solve the racial-discrimination problem, among others, Anglo-American civilization has achieved a high degree of homogeneity in culture and custom. The reasons have been enumerated earlier—mass education and popular culture, which often lack aesthetic values. Many cultural "leaders," especially writers, musicians, and artists, aim their work toward the "average" North American. Refinement in the authentic cultural sense is relatively scarce. Standards are higher among the learned, the professors, writers, and artists, who constitute a link between culture and the people of the United States. The abundance of books in economical editions greatly facilitates their availability to the general public.

A tendency toward rational investigation has always inclined Anglo-Americans toward intellectual flexibility. Philosophical and theological speculation have never "interfered" with inventiveness and scientific achievements. These elements integrate the organic process with cultural development. Their collective dynamism perhaps explains the increasing receptivity to the humanities, which will, it is hoped, counter the utilitarian spirit that still saturates North American life. Instead of being guided by metaphysical speculations, Anglo-Americans use the empirical method as most appropriate to the betterment of their social condition. Anglo-Americans are also advocates of instrumentalism and positivism, systems that are suitable to their creative individuality. Another feature is the minimal nationalism in the United States, in contrast to the nationalistic fervor of Hispanic American—and European—countries.

Salvador de Madariaga and Julián Marías have made acute observations about cultural tendencies in the two Americas. Their judgments also have philosophical and social implications as they are viewed from historical and geographical perspectives.

Madariaga observed in *Latin America Between the Eagle and the Bear* that the Socratic-Christian tradition of Europe is older and stronger in Hispanic America than in Anglo-America. Moreover, the Hispanic ambience tends to produce greater sensitivity to elusive and subtle values than does the empirical and positivistic Anglo-American society. A certain sense of Hispanic superiority to some Anglo-American concepts is implied. However, Madariaga balances the view by contrasting Hispanic emotionalism with North American rationalism.

He believes that the roots of emotionalism lie in a supportive religious devotion that is unfathomable to North Americans. Madariaga has doubts, however, about the depth of Catholicism in Latin America. According to him, religion is observed there more as a rite than as a faith or a moral discipline. He does not, therefore, share the opinion frequently heard that the Catholic atmosphere is a bulwark against communism. He believes that the contrary is true: the Catholic atmosphere can favor the growth of Marxist ideology. He cites as examples Catholic France and Italy, which have the most powerful Communist parties in the free world. (It can be added that in 1970 the Marxist Salvador Allende was elected president of the Republic of Chile. That country, like the rest of Hispanic America, is Roman Catholic.)

Julián Marías, in *Los Estados Unidos en escorzo*, makes original observations about Anglo-American idiosyncrasies and customs. Of those, perhaps the outstanding is homogeneity, which results from common usage, beliefs, ideas, evaluations, and pretensions. This fusion of so many races, religions, tongues, and customs greatly impressed Marías, who wondered why an analogous development had not occurred in Hispanic America.

Another characteristic Marías mentioned is the widespread North American "solitariness." He saw its manifestations in all Anglo-Americans, from the first colonists to the present-day immigrants. Alone, filled with nostalgia for the mother country (which led them to name places in the new land for ones in the old), all were, however, resolved to remain in the new. The observation is not original, but Marías' analysis was accurate: "In North America *a society* has been set up in isolation with respect to Europe and to the indigenous; and that is what expands, grows and in its way keeps on incorporating other small ethnic groups." The immigrant majority was incorporated into an established society, which imposed its way of life on the new citizens. Thus Anglo-American homogeneity increased as the new immigrants gradually drew away from their Old World past. This is in essence the process of Anglo-Americanization that is still going on.

The Anglo-American "separateness" has always been expressed in the large number of citizens who have lived more or less isolated from centers of population, at times even in remote places. An independent attitude is associated with that sort of life. Marías therefore had several reservations about theories of North American conformism, though he did not deny its presence. Customarily that conformity is seen as an attitude of tolerance and acceptance of matters that do not deeply affect the people. But at the same time there exist discrepancies, nonconformity, and independent criteria that are inferred from the forces of the social structure. Marías concluded that "the North American *dissents from within* but depends on society as a whole in order to oppose a fraction of it; consequently there is scarcely anything that cannot be disputed." Marías also had observations about the way of life of Anglo-Americans. He believed that "North American life has had and still has a *minimum of the experience of living together*," which he attributed to the relative isolation from the world in which the Anglo-Americans lived for decades. That isolation also seems to be related to friendships, which are less intimate among Anglo-Saxons than among Hispanic peoples. It also is seen in the intellectual provincialism of many Anglo-Americans.

Marías also made an important observation about the average Anglo-American man. According to him, "The average man in the United States is not a fictional convention with traits taken from the top 10 percent of society but is a composite of the whole population." Marías did not approve the disdainful attitude of many Europeans toward Anglo-American ideas and preferences, because he knew that the European intellectuals do not represent the masses of their countries but small, select minorities. Marías' observation coincides with

Jacques Maritain's. Both authors have pointed out that many Europeans who visit the United States do so with opinions already formed. The same applies to other foreigners.

Anglo-American cultural standards are designed for and tailored to the popular taste of the majority. That assures Anglo-American culture an extensive popularity. By contrast, Hispanic American culture with its excessive idealism and aestheticism remains confined to the educated classes, which gradually enlarge with urban growth. Hispanic American culture, in spite of its "attractiveness," still has a limited audience. It is made up of an extraordinary mixture of doctrinaire elements and reflexive realism, which produces great intellectual vitality. That spiritual state is expressed in the intellectual loftiness of thought of a few. Their view of life and their expression of that view remain beyond popular reach. On the other hand, Anglo-American culture, with its inexhaustible conceptual potential and dynamism, oscillates between the real and the improvised for immediate consumption. It unites a collective consciousness that leads its people to assume certain responsibilities in the world, despite the youthfulness of its cultural and political traditions. Some universal ideas that can be inferred from Hispanic American thought, however excellent they may be, are sometimes lost in the realm of desire or remain in the memory as simply works of theoretical originality.

Some Hispanic Americans have been concerned about this disparity between theory and practice. In 1913, Peru's Francisco García Calderón, in *La creación de un continente*, wrote, "Imperfection in action is the great flaw in the Latin American character, while the lack of preparation for which improvisation is substituted characterizes North Americans." He also observed that in Hispanic America literary personages abounded but technical specialists were scarce. Although the situation has improved in recent decades, the comment is still valid. Nearly a half-century later the Argentinian philosopher Alberto Caturelli, in *América bifronte*, examined the spiritual dualism of Hispanic America. Caturelli saw the spiritual "two-frontedness" in a want of humility that brought a certain alienation of the Hispanic American from his own environment. He noted that attitude particularly in the people of the River Plate region but found it also in other areas, even in Mestizo America. For that reason, Caturelli believed, "Argentina and [Hispanic] America have not yet fully manifested their originality in the cultural sphere."

Civilization has gone through an ideological crisis in recent decades. In North America tremendous scientific and technological progress has been made, while Europe has been mainly concerned with humanistic advances. This unbalanced situation has been all the more serious because Europe and the Americas are the carriers of Western civilization. Two currents have been in conflict in that crisis: technocratic functionalism and humanistic spirituality, each with distinct life-styles and goals. More than a conflict, it has been a rivalry in which humanism has lost much of its vitality, while functionalism, through its practical triumphs, has gained mobility and adherents.

It is not a new controversy; it began with the Industrial Revolution. But now it has acquired new aspects. It has established a hierarchical scale of values in the competing sciences and humanities that keeps them apart instead of bringing them into the close interaction that is indispensable to the very existence of Western civilization. The search is now underway for means of harmonizing the two currents. It is a difficult search, with forces frequently opposed in their objectives.

Considered globally, it is no longer a question of a social evolution or a change "from homogeneity to heterogeneity"—that is, from the simple to the complex in contemporary life. It is a serious challenge to the survival of Western civilization. As such it has been reflected in the deep concern of philosophers from Spengler to Bronowski. Most of them advocate bridging the gap to bring science and the humanities to some sort of working coexistence. In this way strong pressures that emanate from social Darwinism, which favors the "fittest" individuals or groups, may be considerably diminished. It would thus avert Aldous Huxley's overpessimistic vision in *Brave New World*, in which—because of automation—human beings are assigned the slavelike secondary functions. If humanity and its culture are to survive, more internal and external adjustments are needed, not mutual threats. It is hoped that from the present cultural crisis an ideological compromise will result, leading to a renewal of the bases of our civilizations and infusing them with new mobility for the third millennium of our era.

An aerial view of Havana Harbor, Cuba. El Morro Castle is at the upper right; the modern city is at the left. Courtesy Organization of American States.

Columbus Palace in Santo Domingo, Dominican Republic, the restored official residence of Governor Diego Colón, son of America's discoverer. Courtesy Organization of American States.

Harvesting cacao pods in the Dominican Republic. Cacao is one of the main cash crops of the tropical countries of Hispanic America. Courtesy Organization of American States.

Quiché Indians on the steps of the Church of Santa María in Chichicastenango, Guatemala. The Indians pay homage to the Virgin and the saints with incense offerings, while clutching native idols under their robes. Courtesy Organization of American States.

Great plaza of the sacred Maya city at Tikál, Guatemala, being restored by archaeologists from the University of Pennsylvania. Courtesy Standard Oil of New Jersey, Inc.

A jungle Indian of the Guayaquí tribe with his hunting bow and arrow, Ecuador. Courtesy Organization of American States.

A Maya stela at Copán, Honduras. Large numbers of these stelae are scattered throughout southern Mexico, Guatemala, and Honduras. Courtesy Pan American Airline.

A bridge suspended over a swift mountain river in Huatana, Peru. Many such bridges were built by the Incas. Courtesy Organization of American States.

A Mochica polychrome water jug, Peru. Antedating the Inca civilization, the Mochicas belong to an advanced civilization of northern Peru. Courtesy Peruvian Embassy, Washington, D.C.

Palace of the Torre-Tagle family, a good example of Moorish architecture
in Lima, Peru. Photograph by the author.

The patio of the Torre-Tagle Palace with a nineteenth-century colonial carriage, Peru. Courtesy Peruvian Embassy, Washington, D.C.

Solid silver altar in San Francisco Church, Lima, Peru. Courtesy Peruvian
Embassy, Washington, D.C.

Post-Conquest Peruvian native art exemplifying the syncretism of ancient Quechua theogonic beliefs and Christian rites. Left: a small wooden cross with a seashell attached by a short cord. Right: a silver *tupo* (an ornamental pin used to fasten a woman's cap) representing the sun, moon, and stars surmounted by two angels.

Ruins of the Inca fortress at Machu Picchu, Peru, believed to be the last Inca stronghold against the Spanish invasion.

Venezuelan of African descent watching a drum dance, state of Miranda.
Courtesy Creole Petroleum Corporation.

Oil derricks on Lake Maracaibo, Venezuela. Courtesy Creole Petroleum Corporation.

CHAPTER 12

SOCIAL CONDUCT IN THE NEW WORLD

Unmistakable differences mark the behavior of Hispanic Americans and Anglo-Americans. A carefree lack of concern seems to characterize Hispanic Americans, while an almost notorious haste seems to mark the pace of Anglo-Americans. Among the former the words, "Tomorrow is another day," or, "Let's leave it until tomorrow," are often heard. Among the latter a daily theme is, "Time is money." Such concepts, deeply rooted in each society, proceed from different philosophies of life. The need to utilize time for creative work molded the philosophy of the Anglo-Saxons, while a vision of the infinity of time and of the unforseen in human destiny shaped the philosophy of the Hispanic Americans. Those attitudes show a dichotomy in vital objectives. While one group is dedicated to its duties with an almost religious diligence—for Puritanism prohibited idleness—the other is inclined to relaxed contemplation—sometimes, indeed, to passive opposition to any activity. The attitudes are the ancestral attitudes toward labor.

The New England colonies never had an excess of laborers, and therefore most time was spent on something useful or profitable. In Hispanic America abundant native labor freed the ruling class to devote many hours to leisure activities and contemplation. (These conditions could also be found in the southern colonies of North America.) Anglo-American economic ambitions and the Spanish colonists' relaxed attitude toward work grew out of those conditions. Thus were formed two distinct ideologies.

In the United States over the years the Industrial Revolution changed the methods of production and supplanted manual labor with automation, obliging workers to adjust to new methods. Today manufacturing practices require precision and speed of the workers, especially those on assembly lines. Agricultural operations too are almost completely mechanized. Specialization in these and other fields assures good incomes and offers the working classes the opportunity to live well.

North Americans believe that the United States has two closely related sources of wealth: work and natural resources. Many foreigners fail to understand that phenomenon. Once I visited a factory in company with some Hispanic American colleagues. They were overwhelmed by the coordination of the work. Observing the precision with which the tasks were executed, they asked me: "Why do these people work so hard? Don't they have enough money to live on?" To my Hispanic colleagues of a more leisurely world, the workers seemed to be impelled by fanaticism or a "magical" force.

In Hispanic American countries the traditional agrarian structure and the limited industrial development have provided few opportunities for the inhabitants to develop a collective initiative. Manual labor still prevails. The increasing numbers of people moving from the country to urban centers cannot be absorbed in domestic, craft, and community services and are disproportionately numerous for the limited needs of what industry there is. The exodus of workers from rural areas has produced a crisis in agricultural production; vast arable areas are uncultivated, and food costs are high. Agrarian reform, which has been carried out in only a few countries, has not satisfied the hunger for land of the Indian and mestizo peasants in the greater part of Hispanic America. The continuing disproportions in landholding are discouraging to the peasants. It should be noted, however, that even where some reforms have been carried out the agrarian situation has not notably improved. Peasants still tend to work only to satisfy their basic necessities.

The disinterest in material goods seems to arise from extremely modest living needs and a lack of vision of tomorrow. Lack of motivation dates from the Conquest. The subjugation of the Indians and the inhuman treatment weakened the will to work in those subjected to unaccustomed forced labor. Neither did the blacks, uprooted from Africa and enslaved in America, show any great ardor for working under the lash. Creole *latifundistas*, not outstanding examples of industriousness, contented themselves with giving orders and enjoying their ease. The tasks that were carried out could have only a limited economic effect.

The capricious Hispanic American attitude toward work survives to the present time. It is sometimes attributed to lack of energy and to climatic and topographic conditions. Yet immigrants seem capable of working effectively in the same conditions and in the same areas. Moreover, in some industrialized and mechanized agricultural areas the attitude of the workforce has become more positive. Even more encouraging are the economic ambitions displayed by Hispanic American bourgeois society, which has been strengthened by an influx of European and Asiatic immigrants.

The fear that business concerns in Hispanic America may be monopolized by "outsiders" has led some mestizo countries to limit and even exclude immigrants, and there has developed a growing opposition to foreign economic influence. Immigrants who marry native-born citizens are welcomed. Marital ties are considered evidence of integration with the society of the adopted country. Foreign investors who live outside the country are charged with "absentee landlordship." European middle-class immigrants are more likely to become integrated than the less numerous but economically more influential North Americans, partly out of Hispanic snobbery and exclusiveness. These attitudes are manifested in the relative popularity of Europeans and the relative unpopularity of Anglo-Americans, who are still disparagingly referred to as "gringos." By contrast, in the United States, once immigrants have been admitted, they are accepted into business and the professions as equals. Social integration follows—their work is proof of the contribution to national progress. (An exception is the seasonal laborers along the Mexico–United States border, many of whom enter the country illegally and whose presence is resented by native-born workers and their unions.)

Other facets of social conduct in the two Americas are intimately related to circumstances of environment. In Hispanic America the gentleness of the people and the leisurely tempo of life promote an agreeable atmosphere. The courtesy, the amiability seem to assure the visitor that there is nothing to worry about. The etiquette of greeting and of business dealings is effusively cordial.

There is an almost universal tone and mien of humility—even in regions far removed from urban centers. There is also a marked tendency to elaborate gesturing. Unlike some cultures, which look upon it as almost vulgar, gesturing, particularly common at times of intense emotion, is an inseparable feature of the Hispanic American manner. It is but one manifestation of the Latin American temperament, which is very different from the more rigid, controlled personal behavior of individual Anglo-Americans.

In Anglo-America the tempo of life, by contrast, is rapid, even frenzied, and its citizens do not seem to have much time to enjoy activities that have little perceived utility. That tempo, which also emanates from a technological society, carries with it an imposed conventionalism. United States citizens have amiable smiles, which seem more or less standardized from New York to Miami and from San Francisco to Boston. They are fleeting and betray little emotion. Personal courtesy is accompanied by a certain gravity and air of preoccupation with important matters. The almost excessive civility is part of the introversion that controls and regulates Anglo-Americans. It is much like the behavior of other Anglo-Saxon nations—and it is almost incomprehensible to Hispanic peoples.

Foreigners are astonished by the worth Anglo-Americans attach to their words, projects, and daily activities. Conformity is most marked in ways of behaving, living, and dressing. But within that conformity is a wide-ranging diversity. In recent years a freer mode of living among the youth has undermined the posture of conformity. Along with the new life-styles has come a tendency to reevaluate the traditional "American way of life." Aggressiveness in getting things done and intellectual curiosity continue to characterize Anglo-American behavior. That behavior varies between humility and arrogance, between simplicity and sophistication. In the end stereotyping the people of the United States in any single mold is impossible for the impartial observer.

The two Americas are markedly different in their attitudes toward change. Hispanic American civilization promotes a relaxed attitude toward the way people live and think. Changes in that civilization occur only when they emanate from the will of the people, and that will is seldom exercised. The opposite is true in Anglo-America. There rapid technological development exercises tremendous social pressures on the population, subjecting values to rapid transformation.

Various aspects of personality of each society are also reflected in pride and dignity. Hispanic American pride originated from the Indian-Spanish mixture and continues to dominate all aspects of

Hispanic American life. The people are proud of their Spanish lineage, which ties them to the splendor and the past glory of Spain. Unconscious manifestations of that pride are frequent, even among those who are emotionally or intellectually "anti-Spanish." Pride is also reflected in *machismo*, a quality of intense masculinity evidenced in manner and spirit. Perhaps the most profound manifestations of Iberian pride lie in the Hispanic American mental absolutism especially evident among the cultured minority.

Pride is manifested in "I-ism," the conviction that one has possession of the irrefutable truth, from which stems his belief in the correctness of his actions. The attitude borders on arrogance. Pride is apparent also in the extreme sensitivity in the personal relationships of Hispanic Americans, both among themselves and with other peoples. Pride causes discord in public life, for it gets in the way of conciliation among politicians, and it fosters polemicism among intellectuals. It is sometimes expressed in irrational argument and at other times in rhetorical pomposity, even about legitimate differences.

Anglo-Americans, on the other hand, display a dignity that rests on satisfaction with their well-being, which has been achieved through individual and collective effort. Their sense of worth has virtually no ethnic pomposity. Neither can the multiethnic origins, seldom a matter of concern to the average Anglo-American, be readily traced. The overwhelming majority of people come from humble classes and have risen from their former status by their own efforts. They transmit that pride to their children, and their dignity symbolizes social equality. A sense of personal worth has become a common trait among rich and poor, "old" and "new."

When United States citizens travel in countries whose conditions of life they find inferior to their own, they feel—and sometimes show—a sense of superiority that is sometimes labeled pride or even haughtiness. They seem to display an almost arrogant self-confidence that tends to disparage other social and political systems. Foreign observers blame it on the simplistic attitude of the average North American. On the other hand, the same citizens are notably critical of their own country and are willing to listen—though not necessarily respond to—frequently severe foreign criticism. An individual more or less disciplined and satisfied with his way of life, the

Anglo-American is indignant about dictatorial systems that are alien to his democratic persuasions. The only thing, therefore, about which the Anglo-American feels pride is "being" a United States citizen, but without being "nationalistic" in the usual sense of that term.

Also worthy of comparison are the reactions of the societies of the two Americas toward current events. The Hispanic American frequently reacts with an emotionalism that often leads to extremes, though it does not necessarily influence the outcome. Since political, cultural, and social affairs always attract tremendous interest, they produce a great divergence of opinion, often expressed in explosive controversies. Instigators of the controversies are often great polemicists. The press is their arena of battle. Sometimes they know how to capture the attention of the public, who become equally emotional about the controversy. Many of the verbal battles are waged about vital problems; others are purely theoretical.

The "polemic spirit" is a very obvious idiosyncrasy of the Hispanic American. Although it helps discharge emotional pressures, it does not always lead to viable solutions, and it seldom relieves tensions. The polemic tradition in politics is an old one. It is also a feature of literary criticism, the best-known example being the dispute over Romanticism versus Classicism that Domingo Sarmiento and Andrés Bello engaged in in Chile in the mid-nineteenth century. The arena of "academic" controversy is still filled with passionate combatants, many of whom cross pens primarily to advance their careers. Politicized military men cross verbal arms with statesmen—and sometimes carry the conflict into actual battle—uprisings and revolutions. Hispanic Americans do not, however, concede to "strangers" the right to criticize their affairs. They are affronted by negative comments. At the same time they believe that they have the right to criticize other nations, and they do so with an air of superiority. This attitude is incomprehensible to European and United States intellectuals, who are accustomed to "fair play."

Anglo-Americans' attitudes toward national and international affairs tends to be manifested in a collective and often spontaneous manner, rather than in polemics. The reaction assumes a public character. Individuals and groups representing different interests or convictions participate in extensive public debate about matters vital to the community or nation. Congressional debates and public demonstrations on issues involving human rights are typical examples. Commentators of press, television, and radio (which, unlike the media of Hispanic America, are privately owned) express their opinions, raising their voices without fear. The democratic system provides that right. Such practices frequently lead to reconciliation, especially in industrial-labor conflicts. Even radical political demonstrations, which may at first produce overreaction by the people, are ultimately given their hearing in court and often produce a change in national political direction, as witness the Vietnam War demonstrations.

Another trait of Anglo-American society is its bent toward self-criticism, particularly of national social and economic theory and practice. The flexibility of the people of the United States allows them to acknowledge errors of calculation and adjust rapidly to new life situations.

Somewhere between the laissez-faire and activist attitudes of Hispanic America and Anglo-America is the stance of Puerto Ricans, in whom the deeply rooted Hispanic cultural tradition and the influence of the United States have fused in an attitudinal posture that is unique in the Western Hemisphere. The Puerto Ricans are no less "Latin" than their Hispanic American brothers, but because of the very special circumstances there, the intelligentsia has evolved its own perceptions. The literature reveals a moderate, rationalist attitude, flavored with the tone of Hispanic American temperament. Polemics, particularly relating to literature and politics, tend to be more reasoned, less frenzied.

Hispanic Americans are largely resigned to their economic and political condition, which is marked by public apathy. Changes in political regimes rarely arouse them; much less are they impressed by promises of a better future. It is a strange state of indifference, overlying the rebellious spirit that is always present in the Hispanic American subconscious but has few opportunities to express itself in a positive manner. The people find consolation and emotional relaxation through the intense cultivation of social relationships. Family intimacy and friendship are veritable life supports in Hispanic America. An example is the *compadrazgo*. The original meaning of the word was "compaternity" or "godfatherhood." Today it has come to mean a small group of persons who join together for mutual help in business or personal matters. It is characterized by cameraderie and deep feelings of friendship and mutual regard. As such, *compadrazgo* has become a basic ingredient of Hispanic American life.

It should be noted that Hispanic friendships tend to be much more intimate than those in Anglo-Saxon society, which seem to the observer to be more formal, lacking "inwardness." Hispanic "political friendships," on the other hand, are of a different sort. Political alliances masked as friendships are just as subject to corruption or betrayal as those of any other culture rich in human values, despite the sanctimoniousness of the mestizo countries and the *viveza* of the creole countries.

Anglo-American behavior is subject to various social pressures that may be inferred from the accelerated tempo of life and a kind of rigidity that accompanies it. Social life in the United States is utterly unlike the placidity of Hispanic America. The dominant tone is one of nervousness. The United States way of life, with its constant demand for progress and achievement, is accompanied by a tendency to abruptness and impatience, with consequent interpersonal conflicts. The typical Anglo-American is preoccupied with his wristwatch and his daily schedule of activities.

In the view of foreigners Yankees do not take time to enjoy life. Yet it is a fact that Anglo-Americans enjoy their work as much as they do their leisure. The trouble is that there is never enough time for diversion. Other societies enjoy an abundance of spare time. For example, one can compare the small number of legal holidays in the United States with the number celebrated by Hispanic Americans. Anglo-American family life is affected by the involvement in work, especially when both parents are employed. The children of such families are brought up without constant parental supervision, a situation rarely occurring in Hispanic America. Family ties in the United States are thus less strong, in contrast to the strong bonds among Hispanic Americans. Respect for elders is taken less seriously in the United States than in Hispanic America. Political affairs do not attract as much concentrated attention in Anglo-America as in Hispanic America. Political ardor reaches its peak during presidential election campaigns and dies down afterward. The politicization of Hispanic American life is ongoing, centering around the political leaders chosen by or imposed upon the people (the adulation of the Peróns in Argentina is an obvious example).

Other social disparities between the peoples of the two Americas are evident in their different life-styles and diversions. Many middle-class Hispanic American families traditionally occupy the same house for a long time. There they lead a settled life, sharing it with two and sometimes three generations. Their life together is based on mutual respect. There are plenty of adults, and the children do not lack family attention. Families who can afford them have servants to cook, clean, and look after them. Fiestas and other social gatherings are held for family and guests. These affairs are marked by a spirit of cordiality. The children are encouraged to develop friendships in the home environment. The youths may be somewhat pampered, but social closeness is accompanied by respect and a sense of propriety. The accelerated rhythm of urban life is, of course, transforming these traditional life-styles into more "modern" ones.

The typical Hispanic American family has television and from time to time attends concerts and the traditional bullfights. The cinema is especially popular. The women of the house, who take part in volunteer work, sometimes gather in the city to lunch with their friends. Cafés in Hispanic America, like those in Spain, provide pleasant surroundings for leisure hours and for "bohemian" pleasures, principally for men. The men also enjoy pleasant evenings in cabarets without the company of their wives. Many who can afford it keep a *"casa chica"* for extramarital pleasures. These activities do not seem to threaten family seriously; the number of divorces is insignificant, and divorce still produces scandal. It is generally looked upon as a stigma in the Roman Catholic setting and serves as a brake on social behavior.

The Anglo-American family, usually smaller than the Hispanic one, rarely lives with relatives. Because of occupational mobility the average family moves often, and both adults and children are constantly pulling up and transplanting the roots of their family and social life. The sense of "place" is thus weakened; the compensation, of course, is environmental variety. The relatively conventional family life is based on generally accepted behavior, but that behavior does not produce the intimacy of family life that is characteristic of Hispanic America. The Anglo-American's concern with his occupation makes his life scheduled and functional but also provides him with the ingredients necessary to satisfy his needs and ambitions. When both parents work outside the home, the children are often unsupervised, which may affect discipline, although it helps them develop a certain sense of independence.

Domestic service in the United States is costly; consequently, the wife manages the household with the aid of various appliances. The husband sometimes helps with the tasks. Festive occasions in the home are less frequent than in Hispanic American homes. The cocktail party is the standard entertainment. Recreational outlets away from home are clubs, health and sports centers, and stage and motion-picture theaters. The automobile adds to family mobility. In recent decades television viewing is the most important family pastime. Married couples sometimes go together to sports contests, restaurants, theaters, or clubs or visit friends. Not all goes smoothly in family life; there is a high divorce rate. Today divorce is not usually a social stigma.

The status of women in the two Americas is dramatically different. In accordance with the patriarchal concept imbedded in both the Hispanic and the indigenous American traditions, life in the Hispanic American world revolves around the man. He is the head of the family and the repository of all authority in the home. Any transgression against those prerogatives is unthinkable. To the man are left the final decisions about everything, including morality (which he himself sometimes offends). The man exercises his authority without paying much attention to the views of his submissive wife. Yet she is the one who holds the family together, through her self-denial and moral example. Though intelligent, she is not as ambitious as the woman of the North. She takes little part in traditionally masculine activities but concentrates on creating an aura of feminine charm.

Anglo-Americans also inherited from their ancestors the concept of the superiority of the "stronger sex." During the westward movement of the mid-nineteenth century up to the period following World War I, women were perceived as dependent and needing protection. In the modern era they have struggled with some success to gain equal rights. Their active participation in social and economic life assures them a decidedly better position in society than that of their

Hispanic American sisters. They participate in various fields of endeavor, including politics. Their views have influence. The Anglo-American male is less autocratic than the Hispanic American but still usually maintains the role of head of the family.

Customs of courtship differ so markedly in the two societies that comparisons are almost impossible. In some Hispanic American countries the practice of chaperoning young ladies when they go out still prevails. In the Anglo-American setting young people are almost totally unchaperoned and would scoff at the suggestion that adults accompany them on dates. Relations between the sexes are open and casual. In Hispanic America contrast the archaic ceremony of flirtation (*piropeo*), a Peninsular custom of verbal gallantry toward young women. Although young Anglo-Americans do not lack an etiquette of courtship, it is simpler, more casual, and less ostentatious.

It should be mentioned that a moral revolution has taken place in Anglo-America as a result of the social revolution, which is expressed in a change in customs and moral values resulting from increasing prosperity, social mobility, and advances in the legal status of women and of minorities. These factors have contributed to the relaxation of the old code of moral conduct and the adoption of almost unlimited individual liberty, which also affects sexual customs. The old double standard of morality that required chastity of women but not of men is now considered out of date. Religious doctrine to the contrary is largely disregarded or reinterpreted. The emancipation of women and the availability of contraceptives have considerably altered concepts of sexual morality. Early marriages and a high incidence of divorce, of illegitimate births, and of abortions have accompanied the new sexual freedom. In Hispanic America abortion is unthinkable except among the very poor, and Hispanic America has the highest birth rate in the world.[1]

The visitor to the two Americas is struck by the contrasts not only in the pace of life but also in the "climate," or mood, of life. A "gentle" atmosphere is one of the outstanding characteristics of Hispanic American life. It is maintained instinctively and by tradition. The rich calendar of celebrations, festivals, and sports contests

---

[1]According to official statistics, the percentages of population increase during the period 1965–70 were as follows: United States, 1.3%; Canada, 1.9%; Mexico and Central America, 3.2%; and an average of South America, 2.7%.

(bullfighting, soccer, boxing, and horse racing), as well as the mood of the *compadrazgo*, described earlier, with its warm social conventions, is unique. Nothing similar exists in modern-day Anglo-America. The Hispanic cultivation of close relationships is based on the ties of camaraderie—and on a conviction that one should live one's life in the most agreeable manner with as little inconvenience as possible. The Hispanic American ambience seems sometimes to proceed from dissociation from any reality that could cloud it. The Latin American prefers to enjoy today because tomorrow could inflict on him some unexpected annoyance. He frequently assumes an attitude of expectation but becomes passive when it is necessary to make a hard decision. The relatively slow pace of events in contrast to the rapid North American rhythm reinforces that attitude.

Another Hispanic characteristic is ceremoniousness. It is a formality that seems to go beyond standard courtesy. One manifestation is the bureaucratic paperwork (*papeleo*) that attends both government and business dealings.

In contrast to the relaxed tenor of Hispanic American life, the atmosphere in Anglo-America is "nervous," a mood emanating from the fast-paced activity—the drive to achieve new "records." An uninterrupted, clocklike rhythm is sensed in many public sectors. The effort of the individual seems to be subordinated to the rules of an elaborate technology and its social implications. In that process almost every person is forced into competition. Thus he participates in the so-called pursuit of the dollar, accommodating his ambitions to it. That pursuit also seems to influence the "mystique" of work. The average Anglo-American is a victim of the complexities of modern life, although they do not deprive him of his independence in making decisions.

Such conditions seldom lead to close personal relationships. Social contacts, except among the young, tend to be conventional ones. Of course, there are groups bound by common interests who cultivate close friendships. The average Anglo-American lives with his immediate family in a bourgeois monotony. Yet the Anglo-American family experiences all the pains and joys of any family anywhere. The well-known Yankee vigor facilitates socioeconomic mobility, which is tied to the egalitarian feeling and the sense of human worth, attitudes exhibited by both majority and minority ethnic groups. The motivation to achieve equality has nothing of the utopian about it; it is derived from the democratic philosophy. Much emphasis is placed on the young, who enjoy privileged treatment. The generation gap—essentially a discrepancy in ideological criteria—is the subject of much discussion. Pressure groups, both formal and informal, are very active and exercise influence on national and local government authorities to secure new civic and economic advantages. Generally Anglo-Americans strive for their rights and privileges more zealously than people of other nations.

In social conduct the two Americas thus present the following picture: In Hispanic America many aspects of behavior still seem to be tied to the past, though forces of change are appearing. The people of Anglo-America show an obsessive interest in the future, seeing in the process an evolutionary social rhythm.

Disparities in social conduct depend in no small measure on the human-ecology factor, which is closely related to demographic fluctuations. For this reason today more attention is paid to demographic movements as they affect the ethnocultural ambience.

As discussed earlier, the increasing urbanization of Hispanic America is a consequence of a constant influx of *rurales* to metropolitan areas. New nuclei are being established in the suburbs, which often become shanty towns. The well-do-do residential sections that once were on the city's outskirts are gradually becoming urban centers. This demographic shift usually puts new strains on metropolitan life, creates pressing social problems, and complicates urban planning. In an attempt to alleviate the problems, efforts have been made to build new satellite communities around the metropolitan areas. The newcomers tend to observe their old rural customs and, among the Indians, their native languages. Urban assimilation of such groups is a troublesome process.

By contrast, migratory movements in the United States are not to suburbs but to urban centers. The more prosperous inhabitants then move to the suburbs. In the new suburban communities a social exclusiveness similar to that of the well-to-do Hispanic Americans is noticeable. This phenomenon creates what has been called a suburban civilization. The newcomers are gradually absorbed by the more static urban civilization. As the urban dwellers become more prosperous, they also join the exodus. This curious, circular process of population reshifting is, of course, made possible by social mobility. The metropolitan area, which suffers economically from the shifts of progessively poorer populations, undertake urban renewal, a revitalization of the cities through improved facilities and social and cultural services and greater communal cohesion.

Urban-social integration in the United States, although by no means perfect and in spite of its multiethnic structure, is nevertheless more conducive to leveling of disparities than is the population pattern in Hispanic American cities. In the latter serious obstacles are found in the broad economic gap between the old inhabitants and the new ones. This produces not only social but also cultural shock, which makes social integration even more problematical.

Finally, a few words about the manners of the New World ethnocultural groups as reflected in inter-American relations. Ambiability in social behavior and ceremoniousness, around which social and public relations in Hispanic America revolve, have become the traditional manner of the people. In contrast, the firmness of purpose and the speed in carrying it out push Anglo-Americans into decisive action that is sometimes branded commercial coldness. These attitudes, resulting from differences in temperament, produce discernible differences in behavior, particularly in negotiations between the two groups and in procedures. Anglo-Americans, with their pragmatic stance, are free of the metaphysical exercises and oratory Hispanic Americans tend to engage in. Hispanic people often carry on prolonged reflections and consultations that delay the course of negotiations. Anglo-Americans are flexible but firm and express their opinions directly, without flattery, in a manner that may seem somewhat brusque. Meanwhile, Ciceronian luster added to the already entangled problems of Hispanic America, although very impressive, sometimes produces a kind of quixotic vagueness.

It is difficult to close these reflections on New World behavior without noting again that each culture is inseparably tied to its socioeconomic structure. We have already pointed out the enormous difference between the highly stratified society of Hispanic America and the far less stratified one of Anglo-America. This basic difference accounts for the various ways of reacting to social problems. Orthodox capitalism still prevails in Hispanic America, but efforts are being made to tie it to a partly socialized economy through state-run enterprises. Such efforts, no matter how ambitious, are usually beneficial to small groups but cannot raise the average per capita income or equalize the distribution of national wealth. This economic imbalance causes perpetual and widespread discontent. In contrast, owing to the pressure of labor unions and other social forces, Anglo-America's capitalistic system is continuously transforming itself into socialized capitalism. Thus a minimum income level acceptable to most inhabitants has been established. Moreover, in some enterprises workers are also stockholders. They benefit from the profits produced by the industry. This economic concept is still alien to Spanish American enterpreneurs, who have not yet begun thinking of the collective well-being.

The differences in these two socioeconomic systems are especially evident during economic crises, which neither of the Americas escapes. No Hispanic American country has unemployment compensation equivalent to that of the United States, and there are few pension funds for the elderly. Unemployed Hispanic American workers are left to their own fate. In the United States, though public welfare has not been perfected, it is extraordinary in comparison to the systems of Hispanic America. Welfare permits millions of jobless people to survive. Federal subsidies are granted to privately owned industries. In Marxist nations such companies have been nationalized. There are also welfare programs, such as Medicare and Medicaid, for the elderly, food stamps for the poor, free breakfasts for economically deprived school children, and day care for working parents. These programs seem to prove that the United States is slowly becoming a social-welfare state, which is not necessarily antithetical to its traditional principles of free enterprise.

The restlessness caused by economic crises manifests itself everywhere in protests and social unrest. It is interesting to note that such occurrences are most frequent in the United States and Canada. They have little lasting effect in Hispanic America. This is perhaps due to the relative powerlessness of Hispanic labor unions, whose leaders are at times swayed by interests other than union ones. The result is a kind of forced inertia. The psychological reaction to social calamity is, then, different in each group. The conduct of Anglo-Americans is best characterized as collective aggressiveness. When their livelihood is jeopardized, they display an unyielding determination that at times is accompanied by physical violence. In turn, the lack of firmness that is the Hispanic American's "quiet-after-the-storm" attitude stems from experience as well as the cultural and perhaps even religious background.

The Hispanic American working class, which despite its occasional rebelliousness has suffered and been greatly humiliated, has lost faith in the improvement of its economic status and has become almost resigned to its condition. After much spontaneous and rhetorical bravado, these frustrated people immerse themselves in a mental state bordering on passiveness. This frame of mind has been analyzed in a psychiatric study of the "passive-active transcultural dichotomy" of Mexicans and North Americans in times of tension.[2] According to this study, the Hispanic people prefer to endure their lot with passiveness, considering it the optimum behavior for their "internal" defense. Even if such a phenomenon has historic validity, I am not sure that the theory is applicable to all circumstances. After all, in Hispanic American society violence is rather common. However, the people's outbursts of despair are usually suppressed by their governments, which do not acknowledge either the roots or the immediate cause of the rebellion. Thus Hispanic American reaction tends to result in counterreaction. In Anglo-America, on the other hand, this process has its counterpart in the arbitration process carried on by management, labor, government, and the people. It is evident that each approach toward basic human problems emanates from different rationales that are embedded in the texture of each civilization.

Another revealing aspect of social behavior is manifested when national pride is at stake. It takes an extravagant form in Hispanic America, particularly in smaller nations. In border disputes the countries display particularly hostile attitudes and ultrapatriotic feelings. A small border incident provoked by nation A causes an immediate reaction in nation B. The press of the latter magnifies it as international affair and provokes a countrywide outburst of indignation. Such an action leads to counteraction, then frontier skirmishes, and even small-scale wars. Nationalistic emotionalism, frequently ac-

[2]R. Díaz Guerrero, "The Passive-Active Transcultural Dichotomy," *International Mental Health Research Newsletter*, Vol. III, No. 3 (1965).

companied by territorial claims, can delay negotiations for months. Characteristically, the smaller the country in question the longer the period required for reconciliation.

The aggressiveness of smaller nations, like that of big ones, is often motivated by political rivalry for regional domination. This rivalry bears all the characteristics of imperialism, whether or not it is so labeled. In peace or in war it retards economic integration and sociopolitical cohesiveness. Rivalry is an undeniable trait of Hispanic America, along with the hypersensitivity displayed in inter-American relations. Indeed, sensitivity is perhaps *the* dominant Hispanic characteristic, because it is interrelated with ethnic pride and formal rules of courtesy. Outsiders who lack these traits are considered vulgar. Those who have them are looked upon as equals and perhaps even as superior beings. Non-Latin partners of Hispanic America would do well to keep these traits well in mind, both in social and in official contacts.

CHAPTER 13

BETWEEN RELIGIOUS DOGMATISM AND LIBERALISM

Religion is an inseparable component of the Western culture prevailing in Hispanic America and Anglo-America. The spiritual mold imposed by the Christian faith in its historic and moral development merits equal consideration with other civilizing factors in the New World. In view of the moral crisis that for some time has harassed the American nations, an examination of the religious question from historical, theological, and social perspectives is necessary. Not unique in the New World, this crisis is part of the ideological restlessness that is also appearing in other civilizations of the world.

Two branches of Christianity were established in the New World during the colonizing era: Spanish Roman Catholicism, which dominated Hispanic America, and English Protestantism, which spread in Anglo-America. The theologies of the two religions differed as widely as the two societies that were their exponents. The Protestant liberal rebellion that began the Reformation (1512) incorporated Puritan moral extremism in contrast to Roman Catholic conservatism, which reaffirmed its religious fervor through the Counter Reformation undertaken by the Council of Trent (1545–63). Though the Catholic faith prevailed, Protestantism gained a foothold. Through their theological convictions, ecclesiastical practices, and social customs both branches of Christianity had a permanent influence on the religious and moral principles of the New World.

The northern colonies of Anglo-America were settled in large part by people who had been persecuted for religious reasons in their homelands. From the beginning they created conditions favorable to freedom of conscience, which each confession wanted for itself. The Protestant Reformation was not sufficiently radical for some colonists; the moral austerity of the Puritans led them to find refuge in the English colonies. There they were able to cultivate their beliefs in a Christian commonwealth to be established and maintained through hard work in order to achieve redemption. The Calvinists professed a sterner dogmatism, with their doctrines of predestination and the grace of God as the only means of salvation. Their theocratic absolutism and religious inflexibility made them intolerant of other beliefs, though their own freedom to pursue their faith depended on the tolerance of other sects. The Lutherans, who believed that salvation depended on individual faith and contrition, were somewhat less dogmatic. The founders of the Protestant Reformation, they were opposed to papal authoritarianism and clerical corruption in the sale of indulgences. They rejected the Roman interpretation of certain sacraments, as well as celibacy of priests. On separating from the Roman Church, the Lutherans established their own religious doctrines. They and the Calvinists helped give rise to Anglo-American "practical morality."

It is somewhat difficult to relate Protestant doctrinal positions to the Industrial Revolution since the two movements had different aims. Without doubt, however, the Protestant religious revolution, which also brought about a social revolution, changed the character of Christian concepts of the virtues. The change in ethical concepts produced a favorable setting for stimulating economic progress in a Protestant America tied to the Industrial Revolution. Although the Puritans, Calvinists, and Lutherans were dedicated to work and to reading the Bible, their asceticism was secular rather than religious. The mixture of theology and secularism became a part of the Anglo-American tradition that was gradually extended to various Protestant confessions. When the Reformation rejected ecclesiastical authority and thereby weakened the clerical function, the emergence of lay preachers made possible free interpretation of the Scriptures by various groups and the proliferation of confessions with a great variety of beliefs that still characterizes Anglo-American Protestantism.

Puritans, with their austere customs, abhored idleness and had an almost mystical attitude toward work. According to their beliefs, they were worshiping God through their physical efforts and thus were building a Christian community in the new land. Their beliefs also led them to abstrain from diversions and to distrust intellectual pursuits. Life was monotonous, interrupted only by struggles with the Indians and with the wilderness. They did not try to convert the Indians to the Protestant faith and made no effort to attract them to white civilization. Victims themselves of religious persecution, they had no wish to impose their religion on the indigenes. Too, they considered the Indians incapable of assimilating European ideas and mode of life. That attitude may have emanated from the Old Testament Jewish exclusivity. Another criticism that can be made of the Puritans and Calvinists is that, because of their lack of interest in humanistic culture, they neglected the education of their members and thus retarded the cultural progress of the country.

In the seventeenth century the term Protestant was used to refer to Lutherans and Anglicans, but in the course of time it came to include all Christians who did not belong to the Roman Catholic and Eastern Orthodox churches. Protestant adherence to the basic principles of an orderly life, coupled with rationalist precepts, provided the basis for the intellectual liberalism that later stimulated scientific speculation and invention. It may be said that rationalism was one of the foundations of Protestantism, particularly of Anglo-American Protestantism. Rather than being excessively concerned with theological matters, Anglo-American Protestantism was oriented instead toward the well-being of the people. In time it came to be directed toward social welfare rather than religious aspiration—it combined the divine with the worldly. That social accent continued to be an unmistakable trait of Anglo-American Protestantism, which differentiated it from European Protestantism. That is not to say that the Anglo-Americans sacrificed their religious tradition. On the contrary, they observed it in varying degrees and in accord with the opportunities the difficult conditions of frontier life offered them. Their worship services were simple, liturgically less elaborate than the Roman Catholic ones. Their churches were also very simple and functional in design. They believed that work counted for more than complex doctrine. Some, like the Quakers, were deeply engaged in Christian social action, dedicating themselves to the cause of peace and the abolition of slavery.

As the population of Anglo-America increased, new denominations and sects were formed. By and large the groups worshiped among themselves with mutual tolerance. Clashes sometimes occurred among some militant religious groups, but such differences did not produce the grave political and social conflicts that erupted in Europe and later in some Hispanic American countries. The English colonists were determined to maintain freedom of worship. In this they were aided by official English disinterest in the personal consciences of the colonists and freedom from the inquisitorial methods practiced in the Spanish colonies. Moreover, none of the denominations was sufficiently numerous to impose its own form of religion on the other inhabitants. Harmony did not always prevail, for each denomination believed that it was the repository of the authentic faith. There was also discrimination against Roman Catholics, Deists, Unitarians, and Jews, who were sometimes excluded from public office even after independence. Freedom of worship was guaranteed by the Constitution, however, and its practice was made secure by the large numbers of immigrants who arrived with their own creeds and convictions. The separation of church and state—that is, the secularization of the state—greatly fortified freedom of conscience. Secularization also had a profound liberalizing influence on the character of United States society.

Religious life in colonial Hispanic America was far more strict than that in Anglo-America. Its dominant trait was dogmatic conservatism. As in Spain, Roman Catholicism was the official religion in the colonies, where it continued as a traditionalist and rigidly centralized religion. In Roman Catholic daily religious life, prayer and work (*ora et labora*) were the dominant features. Roman Catholic doctrine had a rigidity that was in marked contrast to Protestant flexibility. It also, as a state church, had enormous power over its adherents. The full extent of that power was exercised during the Inquisition, which reached into the Spanish colonies, terrorizing believers and eliminating political enemies and freethinkers. Interestingly, the Inquisition paid little attention to the Indians, considering them powerless and of no threat to the church. In the Portuguese colony of Brazil, where there was a certain laxity in religious matters, the Inquisition also had little effect. But the other colonies felt its weight. There was fear that deviation from dogma and the infiltration of anti-Catholic ideas could undermine the church in the New World. Religious unity was equivalent to political unity, which the Spaniards sought to assure in their colonies, whatever the cost. They imposed restrictions on the importation of literary and scientific works that might threaten the people's loyalty to church and Spain. Even Cervantes' *Don Quixote* was officially prohibited, though a few copies were circulated surreptitiously. The Renaissance celebration of the art and literature of the Greco-Roman pagan world was looked upon as even more dangerous. Because of ecclesiastical opposition, the Renaissance died in its prime, to be succeeded by Baroque pomposity.

One of the aims of the Conquest was the Christianizing of the indigenes. Under the missionary banner the catechism was taught to the Amerindians by various orders, among them the Franciscans, the Augustinians, the Dominicans, and the Jesuits. The missionaries also taught the Castilian language. The extraordinary zeal of the missionary work was a reflection of the religious militancy that had enabled Spain to reconquer its territory after the long occupation by the Arabs. After eight centuries that conflict ended coincidentially with the discovery of America. Echoes of the struggles with the Muslims were fresh in the missionaries' minds as they arrived in the New World. Christianization of the Indians was looked upon as a sort of crusade that would bring new glory to Catholic Spain. In this it is necessary to distinguish between the idealism of the missionaries and the harshness of the conquistadors. While the former endeavored to save the Indians' souls for Christ, the latter subjugated them almost to the point of slavery. That approach was symbolic of Spain's activity throughout the colonial era—a combination of the spiritual and the material. The colonists looked upon the Indians as inferiors, an attitude that provoked theological disputes in Spain itself. Some theologians invoked Aristotle's views about "natural" slavery to justify maltreatment of the natives. The famous dispute between Bartolomé de las Casas and Ginés de Sepúlveda in Valladolid (1550–51) resulted in a moral victory for Las Casas, who contended that "all the races of the world are human beings," but did not alter the Indians' fate. The position of Ginés de Sepúlveda differed little from the attitude of the Puritans of New England, who openly disdained the Indians.[1]

Spanish missionaries working among the Indians had to contend with many deeply imbedded native beliefs. To attract Indians to

[1]Lewis Hanke, *Aristotle and the American Indians*, pp. 38–73, 99; and Lewis Hanke, *La lucha por justicia en la conquista española de América*.

Christianity, the missionaries resorted to such deceptions as carving on church doors and altars triangular façades reminiscent of the Aztec and Mayan pyramids. The Indians were also attracted with native pictorial motifs on baptismal fonts. It was fortunate symbolic coincidence that the stylized solar rays used on the Catholic monstrances also symbolized the Inca sun god for the Quechuas in Peru, Bolivia, and Ecuador. Such symbolism constituted a means of approach to the indigenes. No less important were the theatrical religious performances, in which Indians sometimes participated with native music and dances. Active participation by the Indians and mesitzos increased as they joined the creoles in decorating the churches. The Virgen Morena of Guadalupe, Patroness of Mexico; the Virgin of Chiquinquira, Patroness of Colombia; and Santa Rosa of Lima, Patroness of Peru, were especially revered by the Indians.

The spiritual power of Spain in the colonies had many positive results. The Spaniards were able to make themselves known for their Christianizing, educational, and cultural work. The Spanish orders learned how to attract the Indians to Western civilization, far excelling the Protestant Anglo-Americans in that work. Universities and colleges were maintained principally by the religious, who also controlled the publication of books in the Spanish colonies through the viceregal "license." Those activities took place under the ecclesiastical surveillance that the Roman Catholic Church maintained to assure the steadfastness of its members. The collaboration of the church with colonial authorities, although sometimes marked by rivalry, kept the colonial population isolated from "foreign" ideologies. Of course, that situation changed after independence.

Despite the profession of religious liberty Protestant Anglo-America was not always free of religious conflicts. The colonial era was darkened by the witchcraft trials carried on in New England by some fanatical sects. But they were few compared to the numbers of victims of the Inquisition, and they ceased when superstitions disappeared from Europe. Another matter was the theological weakening, in time, of various confessions. Over the years Puritan dogmatism lost its force, though its principles persisted. Calvinist teachings failed to undermine the inherent Yankee optimism. Calvinists, in spite of their increasing numbers, tended to become indifferent toward religious doctrines.[2] They did not try to refute them but rather ignored them, as did Protestants of other denominations. Parishioners discontented with their ministers' views simply formed new congregations, a procedure their descendants have continued to follow to the present.

The proliferation of new denominations in the United States has to do not only with their moral and intellectual flexibility but also with the national character. Anglo-Americans' individualism permits them independence of judgment. The variety in their thought continues to be reflected in new religious concepts or new interpretations of concepts transplanted from Europe. The result is that today there are more than two hundred North American Protestant denominations, including some that originated in North America, for examples, Mormonism and Christian Science. The proliferation of sects began in the frontier period when geographic isolation prompted the informal organization of churches by settlers. With the growth of urban centers and industrialization the process has diminished. Many denominations join together to speak as one body through the National Council of Churches. Yankees continue to express their belief that their destiny is bound to God, an attitude affirmed by the words "In God We Trust" stamped on United States money.

The fragmentation of Protestantism has today primarily a social significance. Most United States Protestants are almost incapable of distinguishing the differences among the various denominations. Most of them are at least nominal church members and supporters. Its social-consciousness makes Anglo-American Protestantism materially powerful if spiritually somewhat less effective than other branches of Christianity. For its adherents religion has come to be mainly a matter of observing social formalities and endeavoring to do some good. Some therefore call United States Protestantism "socialized Christianity." Discussions of religion are not considered "good form" at middle-class social gatherings.

The Roman Catholic Church in colonial Hispanic America, in addition to its religious domination, had considerable influence through the economic power it acquired from many individual be-

[2]Henry Steele Commager, *The American Mind*, pp. 162–95.

quests of land. Later that circumstance would have an adverse effect on its position. During the independence era, in an effort to preserve its wealth, the church took the side of the creole oligarchy, forming with it a conservative political front. It continued to perform its spiritual role, but its social ties with the masses, most of whom worked on the land, were loosened. The disparity between the spiritual and the social objectives of the church had negative consequences in various Hispanic countries at different times.

Especially deplorable was the intervention of the church in political matters, which provoked turbulent ideological battles. For example, in Ecuador the theocratic dictatorship of Gabriel García Moreno (1860–75) was a strange mixture of political conservatism and religious extremism. His limiting of citizenship to practicing Roman Catholics produced many national outbreaks, with unpleasant consequences that lasted almost to the end of the century.

In Mexico church ownership of agricultural property acquired in the colonial era caused grave internal conflicts after independence. The *antilatifundista* and anticlerical movements were inspired by the War of the Reform and the Reform Law (1857), and also by the later Agrarian Revolution (1910–17). During those internal cataclysms the great church and privately owned latifundias were expropriated. The extreme antireligious politics of General Plutarco Galles (1924–28) brought about the famous Rebellion of the Cristeros.

In recent history even more deplorable events have occurred in Colombia, where religious ideology is represented by the Conservative party and civil ideology by the Liberal party. Their continuous rivalry causes frequent disturbances on a national scale. An instance of this distressing ideological struggle was the undeclared civil war that broke out during the regime of Olaya Herrera (1930–34) and reached its height during the presidencies of Laureano Gómez (1950–53) and General Rojas Pinilla (1953–58). During that long struggle, according to Colombian estimates, about 300,000 peasants died. Apparently the slaughter was promoted by both sides. In the ranks of the guerrillas were some priests with political ambitions who later resumed their religious activities. Still vivid in memory is Camilo Torres, the "guerrilla priest," remembered by some Colombians as a martyr and by others as a symbol of revolution.

In Hispanic America the parties labeled traditional, or conservative, include those of the landowners, the industrialists, the ecclesiastical hierarchy, and the wealthy bourgeoisie. Those who belong to the parties called republican or liberal are mainly the members of the middle and lower classes: the workers, farmers, bureaucrats, and intellectuals with radical tendencies. Military officers often lend their political support to one side or the other as circumstances warrant. Liberals are opposed in general to the vestiges of semicolonial life disguised by democratic slogans and approach the laboring classes in ideology; in sentiment they tend to be freethinkers. Most conservatives, ideologically attached to the economic, social, and religious status quo, are exponents of the creole aristocracy and the Roman Catholic church.

In recent decades ideological fluctuations resulting from social malaise have inclined many formerly conservative and then middle-of-the road intellectuals to turn to Marxist radicalism. Some political groups, motivated by the ideal of Christian justice, have resisted the radical tendencies and organized Christian Democratic parties in support of some programs of the Roman Catholic church. Their principal aim is the cultural and economic integration of Hispanic America based on a still-lacking social cohesion. Christian Democrats consider their progressive movement the better alternative to capitalism, as well as to communism. Political experiences of Christian Democrats in Chile and in Venezuela have not yet demonstrated their practical potential but have indicated a road to genuine reform.

For some time social unrest has been reflected in the moral crisis of the church in Hispanic America, where one-third of the Roman Catholics of the world live. The causes of unrest seem to be the increase in population, which the church blesses while offering no counsel about how to provide for it; the importance of the church regarding the imbalance in the distribution of national wealth and consequent bitterness over social injustice; the growing indifference to spiritual concerns, indicated by the limited number of parishioners who maintain religious practices; and the indecisiveness of the church on important problems affecting the people's well-being, which undermines its moral prestige.

Because of its traditional alliance with the classes in power, the church in Hispanic America finds itself isolated with respect to the "social problem." Papal encyclicals on the subject have been read from the pulpits, but, with few exceptions, action has remained largely theoretical. Agnosticism and communism are censured, but little practical attention is paid to the need for restructuring the social system, a process that has been left to radicals. The ideological crisis consequently grows deeper, carrying possibilities of a social revolution accentuated by antireligious sentiment. Will Hispanic American Roman Catholics act to counter this tendency? It seems that relatively few will do so because religion lacks for them the "interior" quality that can be perceived in Roman Catholics of other countries. Caturelli believes it is a Christianity without charity. It thus, as Salvador Madariaga sees it, becomes a rite rather than a moral discipline.

Other elements of crisis indirectly brought about the changes introduced during Vatican Council II (1962). At that time papal authority was somewhat decentralized; the regional authority of bishops was increased, and so was lay participation in divine services. The new measures diminished the traditional authoritarianism of the church and at the same time opened new roads for social action with a religious orientation. Up to that time there had been no clear Roman Catholic social doctrine in Hispanic America. The new climate stimulated activity by some radical priests and laymen, who, though well intentioned, contributed to dissension among many activists. It should be noted that one-third of Hispanic American clergy are foreigners, owing to the scarcity of native-born priests and the exodus from religious life of young priests and friars. The need for a social revolution (whether violent or peaceful), on the one hand, and the need for a "young church" (as it is called in Chile) suitable for such a task, on the other, produces a tension of the sort that often results in large-scale defections by priests and other religious, who are discontented with the slow pace of reform. The rule of celibacy, one of the pillars of Roman Catholic institutions, is the first to suffer the effects of this trend, as much in Hispanic America as in the United States.

Church-state disputes occur frequently in the ideological struggle, with typical effects and cautious expository statements. In recent years in Bolivia, Colombia, Brazil, Chile, Nicaragua, Peru, and Uruguay that situation prompted groups of priests to issue proclamations censuring social and economic injustice. They expressed alarm at the conservatives' lack of social conscience and also at the excessive emphasis placed on the technocrats, who seldom participate in the government.[3] In response a meeting of bishops, the Consejo Episcopal Latinoamericano (CELAM), was held in Medellín, Colombia. That group judged the circumstances of injustice as institutionalized violence, stating that the present structures "violate fundamental rights," creating conditions that require an over-all and urgent transformation. The bishops also condemned the economic domination of Latin America by "foreign imperialism," a veiled reference to the United States and to European economic powers.

The conclusions of CELAM were audacious and touched on various sensitive points that some bishops had not previously dared discuss in their pastoral letters (such letters were brotherly but ambiguous so as to offend no one). Stimulating parishioners to collaborate in constructive programs, the "Declaration of Medellín" dispelled any suspicion of a possible government-ecclesiastical alliance with respect to the explosive social problems. The church in Hispanic America was thus separated from its practices of the past, and began acting circumspectly to cooperate in the political education of the elite through religious movements and educational institutions. The change in tactics was important for all of Hispanic America. Today only Colombia and Peru protect Roman Catholicism as the state religion. The other countries (with perhaps the single exception of Mexico) consider it an institution of the people. Religious ferment reflects internal political relations, a circumstance that explains the growing "social radicalization" and xenophobia. It is curious that even the material assistance of European and American Roman Catholics, without which the Roman Catholic institutions of some countries would be in a much worse position, is looked upon with suspicion, as though it were an extension of foreign "imperialistic" forces into the spiritual matters of Hispanic America.

Religious issues as such generally play little part in Anglo-American political life. Because of the United States Constitutional guarantees of freedom of religion, there have been no wars over religious issues. Although Protestants are in the majority in the United States, Roman Catholics, Jews, Buddhists, Moslems, and other religious groups worship freely according to their own convictions and traditions. Owing to the extensive variety of denomina-

[3]Mario Einaudi et al., *Latin American Institutional Development: The Changing Catholic Church*, pp. 31–66.

tions, prejudices among them are perhaps less marked than those in countries with only one or two major religions, whose adherents sometimes behave repressively toward minorities of other faiths. These favorable conditions result in a tremendous growth of some minority groups, such as the Roman Catholics and the Jews, who often display more unity than the Protestant majority. Their unity helps maintain the tolerant attitude, since Catholics and Jews today constitute powerful political pressure groups in the United States. No political party can afford to ignore them.

Some nonconformist and traditional practices are carried on simultaneously among United States Protestants and Catholics, mainly those having to do with birth control, divorce, and religious education. Religion is not taught in the public schools but is not prohibited in private schools. Many public assemblies begin with prayer. The Preamble of the Constitution contains mention of the Almighty. The President and other members of the government take the oath of office on the Bible, and the armed forces have chaplains of many faiths and denominations. The principal controversy is about birth control, which most Protestants favor and Catholics oppose. In recent decades, however, a serious division of opinion has taken place within the Roman Catholic community, indicating a growing independence of decision.

Roman Catholics are still intransigent about divorce, which is regarded by Protestants with more flexibility. A good many Roman Catholics leave the church because of ecclesiastic rigidity in this matter. Long ago various minority groups, denied by ecclesiastical authorities the use of their native languages for liturgical purposes, established their own national Catholic churches. Their opposition was aroused when the hierarchy, composed mainly of Irish and Italian elements, ignored their cultural and religious traditions and failed to display an ecumenical spirit. Minority groups who continued faithful to the Roman church were disturbed because bishops were not chosen from among them in proportion to their ethnic numbers.

Better Protestant-Catholic relations are expressed through occasional exchange of ministers and priests for divine services. Dialogues between groups are not unusual. Brotherhood Week, begun in the United States some decades before ecumenism was seriously considered in Europe, is observed each year, with the objective of promoting religious fellowship among people of all creeds. With all this, religious prejudices do exist in the United States. Although such prejudices are rarely verbalized among the better-educated groups, the less well educated do not hide them.

In recent years in the United States social tensions have led to a reexamination of religious values and talk of a "spiritual rebirth." Causes seem to lie in post–World War II skepticism and other international vicissitudes. The Anglo-Americans have begun a search for new human solutions in the metaphysical sphere. Participants in the Protestant revisionism, according to Max Lerner, turn toward theology instead of "social religion." Many young intellectuals follow the pessimistic philosophy of Reinhold Niebuhr and Paul Tillich, who revived the Calvinistic thesis of human corruption. Others who could not find a rational solution for their distress declared that "God does not exist" or "God is dead," sinking even deeper into confusion. These signs indicated that, amid efforts to change the value of things, there was also a search for roads to a religious renewal, exemplified in Harvey Cox's *The Secular City*, a strange mixture of theology, anthropology, and urban studies. Though it offers no concrete solutions, the work displays a revealing revisionism with accents of moral preoccupation. It is also significant that the Bible continues to be sold in great numbers in a wide variety of translations.

Doctrinal as well as social factors are present in the Hispanic American religious crisis. On the one hand, papal infallibility and the inflexible attitudes about abortion and celibacy arouse doubts. On the other hand, the ambiguous attitude of the hierarchy about agrarian reform, which places the future of overpopulated Hispanic America in jeopardy, has been for years a source of much dissatisfaction. Some conservatives among the hierarchy remain emotionally tied to the landholding class and fail to take a decisive position on social reform. The exceptions—notably bishops of Chile and Ecuador—are still too isolated to make it possible to speak of a general transformation of the Hispanic American hierarchy. Progressives are trying to bring about such a transformation by evolutionary and legal means. Guided by religiously inspired motives, they work to bring the Roman Catholic church out of the Middle Ages to save society from economic and social chaos. Some radical elements hope to achieve social reform by revolutionary means, at times supporting the Marxist movement and opposing the church.

Progressives as well as radicals count among their ranks young, militant clergy and idealistic laymen. The first have undertaken their struggle with the expected but so far unrealized cooperation of the ecclesiastical and political sectors, while the latter have depended too much on revolutionary action, which they believed would attract popular support. The future of religion in Hispanic America will depend in no small degree on the victory on of one group or the other. In this prolonged crisis, which has weakened the spiritual force of Catholicism, both agnosticism and anticlericalism have appeared. The agnostics seem convinced that ceremony and ritual are not sufficient to maintain the faith but that moral principles and the conviction of their spiritual validity are necessary. The anticlerical attitude, although not new, reflects the lack of dynamism among some priests who ignore their social role in the community. Some groups of young clergy are trying to assume that role and make the church a meaningful element of society. Whether they will be successful is still doubtful.

Today Roman Catholic dogmatism in Hispanic America, like Protestant liberalism in Anglo-America, is going through a grave moral crisis. Among Roman Catholics the problem of reducing social disparities has grown to great magnitude, and its solution could well restore the lost spiritual cohesion among the various strata of the population. Among some Protestant groups theological concern tends to bring faith back into a balance between the human and the metaphysical, as well as to reconcile them in their spiritual longings. Viewed this way, the concern seems to foretell a religious renewal if the road is taken to restore weakened moral values in daily life. Meanwhile, for Roman Catholics, doctrinal and institutional survival will be a historic feat. The road is a tortuous one, requiring great individual sacrifice. Upon the outcome will depend the direction of Hispanic American Christianity.

A curious effort to meet the religious and social crisis in Hispanic America was the assembly of Christians for Socialism, which met in May, 1972, in Chile. Composed mainly of "progressive" clerical and lay elements of the church, the assembly announced that it favored a Marxist economic and social approach to the socioeconomic transformation of Hispanic America, but without Marxian atheism. The possibility of a Christian-Marxist ideological alliance aroused a good deal of comment. Its viability remains to be seen.

SELECTED BIBLIOGRAPHY

Acosta Saignes, Miguel. *Vida de los esclavos negros en Venezuela*. Caracas, Ediciones Hesperides, 1967.

Adams, Mildred, ed. *Latin America: Evolution or Explosion?* New York, Dodd, Mead and Company, 1963.

Aguilar, José. *Historia de la Cartografía*. Buenos Aires, Editorial Codex, 1967.

Alba, Duque de, ed. *Mapas españoles de América*. Vols. XV-XVII. Madrid, 1951.

Alcina Franch, José. *Floresta literaria de la América indígena*. Madrid, Ediciones Aguilar, 1957.

Alegría, Fernando. *Historia de la novela hispanoamericana*. Mexico City, Ediciones de Andrea, 1966.

Alexander, Robert J. *The Bolivian National Revolution*. New Brunswick, Rutgers University Press, 1958.

Anderson Imbert, Enrique. *Historia de la literatura hispanoamericana*. Mexico City, Fondo de Cultura Económica, 1966.

Andreski, Stanislav. *Parasitismo y subversión en América Latina*. Buenos Aires, Editorial Americana, 1967.

Arboleda, Sergio. La colonia: *Su situación política y económica*. Bogotá, Biblioteca Popular de Cultura Colombiana, 1951.

Arciniegas, Germán. *América: Tierra firme*. Santiago de Chile, Ediciones Ercilla, 1937.

————. *El continente de siete colores*. Buenos Aires, Editorial Sudamericana, 1965.

————. *Entre la libertad y el miedo*. Santiago de Chile, Ediciones Ercilla, 1954.

Arguedas, Alcides. *Pueblo enfermo*. La Paz, Editorial Futuro Lda., 1967.

Arrom, José Juan. *Criollo: Definición y Matices de un concepto*. Bogotá, 1951.

————. *Hispanoamérica: Panorama contemporáneo de su cultura*. New York and London, Harper and Row, 1969.

Ayala, Felipe Guamán Poma de. *Nueva Crónica y buen gobierno*. Paris, 1936.

313

Bagrow, Leo. *History of Cartography*. Cambridge, Harvard University Press, 1964.

Basave Fernández del Valle, Agustín. *Visión de Estados Unidos*. Mexico City, Editorial Diana, 1974.

Baudin, Louis. *La vie quotidienne au temps des dernier Incas*. Paris, Librairie Hachette, 1955.

Bennett, W., and J. Bird. *Andean Culture History*. New York, American Museum of Natural History, 1960.

Biblioteca Nacional. *Catálogo de la Exposición "Cartografía de los descubrimientos."* Madrid, 1974.

Caballero Calderón, Eduardo. *Americanos y europeos*. Medellín, Ediciones Bedout, 1963.

Cambours Ocampo, Arturo. *El problema de las generaciones literarias*. Buenos Aires, A. Peña Lillo, Editor, 1963.

————. *El pueblo del sol*. Mexico City, Fondo Cultura Económica, 1954.

Caso, Alfonso. *The Aztecs: People of the Sun*. Trans. by Lowell Dunham. Norman, University of Oklahoma Press, 1959.

Castro, Américo. *España en su historia: Christianos, moros, y judíos*. Buenos Aires, Editorial Losada, 1948.

Caturelli, Alberto. *América bifronte*. Buenos Aires, Editorial Troquel, S. A., 1961.

Chang-Rodríguez, Eugenio. *La América Latina de hoy*. New York, Ronald Press Company, Inc., 1961.

Clark, Gerald. *América en llamas*. Barcelona, Editorial Bruguera, 1964.

Cline, Howard F. *Mexico: Revolution to Evolution*. London and New York, Oxford University Press, 1962.

Collier, John. *Indians of the Americas: The Long Hope*. New York, New American Library, 1956.

Comas. Juan. *Anthropología de los pueblos iberoamericanos*. Barcelona, Editorial Labor, S.A., 1974.

————. *Razas y racismo: Trayectoria y antología*. Mexico City, Editorial Sep-Setentas, 1972.

————. *Relaciones interraciales en América Latina: 1940–1960*. Mexico City, Universidad Nacional de México, 1961.

Commager, Henry Steele. *The American Mind: An Interpretation of American Thought and Character Since the 1880's*. New Haven, Yale University Press, 1950.

Cortesão, Armando. *Cartografía e cartógrafos portuguese dos séculos XV e XVI*. Lisbon, Edicão da Seara Nova, 1935.

————. *The Nautical Chart of 1424*. Coimbra, 1954.

————, and Avelino Teixeira da Mota. *Portugaliae Monumenta Cartographica*. 5 vols. Lisbon, 1960.

Cossío Villegas, Daniel. *Extremos de América*. Mexico City, Edit. Tezontle, 1944.

Coulthard, G. R. *Raza y color en la literatura antillana*. Seville, Escuela de Estudios Hispano-Americanos, 1958.

Cumming, W. P., R. A. Skelton, and D. B. Quinn. *The Discovery of North America*. New York, American Heritage Press, 1972.

Davis, Harold, ed. *Latin American Foreign Policies: An Analysis*. Baltimore, Johns Hopkins University Press, 1975.

Díaz Guerrero, Rogelio. *Estudios de psicología del mexicano*. Mexico City, Antigua Librería Robredo, 1961.

Einaudi, Mario, et al. *Latin American Institutional Development: The Changing Catholic Church*. Santa Monica, 1969.

Escalante, Aquiles. *El negro en Colombia*. Bogotá, Universidad Nacional de Colombia, 1964.

Estupiñán Tello, Julio. *El negro de Esmeraldas*. Quito, Talleres Gráficos Nacionales, 1967.

Franco, Jean. *The Modern Culture of Latin America: Society and the Artists*. London, Pall Mall Press, Ltd., 1967.

Frankowska, Maria. *Podstawy gospodarki wiejskiej w Peru*. Poznań, Uniwersytet im. Adama Mickiewicza, 1967.

Fussell, Edwin. *Frontier: American Literature and the American West*. Princeton, Princeton University Press, 1965.

García Calderón, Francisco. *La creación de un continente*. Paris, Editorial Ollendorf, 1913.

Gil, Federico G. *Instituciones y desarrolo político de América Latina*. Buenos Aires, INTAL, 1966.

Gillin, John. *The Social Transformation of the Mestizos*. Mexico City, 1961.

Gómez-Gil, Orlando. *Historia crítica de la literatura hispanoamericana*. New York, Holt, Rinehart and Winston, 1968.

González, Fernando. *Los negroides: Ensayo sobre la Gran Colombia*. Medellín, Editorial Bedout, 1970.

Gumplowicz, Luis. *La lucha de razas*. Buenos Aires, Editorial Fas, 1944.

Gunther, John. *Inside Latin America*. New York, Harper and Brothers, 1941.

Haiman, Miecislaus. *Poland and the American Revolutionary War*. Chicago, Polish Roman Catholic Union of America, 1932.

Hanke, Lewis. *Aristotle and the American Indians*. Bloomington, Indiana University Press, 1959.

———. *La lucha por justicia en la conquista española de América*. Buenos Aires, Editorial Sudamericana, 1949.

Harris, Marvin. *Pattern of Race in the Americas*. New York, Walker and Company, 1964.

Henriquez Ureña, Pedro. *Las corrientes literarias en la América Hispánica*. Mexico City, Fondo de Cultura Económica, 1954.

————. *Historia de la cultura en la América Hispánica*. Mexico City, Fondo de Cultura Económica, 1947.

Herring, Hubert. *History of Latin America*. 3d ed. New York, Alfred A. Knopf, Inc., 1968.

Hilton, Ronald. *La America Latina de ayer y de hoy*. New York, Holt, Rinehart and Winston, 1970.

Howse, Derek, and Michael Sanderson. *The Sea Chart*. Norwich, 1973.

Inan, Afet. *Life and Works of the Turkish Admiral Piri Reis: The Oldest Map of America*. Ankara, 1954.

Instituto Panamericano de Geografía e Historia. *El mestizaje en la historia de Ibero-América*. Mexico City, 1961.

James, Preston E. *Introduction to Latin America: The Geographic Background of Economic and Political Problems*. New York, Odyssey Press, 1964.

Jiménez Moreno, Wigberto. *El mestizaje y la transculturación en Mexiamérica*. Mexico City, 1961.

Kalijarvi, Thorston. *Central America: Land of Lords and Lizards*. Princeton, N.J., D. Van Nostrand Co., 1962.

Kauffman Doig, Federico. *El Perú arqueológico*. Lima, 1963.

Kohl, Johann Georg. *Asia and America*. Worcester, 1911.

Konieczny, Feliks. *On the Plurality of Civilisations*. London, Polonica Publications, 1962.

Kroeber, Alfred L. *Style and Civilizations*. Ithaca, Cornell University Press, 1957.

Lagos, Ramiro. *Mester de rebeldía de la poesía hispanoamericana*. Madrid and Bogotá, Ediciones Dos Mundos, 1973.

Latcham, Montenegro Vega. *El criollismo*. Santiago de Chile, Editorial Universitaria, Colección Saber, 1956.

Leal, Luis. *Breve historia de la literatura hispanoamericana*. New York, Alfred A. Knopf, Inc., 1971.

————. *Mexico: civilizaciones y culturas*. Boston, Houghton Mifflin Company, 1971.

————, and Frank Dauster. *Literatura de Hispanoamérica*. New York, Harcourt, Brace & World, Inc., 1970.

León-Portilla, Miguel. *Aztec Thought and Culture: A Study of the Ancient Nahuatl Mind*. Norman, University of Oklahoma Press, 1963.

————. *Pre-Columbian Literatures of Mexico*. Norman, University of Oklahoma Press, 1969.

Lepkowski, Tadeusz. *Azjatycka i afrykańska Ameriyka*. Warsaw, Wydawnictwo Czytelnik, 1969.

Lerner, Max. *America as a Civilization*. 2 vols. New York, Simon and Schuster, 1957.

Madariaga, Salvador de. *Latin America Between the Eagle and the Bear*. New York, Frederick A. Praeger, 1962.

Mafud, Julio. *Psicología de la viveza criolla*. Buenos Aires, Editorial Américalee, 1965.

Malinowski, Bronislaw. *Una teoría científica de la cultura*. Buenos Aires, Editorial Sudamericana, 1948.

Mallea, Eduardo. *Historia de una pasión argentina*. Buenos Aires, Editorial Sudamericana, 1961.

Marías, Julián. *Los Estados Unidos en escorzo*. Buenos Aires, 1964.

Mariátegui, José C. *Siete ensayos de interpretación de la realidad peruana*. Lima, Editorial Amauta, 1958.

Maritain, Jacques. *Reflexions sur l'Amérique*. Paris, A. Fayard, 1958.

Martinez Estrada, Ezequiel. *La cabeza de Goliat: Microscopía de Buenos Aires*. Buenos Aires, Editorial Nova, 1957.

————. *Diferencias y semejanzas entre los países de la América Latina*. Mexico City, Universidad Nacional Autónoma de México, 1962.

————. *Radiografía de la pampa*. Buenos Aires, Editorial Losada S. A., 1957.

Mathews, Herbert L., ed. *The United States and Latin America*. Englewood Cliffs, N.J., Prentice-Hall, Inc., 1963.

Mellafe, Rolando. *La esclavitud negra en Hispanoamérica*. Buenos Aires, Editorial Universitaria de Buenos Aires, 1964.

Métraux, Alfred. *Problema racial en América Latina*. Paris, UNESCO, 1960.

Milewski, Tadeusz. *Aztek Anonim: Zdobycie Meksyku*. Wroclaw-Kraków, Zaklad Narodowy im. Ossolińskich, 1959.

Morales, Ángel Luis. *Literatura Hispanoamericana. Épocas y figuras*. San Juan, P.R., Editorial D.I.P., 1967.

Morison, Samuel Eliot. *The European Discovery of America: The Northern Voyages, A.D. 500-1600*. New York, Oxford University Press, 1971.

————. *The European Discovery of America: The Southern Voyages, 1492-1616*. New York, Oxford University Press, 1974.

Mörner, Magnus. *Race Mixture in the History of Latin America*. Boston, Little, Brown and Company, 1967.

Murena, H. A. *El pecado original de América*. Buenos Aires, Editorial Sur, 1965.

Needler, Martin C., ed. *Political Systems of Latin America*. Princeton, N.J., D. Van Nostrand Company, 1964.

Nocoń, Rudolf H. *Dzieje, kultura i upadek Inków*. Wroclaw, Wydawnictwo Ossolineum, 1958.

Nordenskiold, A. E. *Facsimile-Atlas to the Early History of Cartography*. Stockholm, 1889.

O'Leary, T. J. *Ethnographic Bibliography of South America*. New Haven, Conn., Human Relations Area Files, 1963.

Ortega y Gasset, José. *Obras: El espectador*. Madrid, Espasa-Calpe, 1943.

Ortiz, Adalberto. *La negritud en la cultura latinoamericana*. Quito, Centro Andino de la Universidad de New Mexico, 1972.

Paz, Octavio. *El laberinto de la soledad*. Mexico City, Fondo de Cultura Económica, 1963. (Originally published in 1950.)

Picón-Salas, Mariano. *De la Conquista a la Independencia: Tres siglos de historia cultural hispanoamericana*. Mexico City, Fondo de Cultura Económica, 1944.

————. *Europa-América: Preguntas a la esfinge de la cultura*. Mexico City, Editorial Cuadernos Americanos, 1947.

Plaza, Galo. *Latin America Today and Tomorrow*. Washington, D.C., Acropolis Books, Ltd., 1971.

Prokosch Kurat, Gertrude, and Samuel Marti. *Dances of Anahuac: The Choreography and Music of Precortesian Dances*. Chicago, Aldine Publishing Company, 1964.

Ramos, Samuel. *El perfil del hombre y la cultura en México*. Buenos Aires, 1952.

Restrepo Jaramillo, Gonzalo. "Norteamérica: signos de interpretación," *Revista Universidad Católica Bolivariana*, Vol. II (1938).

Reyes, Alfonso. *Obras completas*. Vol XI. Mexico City, Fondo de Cultura Económica, 1960.

Rockefeller, Nelson A. *The Rockefeller Report on the Americas*. Chicago, Quadrangle Books, 1969.

Romero, Francisco. *El hombre y la cultura*. Buenos Aires, Espasa-Calpe Argentina, 1950.

Rostworowski de Díez Canseco, María. *Pachacutec Inca Yupanqui*. Lima, Imprenta Torres Aguirre (Premio Nacional de Fomento de la Cultura Inca Garcilaso de la Vega), 1953.

Sánchez, Luis Alberto. *¿Existe América Latina?* Mexico City, Fondo de Cultura Económica, 1945.

Sanders, Thomas E., and Walter W. Peck. *Literature of the American Indians*. Beverly Hills, Calif., Glencoe Press, 1973.

Scalabrini Ortiz, Raúl. *El hombre que está solo y espera*. Buenos Aires, Editorial Plus Ultra, 1964.

Snowden, Frank M., Jr. *Blacks in Antiquity*. Cambridge, Mass., Harvard University Press, 1970.

Soustelle, Jacques. *La vie quotidienne des Azteques à la veille de la conquête espagnole*. Paris, 1955.

Spinden, Herbert J. *Ancient Civilizations of Mexico and Central America*. New York, American Museum of Natural History, 1946.

Stevenson, Edward L. *Portolan Charts: Their Origin and Characteristics*. New York, 1911.

Stokes, Phelps. *The Iconography of Manhattan Island*. New York, 1915–1928.

Szulc, Tad[eusz]. *The Winds of Revolution: Latin America Today and Tomorrow*. New York, Frederick A. Praeger, 1963.

Szyszlo, Vitold de. *La Naturaleza en la América Ecuatorial*. Lima, San Martí y Cía., 1955.

Tannenbaum, Frank. *Mexico: The Struggle for Peace and Bread*. New York, Alfred A. Knopf, Inc., 1950.

———. *Ten Keys to Latin America*. New York, Alfred A. Knopf, Inc., 1962.

Thompson, J. Eric S. *Maya Archaeologist*. Norman, University of Oklahoma Press, 1963.

———. *The Rise and Fall of Maya Civilization*. 2d ed. Norman, University of Oklahoma Press, 1966.

———. *Maya History and Religion*. Norman, University of Oklahoma Press, 1970.

Thrower, Norman J. W. *Maps and Man*. Englewood Cliffs, N.J., Prentice-Hall, Inc., 1972.

Tooley, Ronald V. *Maps and Map-Makers*. New York, Crown Publishers, 1952.

Torres-Ríoseco, Arturo. *The Epic of Latin American Literature*. New York, Oxford University Press, 1946.

Urbanski, Edmund S. *Angloamérica e Hispanoamérica: Análisis de dos civilizaciones*. Madrid, Ediciones Studium, 1965.

———. *Hispanoamérica: Sus razas y civilizaciones*. New York, Torres and Sons, 1973.

———. *Studies in Spanish American Literature and Civilization*. Macomb, Western Illinois University Press, 1964.

Uslar-Pietri, Arturo. *Breve historia de la novela hispanoamericana*. Caracas and Madrid, Ediciones Edime, 1954.

———. *En busca del Nuevo Mundo*. Mexico City, Fondo de Cultura Económica, 1969.

Valadés, E., and L. Leal. *La Revolución y las letras*. México, Instituto Nacional de Bellas Artes, 1960.

Valle, Manuel M. *Biological Bases of Race, Culture and History*. Lima, Pacific Press, S.A., 1964.

———. *Dualismo Racial*. Lima, Editorial Lumen, 1961.

———. *Observaciones sobre geografía ecológica del hombre*. Lima, Editorial Lumen, 1953.

Varallanos, José. *El cholo y el Perú*. Buenos Aires, Imprenta López, 1962.

Veblen, Thorstein. *The Place of Science in Modern Civilization*. New York, Viking Press, 1919.

Vindel, Francisco. *Mapas de América en los libros españoles de los siglos XV-XVII*. Madrid, 1955.

Wagley, Charles, and Marvin Harris. *Minorities in the New World*. New York, Columbia University Press, 1964.

Wagner, W. J. *The Federal States and Their Judiciary*. The Hague, Mouton and Company, 1959.

Wendt, Herbert. *Der Schwartz-Weiss-Rote Kontinent*. Oldenburg, Gerhard Stalling Verlag, 1965.

Wieder, F. C., ed. *Monumental Cartographica: Reproduction of Unique and Rare Maps*. The Hague, 1925–33.

Withers, William. *The Economic Crisis in Latin America*. Glencoe, Ill., Free Press, 1964.

Worchester, Donald, and Wendell Schaefter. *Culture in Latin America*. 2 vols. New York, Oxford University Press, 1971.

Wyrwa, Tadeusz. *Les Républiques Andines*. Paris, Pichon et Durand-Auzias, 1972.

Zapata Olivella, Manuel. *El Hombre Colombiano*. Vol. I. Bogotá, Canal Ramírez-Antares, Enciclopedia del Desarrollo Colombiano, 1974.

Zavala, Silvio. *Filosofía de la Conquista*. Mexico City, Fondo de Cultura Económica, 1947.

Zea, Leopoldo. *América en la historia*. Mexico City, Fondo de Cultura Económica, 1957.

———. *Dos etapas del pensamiento en Hispanoamérica*. Mexico City, El Colegio de México, 1949.

———. *The Latin-American Mind*. Tr. by James H. Abbott and Lowell Dunham. Norman, University of Oklahoma Press, 1963.

———. *Latin America and the World*. Tr. by Frances K. Hendricks and Beatrice Berler. Norman, University of Oklahoma Press, 1969.

INDEX